The economic function of futures markets

The economic function of futures markets

JEFFREY WILLIAMS

Brandeis University

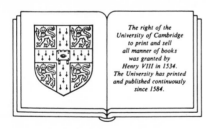

The right of the
University of Cambridge
to print and sell
all manner of books
was granted by
Henry VIII in 1534.
The University has printed
and published continuously
since 1584.

CAMBRIDGE UNIVERSITY PRESS

CAMBRIDGE
NEW YORK   NEW ROCHELLE
MELBOURNE   SYDNEY

Published by the Press Syndicate of the University of Cambridge
The Pitt Building, Trumpington Street, Cambridge CB2 1RP
32 East 57th Street, New York, NY 10022, USA
10 Stamford Road, Oakleigh, Melbourne 3166, Australia

First published 1986
Reprinted 1987

Printed in the United States of America

Library of Congress Cataloging in Publication Data
Williams, Jeffrey, 1953–
The economic function of futures markets.
Bibliography: p.
1. Commodity exchanges. I. Title.
HG6024.A3W54   1986   332.64′4   85–6653
ISBN 0 521 26591 6

British Library Cataloging-in-Publication applied for

Contents

v

Preface

The recent boom in futures trading has sparked in turn a surge in books on speculation in futures contracts, on the historical patterns in commodity prices, and on the mechanics of futures trading. I hope with this book to contribute something different. I have not tried to set up a system that would predict the prices for different delivery dates and locations but have instead concentrated on explaining the patterns among them. I have done so by connecting these patterns to general economic principles rather than by taking an empirical approach. The reader should not expect, therefore, to find interviews with processors and commodity dealers, nor surveys of the ways they use futures markets. Still, I hope it is clear that these handlers of commodities remain the centerpiece of my study, because they, rather than speculators or brokers, have the greatest effect on the patterns in prices and on the viability of futures markets.

This book offers a new explanation of the function of futures markets: that dealers use them as part of an implicit method of borrowing and lending commodities. My argument counters the heretofore accepted wisdom that dealers in commodities employ futures markets to insure their inventories against the risk of fluctuating prices. Futures markets are believed to be most closely related to insurance markets, yet the appropriate analogy should be money markets. Futures prices for different delivery dates serve to express a term structure of commodity-specific interest rates, in much the same way money markets do for money.

Futures markets have too often been examined in isolation from other markets in the economy. Although such an emphasis on futures markets' special characteristics is appropriate for grasping the mechanics of futures trading, it is nonetheless myopic, and it inadvertently misrepresents the economic function of futures markets. That more fundamental subject is better comprehended through studying what futures markets have in common with other institutions. This book establishes many parallels between them, by demonstrating the economic effect of complex trades whatever their names, by applying to dealers in commodities models long used in other areas of economics, and by considering the variety among commodity markets themselves.

Some readers may resist the notion of loans in and interest rates for commodities. Precisely because it is so wrenching to discard the perspective of price insurance, this book includes a chapter demonstrating the internal inconsistencies of the prevailing theory. The book also contrasts the competing explanations of several specific topics, such as the subject of why futures markets exist for particular commodities and not for others.

Other readers will note that my perspective is not entirely novel, that it is related to the earlier arguments of the economist Holbrook Working. Indeed, I am attempting to provide a comprehensive theory linking Working's concept of the supply of storage with his observation of firms using futures contracts as temporary substitutes for specific merchandising contracts.

One might well ask what practical difference it makes to understand better the function of futures markets. In truth, the markets would operate much the same whatever economists might say about them. But the motives of futures traders have never been clear to those not actively trading, even when the effect of nontraders on the markets is substantial. For that reason it is essential to articulate the larger function of futures markets to bankers, to regulators, and most important of all, to those who desire, as has happened periodically, to outlaw futures trading. A clearer perception of the economic contribution of futures markets also ought to redirect the efforts of the many economists who study them. I believe there is much to be learned – about both commodity markets and money markets – from recognizing their fundamental parallels.

This book developed from my doctoral dissertation at Yale University. I would, therefore, like to thank my committee, William Parker, Martin Shubik, and Brian Wright, who heard out the first formulations of the ideas presented here. I am particularly grateful to Brian Wright for his insights into futures markets that have arisen in the course of our research on commodity storage. Working on a subject with such perplexing vocabulary and customs, I owe special thanks to those who insisted on the many revisions between my dissertation and the current version: my editor Katherine Banks, my colleagues Robert Lurie, Stephen DeCanio, and especially Victor Goldberg, and my wife Diana Strazdes. Each has a strong claim to be coauthor.

CHAPTER 1

An introduction to futures markets

The hurly-burly of futures markets provides economists with a prime example of order arising from seeming chaos. The workings of commodity exchanges, such as margin rules, clearinghouses, and arcane terminology, result from the unplanned evolution of complex institutions. Futures prices are likewise the result of the interaction of brokers, speculators, and dealers in commodities, with no one firm or individual able to control prices. Yet the institutional features display compelling logic and futures prices remarkable consistency in their patterns. Because they exemplify competitive markets, futures markets bring into focus many areas of theoretical interest in economics, such as the role of risk aversion in people's decisions, the behavior of those storing commodities, and the market system's ability to digest information.

A study of the function of futures markets, therefore, can investigate the operation of actual markets as well as broader theoretical topics. This particular study aims mainly at theoretical topics rather than purely institutional questions such as the response of futures markets to changes in legal precepts. This study begins with the premise that understanding the motives of handlers of commodities is central to understanding futures markets. Without the business of handlers of commodities, futures markets wither away (Working 1954), contrary to the popular impression of the importance of speculation. Concentration on handlers of commodities illuminates two fundamental issues in particular: the reasons why futures prices have the patterns they do and the reasons why so few futures markets exist.

Handlers of commodities range from flour millers and soybean exporters to dealers in Treasury securities and mortgages. Because industries processing agricultural commodities or minerals are often easier to comprehend, the examples used here will mainly be about conventional primary commodities. The insights gained about agricultural processors' use of futures markets apply with little modification to those handling financial instruments.

Currently, economists draw on an analogy with insurance markets, where risk aversion takes center stage, for their understanding of why dealers in commodities use futures markets. This study seeks to replace that analogy with one of money markets. Dealers use futures markets as an implicit method of borrowing and lending their commodities. Because of the inflexibilities of transporting and processing commodities, they have sufficient reason to use futures markets even if they are neutral toward risk. Economists should approach firms' use of futures markets with the tools they have developed to study financial intermediation rather than the tools they have developed to study risk aversion. The patterns among futures prices can best be comprehended from the perspective of interest rates rather than insurance premiums. Economists have misunderstood the function of futures markets.

Of course, these theoretical discussions should never ignore the institutional realities. For example, a theoretical analysis can determine which commodities have the potential to develop futures trading, but the success of an actual market still depends crucially on such factors as the proper design of contractual terms for delivery, the trust traders need for dealing with one another, and the number of interested speculators. Accordingly, this first chapter introduces both the mechanics of futures trading and the theoretical subjects to be explored at length in later chapters.

To the individual unfamiliar with commodity exchanges, the jumble of figures and terms found in newspaper coverage of futures markets must be a cryptogram. Indeed, "cash price," "futures," "shorts," and "longs," terms whose meanings are not immediately apparent, are parts of a code that must be broken in order to understand futures markets.[1] Cash price, for example, does not refer solely to transactions requiring immediate payment of cash. Although most often "cash" refers to the immediate transfer of ownership of goods already at a specific location, some trades in the cash market are on credit, and others call for goods to be delivered and paid for several months later. A common synonym for cash price is "spot price," the word "spot" abridging the best description of the transaction – an exchange of cash for a commodity on the spot. Similarly, the terms "futures" and "futures markets" are difficult to decipher. "Futures," formally an abbreviation of the phrase "contract for future delivery," refers to contracts calling for delivery of a standard quantity and quality of a commodity to a particular location during a specified period in the future. Although the contracts stipulate the month for delivery, the seller chooses the exact day of

---

[1] These and many other terms are explained in detail in the Glossary.

delivery.[2] Futures markets like the Chicago Board of Trade are institutions that allow for such standardized contracts to be traded at
high volume with low cost, in part because such contracts can be
canceled before the time of delivery simply by negotiating an offsetting contract. In effect, the contracts themselves are bought and
sold. A trader who has sold a contract, that is, has committed himself
to deliver, is called a "short." A trader who has bought a contract,
which commits him to accept delivery, is a "long."[3]

The pressure of finding trading partners, simplifying negotiations, and reducing operating expenses of the exchange all work to
keep the number of distinct contracts for a particular commodity to
a minimum. Usually the exchanges, sometimes in their bylaws, limit
the number of contracts to six or eight different delivery months.
But actually the exchanges show far greater concern with promoting
trading, there rarely being from their perspective sufficient trading
over the full range of contracts and commodities.

For the market in a particular commodity to be legitimately called a
futures market, contracts in several delivery months must be traded
simultaneously in reasonable daily volume, say at least a few hundred
per delivery month and several thousand collectively. The daily volume of the most active futures markets is on the order of 50,000
contracts, occasionally reaching 100,000 contracts. The majority of
functioning futures markets, forty or fifty in number, are for agricultural products like corn, feeder cattle, cotton, and cocoa, or for metals
such as gold and copper. The mid-1970s saw the beginning of a boom
in new contracts calling for delivery of financial instruments like Swiss
francs or U.S. Treasury bonds. Although dealings in contracts for
such financial instruments have endured, attempts by the major exchanges to establish markets for many commodities, from frozen
turkeys to silver coins, have failed. Other once active markets, such as
the egg market on the Chicago Mercantile Exchange and the wool
tops market on the New York Cotton Exchange, have died.

Despite the large number of contracts bought and sold on an
active futures market during a typical day, the change in the total
open interest, the number of contracts outstanding at the close of

[2] In the 1860s and 1870s, early in the history of the Chicago Board of Trade, parallel
contracts existed calling for delivery at the buyer's option as to time.
[3] The use of "he" and "his" is not meant to imply that a trader of futures contracts
must be a male (although the overwhelming majority of members of futures exchanges are men). Nor is that usage meant to imply that a trader cannot be a
corporate entity. Millers, exporters, processors, and other hedgers are most often
impersonal firms. Although such a firm should be referred to as "it" and "its," it
seems less confusing to accede to the dictates of grammar.

the day's trading, is small, usually within a range of −500 to +500
contracts. The open interest changes slowly because many traders
taking a position in the market just replace those who are leaving.
Meanwhile, other traders called "day traders" and "scalpers," whose
volume of trading is high, close out their positions at the end of each
day by obtaining contracts that offset the holdings they have already
accumulated. Viable futures markets typically have average daily volume on the order of one fifth or one fourth their open interest,
although the most active markets by attracting many day traders and
scalpers sustain daily volume of one half their open interest.

Contracts for delivery in more distant months generally have a lower
volume and smaller open interest.[4] The exception is the contract calling for delivery in the current month. Before a contract becomes eligible for delivery, most traders offset it entirely or "roll over" their position into a more distant delivery month. Indeed, surprisingly few contracts for future delivery end in delivery. In the more actively traded
commodities, usually less than one or two percent of the peak open
interest in a contract culminates in delivery.[5] A formal exchange like
the Chicago Board of Trade greatly facilitates this practice of canceling
contracts by devoting much of its energy to the settlement of contracts
through offset rather than delivery of the physical commodity.

1.1.   Clearinghouses

Instrumental in the process of offsetting contracts before delivery is
the clearinghouse associated with each futures exchange. A clearinghouse effectively transforms a contract for the future delivery of
some commodity into a good itself. A sale of a futures contract
immediately and exactly cancels the purchase of a contract for the
same delivery month.

The contribution of a clearinghouse can best be appreciated by
tracing its development. Actually such a historical perspective can
often elucidate futures markets. Even though trading now takes
place in many more commodities, futures markets took on their
modern form by 1900 if not earlier. The experimentation during

[4] For agricultural commodities, open interest in all delivery months combined also
follows a pronounced seasonal pattern, peaking just after the start of the crop-year
(Irwin 1935).
[5] Even if few contracts culminate in delivery, delivery is not conditional on either
party's choice or any particular event. Sometimes actual futures contracts are con-
fused (e.g., Shefrin 1979 and 1981) with the hypothetical contracts of general equilibrium theory in which delivery is only made if some state of the world comes to
pass, such as whether it has rained.

their period of most rapid development, the 1870s and 1880s, is especially revealing of their workings as institutions. In much the same way, despite tremendous advances in technology, the fundamental economic predicament of handlers of commodities has changed little in 150 years. Therefore, examples from the nineteenth century can often be profitably used alongside modern ones. A diversity of examples is worth the risk of taking them too much out of their historical contexts.

Official clearinghouses are a natural evolution of the informal clearing first done among "rings" of members of an exchange, and an extension of the common funds they set up for payment of money due on futures contracts. Clearinghouses, rings, and common funds are all founded on one principle: the economy and convenience achieved through settlement of contracts by the payment of differences. The development of a clearinghouse involved increasingly more sophisticated applications of the principle of settlement by the payment of differences.

Long before the emergence of modern futures markets, settlement by the payment of differences was used in commodity markets between two parties to simplify the fulfillment of contracts. For instance, if two parties have contracted to deliver the same amount of cotton to each other, but at different prices, they can conclude their negotiations by having the party who bought at the higher price pay to the other the difference in price. Although in this example the method of settlement is taken to mean the payment of monetary differences, the same logic applies to the payment of differences in the quantity of a commodity. If one party has promised to deliver to another party 1,000 bales of cotton on the tenth day of the next month, while a few days later in the course of business the second party contracts to deliver 500 bales of similiar cotton also on the tenth day of the next month to the first party, it makes no sense for the first party to deliver the whole 1,000 bales while the other is delivering 500 bales to him. Rather, settlement of both contracts is achieved when the first party delivers the difference in obligations, 500 bales, to the second party.

This practice of payment of differences need not be confined to two parties; in fact, in the 1860s and 1870s members of the newly founded futures exchanges extended this logic to a group.[6] Called a

---

[6] Although there was futures trading in the 1840s if not earlier, settlement through rings seems to have developed in the 1860s and 1870s simultaneously with the first official recognition and encouragement of futures trading by the Chicago Board of

ring, such a group was composed of many traders who dealt in the same commodity and who collectively had counterbalancing positions. The advantage of "ringing up" over many actual deliveries of the same commodity is obvious. Imagine that four parties have contracted deals among themselves. Party A has bought a particular amount of cotton from B and B, in turn, has bought the same amount from C. Party C has bought the same amount from D and D from A. Regardless of who makes the first delivery, after an expensive and time-consuming journey, the cotton and most of the money as well will return to where it started. Rather than send the cotton and the money around the ring, it is much easier and cheaper to settle by the payment of monetary differences.

Frequently, members of a ring did not deal for their own accounts but as agents for others, who as the principals were legally responsible for the fulfillment of the contracts. The extension of the idea of rings to the cases in which different customers were involved increased substantially the number of futures contracts ended by offset rather than delivery. When, as in the supposed ring, A had bought from B and sold to D, he was ordinarily buying for one customer, say X, and selling for another, say Y. With this in mind it might seem from a legal perspective that A, as well as the other brokers, would be obliged to refrain from forming a ring until the same customer made an offsetting trade. After all, the contract negotiated by A with B is held for X's benefit. And A when he participates in a ring releases B from the contract and substitutes another principal, his own customer Y, thereby changing X's contract since Y might be more likely to default than B. Whatever the legal arguments in regard to the substitution of principals without consultation, commission merchants early on formed rings in which they were acting as brokers for different customers. The New York Cotton Exchange, an ideal example, allowed such substitution as long as the futures commission merchant himself was responsible for the strict fulfillment of contracts.

Members of an exchange were themselves responsible for discovering the existence of rings. Rings, however, were far from obvious to find. Even if Party A knew he had bought from one person and sold to another, he could not be sure the others had ever offset their positions. Clerks had to travel from office to office in search of rings. Once a ring was discovered on the Chicago Board of Trade,

Trade and the New York Cotton Exchange. For a discussion of the origins of futures trading, see Williams (1982).

ringing up was strictly voluntary, but on the New York Cotton Exchange (1891: Rule 4), discovery of a ring made ringing up compulsory if the differences required for immediate payment were small.[7]

In forming a ring it is convenient if all the parties involved pay into a common fund from which they get back the appropriate amount due them. In effect, a common fund applies the principle of settlement by the payment of differences to a ring. The ringing up itself eliminates the need for the commodity to travel around the ring; rather, only monetary differences travel around the ring, A paying an amount to B and receiving some of that back from D. A common fund eliminates the duplication in the monetary differences, so that only the differences in the monetary differences change hands.[8] Instead of calculating and paying differences in turn around the ring, in which case each party pays and receives a total of two checks, a common fund enables all to pay or receive, as the case may be, one check for the balance of their transactions. Traders will be able to conserve on their inventory of cash, not needing to worry about checks clearing through the banking network. Not only are smaller checks moving back and forth much less likely to be misprocessed by banks, but they also give greater confidence in traders in their dealings with one another. A trader will feel more secure in writing a check for $1,000 to another trader than in issuing a check for $50,000 while receiving a check for $49,000 in return. An advantage of a common fund is obvious when the net effect of the transactions around a typical ring is for just a few parties to receive small amounts. But the real advantage of a common fund surfaces when each contributor is a member of several rings. Then, instead of issuing to or receiving a check from every ring, each party pays to or receives from a giant common fund only one check.

At the point when traders are dealing with one giant common fund, the informal practice of ringing up becomes much like that of clearing through a clearinghouse. In fact, as soon as the Chicago Board of Trade reached this stage, in the early 1880s, proposals

---

[7] Early rules of the New York Cotton Exchange required discounting of the monetary differences, since the contracts called for payment in the future with money worth less than current money by the interest it would earn over the interim.

[8] As a further convenience, all the parties to a ring can calculate their differences in reference to a standard settlement price. The settlement price is purely an accounting convenience. If it overstates the true market price, on some transactions a trader will be responsible for more than he should owe, on others, less. His net due will be the same regardless of the settlement price. For this reason, some exchanges in the past have used whole numbers for the settlement price because they simplify computations.

were put forth for an actual clearinghouse. At first, officials of the clearinghouse of the Chicago Board of Trade, founded in 1883, were only spectators to the actual settlements. The new clearinghouse's main contribution, which was considerable nonetheless, was to provide a central location for its members' clerks. In addition, at the close of business each day, every member of the clearinghouse submitted a list of his transactions. The clearinghouse combined these lists into one grand roster, which it presented each morning to the clerks of the member firms who met together in a "settling room." Aided by this grand roster, the clerk of a house with a bought contract not yet offset looked for the clerk of the firm that had sold to it. That clerk, in turn, was looking for a clerk representing a firm from which his firm had bought. This search expanded until the original buyer was found to have sold to someone on the circuit, at which point the ring was complete. The clerks would then mutually cancel the trades or "ring out the deals." All differences would be paid in reference to an official settlement price, as posted by a committee of the exchange during the day. Those firms whose clerks had arranged many rings would pay all in one lump the many differences, the giant common fund being looked after by the clearinghouse.[9]

Despite searches for rings, however greatly facilitated by the clearinghouse's grand lists, many contracts actually offset would remain outstanding at the time of delivery. This necessitated considerable delivery and redelivery of commodities, which fortunately was done through the exchange of warehouse receipts rather than the actual commodity. At the Chicago Board of Trade, a warehouse receipt had to be delivered to a member's office, a stipulation that created problems when the volume of deliveries was large. For example, during the delivery of wheat in August of 1881,

Settling clerks rushed from one office to another and chucked in warehouse receipts which were immediately passed to another firm – sometimes through ten or even twenty-five firms – without any memoranda. . . . Some houses received receipts in fulfillment of contracts they never made.[10]

Later in 1881, a new rule provided for all deliveries to occur at one time in the main hall of the Board of Trade. In accordance with this provision, clerks sat at tables, alphabetically, according to their firm's name, and in this manner, huge quantities of grain changed hands within an hour (Taylor 1917: 623, 692). This assemblage of all clerks

---

[9] This description follows Starr (1886).   [10] Quoted in Taylor (1917: 622).

together was the first step toward delivery of only the net amount of a commodity.

Even if all clerks conducted their business at the central location, there was still considerable duplication of effort among those passing warehouse receipts or looking for rings. This duplication of effort could be eliminated if only one clerk, say that of the clearinghouse, checked all lists simultaneously. Not surprisingly, members of the exchanges noted this advantage of increased centralization and the role of clearinghouses in the process of settlement of both monetary differences and differences in the quantities of commodities expanded.

As a result of the further reductions in duplication of effort, modern clearinghouses actively interpose themselves among parties to trades. At the close of trading each day, firms still submit a list of their transactions to their clearinghouse, and the clearinghouse still checks these lists for discrepancies. Then the clearinghouse pays or asks for the balance due on all the transactions of each of its members.[11] Thus, in a modern futures market a trader deals with the clearinghouse, not his fellow members of the exchange. Yet, the clearinghouse is still operating under the principle that motivates ringing up among individual traders. In effect, the clearinghouse forms a giant ring of all the members of the exchange for all their transactions. Further, it applies the principle of settlement by the payment of differences to both quantity and price, so that after settling all the trades, the clearinghouse leaves the member with an outstanding balance of contracts, sold or bought, and an outstanding balance of money, to be paid or received.

As an example of the operation of a modern clearinghouse, suppose a member firm has bought 100,000 pounds (2 contracts) of December cotton at 60.0¢ per pound and sold 50,000 pounds (1 contract) also for delivery in December at 60.3¢ per pound, and that exchange officials set that day's settlement price at 60.2¢ per pound. Having bought at a lower price than the settlement price, the firm will receive 0.2¢ per pound for the 100,000 pounds it bought, or $200.00. Having sold at a price above the settlement price, the firm will receive 0.1¢ per pound for the 50,000 pounds it sold, or $50.00 At that point, the firm's account will read, Bought 100,000 pounds at 60.2¢, sold 50,000 pounds at 60.2¢, with $250.00 due from the clearinghouse. Of course, only the difference in the amount of cotton bought and sold matters, so the final account will read, Bought

---

[11] Generally speaking, clearinghouses are nonprofit associations.

50,000 pounds at 60.2¢ per pound with $250.00 due from the clearinghouse.[12] The original transactions are forgotten, the sale of 50,000 pounds having offset half the purchase of 100,000 pounds.

Thus, after each day's trading, clearinghouses cancel all obligations where a member firm has bought and sold the same commodity for delivery in the same month. That futures contracts are so highly standardized, effectively leaving only the month of delivery and the price open for negotiation, is the reason that so many can be offset before they mature. And because so many are offset and canceled ahead of delivery, futures contracts are effectively traded as if they themselves were a good.

1.2.   Margin money

Modern clearinghouses are concerned not only with the offsetting of contracts, but also with the collecting and disbursing of margin. Margin ensures the proper execution of futures contracts. Although margin is at present associated with clearinghouses, members of futures exchanges like the Chicago Board of Trade collected margin from one another many years before establishing a clearinghouse. And for its part, the clearinghouse of the Chicago Board of Trade had nothing to do with margin for the first forty-odd years of its existence. Thus, clearing and margin can, and should, be kept analytically distinct even if they are intertwined in modern clearinghouses.

Fundamentally, margin enforces performance of futures contracts. The risk of failing to perform a contract arises from swings in the price of commodities. For example, if two parties have contracted for wheat at $4.00 a bushel, the short might refuse to make delivery if the price has risen above $4.00 by the time of delivery, because he could sell his wheat to someone else at a higher price. Likewise, the long might refuse to accept delivery if the price has fallen below $4.00, because he could buy it elsewhere more cheaply.

Futures contracts are protected against fluctuations in price first by original margin and then by variation margin. Original margin is the amount a trader must deposit in order to open a position in a futures contract. In effect, it is a bond for the execution of a contract. It is not, however, a down payment. The person obliged to deliver the commodity must, like the buyer, deposit original margin. If the seller were to make a down payment, he would deposit not the

---

[12] This one contract for 50,000 pounds will be recorded as open interest.

money required for a performance bond but some of the physical commodity.

The amount of original margin a trader must post depends on both the commodity and the size and type of positions he holds. For most futures contracts, original margin is on the order of $1,000 to $2,000 on a contract typically calling for the delivery of $15,000 to $30,000 worth of the commodity.[13] Hence, the performance bond is on the order of a few percent of the value of the contract. Clearinghouses, like individual traders before them, adjust the original margin they require according to the value of the contract and their estimate of the volatility of prices. Whenever prices are skittish because of conflicting reports about the damage from frost, drought, or heat, the clearinghouses raise the original margin.[14] If a member of the clearing association holds an inordinately large portion in one contract or commodity such that liquidating his position might affect the price substantially, the clearinghouse may ask for "super margins," that is, original margin above that required of small traders.

It is often heard how the small amount of original margin provides tremendous "leverage" to investments in futures contracts. A speculator can find his $1,000 doubled or wiped out with just a few cents change in the price of the commodity. This perspective of leverage is a most misleading view of original margin, for two reasons. First, original margin does not represent an investment, against which the speculator measures the profit or loss of his trade by comparing the return to alternative uses for his original margin. At most exchanges, original margin can be deposited as Treasury bills or similar secure, but interest-earning, assets (Edwards 1983). Provided the speculator intends to hold a reasonable number of Treasury bills anyway, he does not care whether the original margin is $1,000 or $10,000 per contract. Second, futures contracts provide leverage to an individual speculator because they involve a large quantity of a commodity, not because of original margin. Moves in the whole position, that is, whether the contract is now worth $20,500 instead of $20,000, are the proper measure of the risk involved in futures contracts. This risk remains the same whether the original margin is $10 or $10,000, and whether the percentage return as measured against the standard of that original margin is 5,000% or 5%.

---

[13] Financial futures usually involve larger lots, on the order of $100,000 worth of the instrument.

[14] Usually this higher requirement applies only to positions initiated subsequently. It should, however, apply retroactively to existing positions as well since both new and old positions are exposed to the same risk of large moves in price.

That original margin for futures contracts can be set so low is due to the existence of the second type of margin, namely variation margin. If prices move against one party to a contract, the original performance bond no longer provides the same degree of protection. The other party, not surprisingly, asks for additional margin, most likely an amount that restores the original margin. For example, if a contract to deliver 5,000 bushels of wheat, requiring $1,000 in original margin, was made at $4.00 a bushel, an increase in price above $4.20 might provoke the short to default on his contract. If this were to happen, the long would have to replace his wheat at say $4.25, paying $4.05 net instead of $4.00.[15] To avoid such default, as the price rose above $4.00, say to $4.10, the long would demand the additional 10¢ per bushel to restore the degree of protection given by the original margin.

The legal right to sell out a trader who fails to keep his margin account current underpins the whole system of enforcing futures contracts.[16] If a short fails to deposit variation margin in a timely manner after a rise in price, the long has the right to purchase the equivalent contract on the open market at the prevailing price, in effect canceling his contract with the defaulting short and replacing him with another party. The short's original margin would be applied to make up for any discrepancy between the current market price and the price stipulated in the contract.

Generally speaking, the party calling for the variation margin asks the other party to make up the difference between the price stipulated in the contract and the market price, or if some variation margin has already been deposited, between the price protected by the previous variation margin and the new market price. Consequently, the system of variation margin is often called "marking to market." Although it could be done more or less frequently, the common practice is to mark to market once a day, except in periods of extreme fluctuations in price, when calls for variation margin will be made several times a day. A convenient estimate of the market price is the settlement price used for the payment of monetary differences. If this settlement price is used as a basis for marking to market, variation margin flows between the accounts of longs and shorts, the direction depending on whether the settlement price is higher or lower than that of the previous day.

---

[15] On 5,000 bushels, $1,000 is 20¢ per bushel, and would go to the long in this case.
[16] Not suprisingly, this legal right was contested at first. See *Corbett* v. *Underwood*, 83 Ill. 324 (1876), *Gregory* v. *Wendell*, 39 Mich. 337 (1878), *Union National Bank of Chicago* v. *Carr*, 15 Fed. Rep. 438 (1883).

Strictly speaking, the system of original and variation margin applies only to members of the exchange, or to be even more precise, to members of the clearing association. Usually clearing members duplicate the system with their customers, but there are some exceptions. For one, although the exchanges (rather than the clearing associations) now set minimum requirements, each futures commission merchant is free to demand, within the limits of the minimum, different levels of original margin from different customers for whom he serves as broker, depending on his judgment of their ability to fulfill their contracts. To protect themselves in especially volatile markets, futures commission merchants often take advantage of this freedom, as witnessed in the fall of 1979 when the price of silver rose extraordinarily. Some brokerage firms required original margin for silver trades several times that of the Commodity Exchange in New York's Clearing Association, which had itself raised original margin considerably. Another exception concerns the frequency with which customers must post additional margin whenever prices move against them. Rather than approach a customer every day for variation margin, futures commission merchants often request a larger amount to begin with, requiring that amount be supplemented only when the balance after payments of variation margin falls below a level designated as maintenance margin. But the biggest difference in the procedures of margin between futures commission merchants and their customers from the operation of margin among clearing members is that while each customer is responsible for margin to the commission merchant, the commission merchant himself is responsible to the clearinghouse only for the net position of all his customers combined. If he has equal numbers of short and long customers, he deposits no original margin with the clearinghouse. The difference between the gross margin he collects and the net margin he himself deposits provides him with considerable sums. Depending on the futures commission merchant, the interest on the original margin, paid in cash more frequently than margin given to the clearinghouse, accrues to its customers' accounts or to its own. Obviously, those commission merchants who retain the interest for themselves must offer other inducements (e.g., lower charges for executing trades) to entice customers.

Although defaults on futures contracts, or what is more symptomatic, failures to keep current with calls for variation margin, are rare, the system of original and variation margin is not certain to protect the integrity of contracts. If a move in price is large and sudden, as with a currency devaluation, the imposition of an embargo, or the collapse of a corner, the original margin may be exhausted before variation margin can be called. Without margin, however, if the party against whom prices moved were to walk away from his contract, the other party's sole recourse would be the time-consuming disciplinary machinery of the exchange and the courts. If the defaulting party declared bankruptcy, the prospect for restitution would be even more problematical. In a sense, the purpose of margin is to avoid the delays and expenses of these other ways of enforcing contracts as much as possible.

For much of the early history of futures exchanges, if a party became bankrupt the person with whom he contracted absorbed any loss left unprotected by margin. Beginning in the 1920s, however, the clearing associations of the major exchanges accepted the responsibility, often unwillingly, of collecting margins and interposing themselves as a party to the trades. Hence, they became responsible for the performance of contracts made between their members. In today's market, even though two members contract between themselves, the identity of the opposite party is lost as soon as the clearinghouse receives notice from them of the transaction after the close of trading. Once the clearinghouse processes the transaction, the long is responsible to the clearinghouse for margin and for accepting delivery, while the short is responsible to the clearinghouse for margin and making delivery. Presumably, the collective backing of all members of the clearing association makes contracts more reliable than dependence on one member alone. Because no large-scale default has tested a clearing association's promise to make good all contracts, it is difficult to judge the value of this collective endorsement.[17] The clearing association's assumption of responsibility for contracts is likely to help most in those cases where the default is isolated, say, because it has more to do with a member's commitments outside the futures market. But because movements in price are marketwide, the clearing association cannot ensure the performance of contracts in all circumstances.

From a broader perspective, the clearinghouse's assumption of responsibility for contracts is a natural evolution of a previous achievement of futures markets. The performance of contracts is assured to a great extent because members of an exchange deal with one

---

[17] During the turmoil in the silver market in late 1979 and early 1980, first the principal shorts and then the principal longs experienced trouble paying variation margin. Had a clearinghouse needed to assess its members for losses of such magnitude (hundreds of millions of dollars), they surely would not have paid without a protracted legal battle.

another as principals, even when they are actually acting as agents for others. Even if a commission merchant's customer were to default, the futures commission merchant would still be responsible to another member of the exchange, or to the clearing association, for the performance of that contract. Upon offering to trade, a member could announce that he was acting as an agent for one of his customers. Other members, however, would naturally prefer to deal with him as a principal because they are in a much better position to judge his financial resources and integrity than those of his customer, especially during the few seconds required to enact a transaction in futures. Moreover, they know he is especially inclined to fulfill his contracts because his livelihood as a futures commission merchant depends on his ability to trade with them.[18] The practice of treating a commission merchant as agent to his customer and principal to his fellow members places the responsibility of monitoring customers' credit ratings and margin accounts on the shoulders of the person in the best position to do so – their broker. For the same reason, the clearinghouse is probably more vigilant in calling margin from members than are individual members themselves for it avoids much duplication in gathering information on financial standing.

In practice, the payment of variation margin to the clearinghouse alters slightly the settlement of contracts by the payment of differences through the clearinghouse. Consider what happens if a clearing member establishes a short position in soybeans. He must first deposit original margin with the clearinghouse of the Chicago Board of Trade. Then, every day he pays or receives variation margin depending on the direction in which the settlement price for soybeans has moved. If he receives variation payments, the money is his free and clear.[19] If he must pay, he is responsible for the prompt depositing of cash or a certified check, or the clearinghouse closes out his position. If he himself takes on a long position, his original position is offset. The payment of differences, however, will not be calculated from the original price of his short position. Rather, it will be calculated from the previous day's settlement price, since the effect of variation margin is to renegotiate the price of the contract

---

[18] The Directors' Papers in the Archives of the Chicago Board of Trade at the University of Illinois in Chicago are filled with requests by members to suspend others from membership until they pay their obligations. Often this threat of suspension persuaded those owing money to pay immediately.

[19] When margin was between individual members, the sum was held in escrow until the contract was executed or rung out.

every day. In any case, all of his obligations end when he offsets his position. Were he to settle his contract by delivery rather than offset, he would deliver his warehouse receipts to the clearinghouse, which would assign them to the long on its books who had held a long position for the greatest amount of time. The identity of the buyer with whom he originally contracted will have long since been forgotten.

1.3.   The spreads among futures prices

Although many people exposed to futures markets for the first time have trouble comprehending the mechanics of initiating a position in futures contracts, paying margin, and closing the position, per- haps what is most confusing to them is the multitude of delivery dates and prices. Yet these prices and the patterns among them are the most interesting aspect of futures markets. Accordingly, now that the rudiments of the mechanics of trading in futures markets have been discussed, the remainder of this chapter will introduce the patterns of prices that emerge from such trading. They have many features difficult to understand at first.

Table 1.1 presents the closing prices of wheat on the Chicago Board of Trade on 6 September 1979, a day and commodity picked to be representative. On that day were traded more than 16,000 wheat contracts calling for delivery in six different months: contracts calling for delivery of 5,000 bushels in September or December '79, or in March, May, July, or September '80.[20] Even though such con- tracts provide for delivery far into the future, by which time many circumstances will have changed, the closing prices in Table 1.1 are in no sense uncertain. At that moment on 6 September, the price was exactly 422¢ per bushel for July delivery. Yet whether a buyer or seller on 6 September has traded at an opportune moment will only be known after time has passed (as with any contract whether for immediate or future delivery).

There is an important distinction between the price of wheat in September and the price as of the previous April for delivery in September. Obviously, it is of interest how these prices compare. The same is true of the price as of April for December delivery and the price prevailing in December. It is also of great interest how the price for September delivery is related to that for December deliv-

---

[20] The use of "September '79" instead of "September 1979" is meant to emphasize that a contract with its own identity is involved; the calendar year is not too important.

Table 1.1. *Spreads in wheat on 6 September 1979*

Month of delivery	Closing price (cents per bushel)	Spread between months (cents per bushel per month)
Immediate	417-½	
September	423-½	3[a]
December	432-¼	2-⅞
March '80	440-¼	2-⅜
May	439-¾	−¼
July	422	−8-⅞
September	428	3

[a]This spread was approximately 3¢ per month after making allowance for the conditions of delivery for spot wheat.

ery, both as of April or both as of early September. Although the behavior of prices as they unfold over time is connected to the relationships among the prices for different dates of delivery as of one moment in time, clearly they are distinct subjects. The study of futures markets concerns, mainly, the relationship among the latter.

Prices for various dates of delivery as of the same moment in time can best be grasped as an array. The spot price for wheat should also be considered part of the array, representing as it does the price of a contract for immediate delivery. On 6 September 1979, wheat for delivery that September sold for 423-1/2¢ per bushel. On that day within the array of futures prices, prices rose through the contract for March '80, where they peaked at 440-1/4¢ per bushel. Wheat for delivery in May was priced slightly less than March, but there was a large drop between the May and July futures, the period during which American farmers harvest wheat. After the conditions within the futures contract for grade and place of delivery (the quoted spot price is for wheat in boxcars rather than elevators) had been accounted for, the September '79 futures price was nearly the spot price, which was 417-1/2¢ per bushel. As September wound down, the spot price and September contract moved ever more closely together.[21]

The relationships among the prices in the array can be seen most easily as spreads. A spread is the price of a more distant month minus the nearer month, adjusted here in Table 1.1 for the span between the times of delivery in order to make them comparable.

[21] Consequently, the expiring contract is often called the "spot month."

For example, if someone bought a December contract and simultaneously sold a March contract at the market's close on 6 September, he would earn 2-5/8¢ per bushel per month by taking delivery in December and redelivering in March. Although few traders actually follow this sequence of first taking delivery and then making delivery, the potential for such action is always present in futures markets. Hence, the spreads between futures prices are related to the costs of holding commodities over time, and they are often called "carrying charges" as a result.[22]

In all futures markets, many traders take on simultaneous positions in two delivery months, buying one month and selling another. Because what matters to these simultaneous positions are the spreads between futures prices rather than the futures prices themselves, their combination of positions in different months of delivery has come to be referred to as a "spread." In some futures markets, such as the Commodity Exchange (Comex) in New York, spreads in the sense of market positions are called "straddles." Of course, a trader could also sell a spread or a straddle, or in other words he could sell a near-term contract and buy a more distant contract. Among some traders the name "bull straddle" is given to a pair of contracts in which the near-term contract is the long position, while in a "bear straddle" the near-term contract is the short position.[23] Straddles and spreads are not restricted to contiguous contracts. A trader could hold a long position in a September contract and a short position in the subsequent July contract, a straddle covering almost a whole year.

The interpretation of a spread as the return to holding commodities illuminates another transaction fundamental to futures markets, that of hedging. Broadly speaking, a hedge is the purchase or sale of a futures contract by a handler of commodities. Thus, it is this type of use of futures markets that this study seeks most to explain. Among handlers of primary commodities, hedgers usually are middlemen and processors. Rarely are farmers hedgers, at least not directly.[24] Flour millers, cotton spinners, coffee roasters, copper fab-

[22] The Chicago Board of Trade (1982: 39-45) provides a good introduction to the concept of "carrying charges."

[23] C. Smith (1982) introduces spreads and straddles, while Jones (1981) describes some of the arcane combinations of positions. Thiessen (1982) discusses spreads from the perspective of the professional speculator.

[24] Farmers often use futures markets indirectly. After a harvest a farmer will bring his grain to his local elevator, intending to wait some time before he sells it to the elevator. Rather than store the grain, the elevator prefers to sell the grain forthwith to someone farther down the line of distribution, its real business being the loading

ricators, and similar processors frequently sell a futures contract while holding inventories of their inputs; these dealers are called "short hedgers." Other dealers, especially exporters, make deals with their customers several months in advance. Because these dealers often buy a futures contract, they are known as "long hedgers." Most hedgers are short hedgers.

A short hedger normally sells a futures contract at the same moment he buys his inventory in the spot market. Likewise, a long hedger most often takes his position in futures simultaneously with his commitments in the cash market. These combinations of two simultaneous transactions are best called hedging operations.

Hedging operations, which comprise one transaction in a futures market and a simultaneous transaction in the cash market, are central to futures markets. From the very word itself, it can be seen that hedging is commonly associated with risk aversion. That association, however, results from confusion on the part of observers who have failed to understand the nature of hedging as one of two simultaneous transactions. The function of futures markets is intimately connected to the function of hedging operations, rather than one of the component transactions, the "hedge." It is by no means obvious that risk aversion motivates dealers' hedging operations.

A hedging operation is like a straddle, a short hedger being simply in the broader class of traders who contract to take delivery at some point in time and promise to redeliver at an even later time. The spread between the spot price and the contract in which the hedge is placed is the short hedger's return for carrying the commodity over the interim.

When examined in relation to spreads, futures prices display many paradoxical features. For instance, as of 6 September 1979 for wheat, the spreads between delivery months, including immediate delivery, although typical, are counterintuitive to a person not familiar with futures markets. In the first place, they were not the same between each set of months. Someone holding wheat in September with a contract to deliver in December would have received 2-7/8¢ per bushel for each intervening month. Similarly he would have received 2-5/8¢ per bushel for each month as the return for wheat

---

of grain into railcars. The elevator substitutes a long position in the futures market for the grain it holds for the farmer. When the farmer decides to sell his already sold grain, the elevator offsets its long position in futures. The farmer does not himself sell originally, substituting a futures contract for his grain, because tax considerations often make it advisable for him to "own" his grain until the next tax year.

taken in delivery in December and held until delivery on the March contract. On the other hand, all wheat contracted to be held between March and May would not only have earned nothing but in fact would have cost 1/4¢ per bushel because the spread was negative. The spread between May and July, −8-7/8¢ per bushel per month, was even more negative than that between March and May. A negative spread has long been called a "backwardation" in the trade, since a negative return to holding wheat seems so contrary to what would commonly be expected given the obvious expenses of storing wheat. Yet backwardations, or "inverse carrying charges" as they are also known, are common to arrays of futures prices.

Another paradoxical feature is that these spreads change day to day and hour to hour. For example, the spread between May and July '80 changed from −8-7/8¢ per bushel per month on 6 September 1979 to only −1/8¢ on 2 November, even though the May contract sold for the same amount as on 6 September. (That is to say, the July futures price rose while that for the May contract did not.) By early January 1980, the May-July spread had moved to −5-1/4¢, and by May, when the May contract expired, it was at a positive 1-1/8¢.

1.4.   The importance of spreads to futures markets

Spreads are the key to understanding futures markets. In fact, if spreads were not different for each pair of delivery months and did not vary from hour to hour, there would be no reason for futures markets to exist. For there to be futures markets for many commodities, something must be special to the spreads for each.

To see the importance of variable spreads to futures markets, consider the simple situation where a competitive economy can consume a finite stock of a natural resource like copper. Suppose it is costless to store the copper. According to well-established models of natural resources, in this world of perfect certainty the equilibrium array of prices at any moment in time, and the realized path of the spot price as well, would be such that the prices for later delivery dates would increase at the rate of interest.[25] If the rate of interest is zero percent per annum, the price of copper for delivery tomorrow would equal that for delivery six days, thirty days, or ten years

---

[25] Strictly speaking this is true only if the marginal cost of extraction is constant. But even if this condition does not hold, the point remains that knowledge of the cost of extraction and the interest rate determines the full array of futures prices. See Fisher (1981) for a survey of this literature.

hence. By simple calculation, the spreads between pairs of futures prices would also be the same, namely zero.

But would a futures market exist under such circumstances? The answer is no. Since prices would be the same regardless of the time of delivery, there would be no need to quote prices for different delivery dates. Any one price would suffice. Such a situation would hardly be what is meant by a futures market, since an active market has not one but several contracts traded in substantial volume (counting a contract for immediate delivery as one in the array of contracts). By extension, from the perspective of spreads, contracts are superfluous whenever spreads are constant.

Of course, this example of constant spreads relies on unique conditions: certainty, constant extraction costs, the absence of storage costs, and an interest rate of zero. Yet the main conclusion would not change if these assumptions were relaxed (Pindyck 1980). Futures markets are necessary only when some spreads cannot be deduced from other spreads.[26]

Imagine what would happen if there were a positive interest rate, with all other conditions remaining the same. With a positive interest rate, the futures price would rise in progression from that for immediate delivery to that for delivery thirty days hence and beyond. Spreads could even be different if there were a term structure to the interest rate (which would imply that the forward interest rate for the day beginning on the twenty-ninth was not the same as the immediate one-day rate). Yet, from the spot price for copper and the interest rates on loans of various durations, it is an easy matter to calculate the full array of futures prices. Consequently, a full array of futures prices is not necessary. For example, the spot price and the interest rate on a thirty-day loan determine, precisely, the price for a contract calling for delivery in thirty days. For that matter, the spot price could be computed from a fifteen-day futures contract with the aid of the fifteen-day loan rate. As long as the only content of spreads is the interest rate over the appropriate period, a fully formed money market makes a copper futures market superfluous.

Conversely, if all variation in spreads could be attributed solely to

---

[26] The absence of forward markets in foreign exchange when exchange rates are fixed also demonstrates that a full array of delivery dates is unnecessary when spreads are constant. Only when the rate for delivery in thirty days differs from the rate for ninety days, say $1.40/£ versus $1.38/£, and moreover only when that relationship could just as well be $1.40/£ versus $1.43/£, is a futures market likely to emerge. Of course, saying that the thirty- and ninety-day rates are no longer locked together is equivalent to saying that the spread between them is volatile.

interest rates, a futures market in copper would make a money market superfluous, since the interest rates could be deduced from the spreads in the array of futures prices. Further, if a copper futures market existed as a replacement for a money market, there would be no place for futures markets in other commodities; the copper market would suffice to convey the interest rates common to the spreads in all markets. Hence, there must be something besides interest rates on money determining spreads or there would not be so many actual futures markets.

By the same reasoning, physical storage costs, which are closely related to interest expenses, cannot explain why so many futures markets are active because physical storage costs can be deduced from other sources. For example, all the grains, including wheat, corn, oats, rye, and soybeans, compete for the same storage space, and as a result the storage rate for all can be deduced from one.[27] Indeed, public elevators usually charge a flat rate per bushel regardless of the particular grain. Consequently, if storage costs were the sole component of spreads, the spreads in any one of the grain futures markets would convey all price information, making other grain futures markets superfluous. For there to be futures markets in many commodities, something must be unique to the spreads of each.

In sum, if spreads for a particular commodity were easily calculated from prices in other markets, there would be no reason for an active futures market in that commodity. For much the same reason, if the spreads between a particular pair of contracts remained the same from period to period, one of the two prices could effortlessly be deduced from the other, eliminating the need to quote both. Thus, to return to the central theme, volatile, distinct spreads are a necessary condition for a viable futures market. From this, it follows that the study of futures markets must ultimately become a study of spreads, and by extension, a theory of futures markets must rest upon an explanation of spreads.

1.5.   The behavior of spreads

Compelling as the theoretical argument for the importance of different and volatile spreads to the existence of futures markets is, it

---

[27] Although all of these grains are rarely grown in the same locality, if corn competes with oats for storage space on one fringe of the corn belt and with soybeans on another, oats effectively compete with soybeans (Paul 1970).

Table 1.2. *Spreads in wheat, 1973-1982 (closing prices as of the first business day in October; spreads expressed in cents per bushel per month)*

Period of spread	1973	1974	1975	1976	1977	1978	1979	1980	1981	1982
Spot-December	-3.7	3.3	6.7	8.0	8.3	-3.0	5.3	8.3	11.7	8.7
December-March	-1.3	4.3	4.8	4.0	3.3	-1.8	5.7	6.3	8.5	6.8
March-May	-10.5	-1.8	1.3	3.3	3.0	-2.3	6.1	4.0	4.3	4.9
May-July[a]	-26.0	-15.8	-7.6	3.3	2.5	-6.3	-10.4	-2.5	-1.8	1.5
July-September	-.5	2.0	2.5	2.3	3.6	1.5	2.8	4.3	9.8	4.5
Price of September contract ($)	3.77	4.58	4.36	3.13	2.83	3.26	4.79	5.22	4.64	3.59

[a]Officially, new-crop contracts begin with July.

remains to be shown whether spreads in actual futures markets are, in fact, volatile and different over each pair of contracts. It has already been demonstrated (Table 1.1) that in 1979 spreads in wheat did, indeed, vary. But is this behavior exceptional, or typical of other years and other commodities? The answer is that spreads in all futures markets are volatile and different for each pair of contracts. Table 1.2, for example, displays the spreads in wheat as of the first day in October for a period of ten years, 1973-1982.[28] Similar tables (1.3 and 1.4) will be presented for two other commodities, soybean oil and copper.

The most cursory examination of Table 1.2 confirms the behavior of spreads seen in Table 1.1 for wheat as of 6 September 1979. Rarely are the spreads between two sets of pairs the same. Likewise, the value for a particular pair, say December-March, never repeats. This pattern of different and volatile spreads is not an artifice of a general trend over the decade. Compare 1 October 1976 to 1 October 1978, dates on which the prices of wheat for delivery the following September were nearly equal. In 1976 the spreads were all positive; in 1978 four of five were negative. That is to say, in October 1976 the spot price stood well below the price for delivery the following September, while in 1978 it was well above that contract's price. A comparison of 1979 to 1981 also reveals a considerable diversity in the spreads despite the September contracts selling for much the same price.

A striking feature of the wheat spreads in Table 1.2 is the number of negative values. Fifteen out of the fifty listed display a backwardation, some decidedly so. In October 1973 the backwardation was so pronounced that the March contract sold for $4.52 while the July contract sold for $3.78. If the significance of such values is not immediately obvious, consider this perspective: Over those four months in 1973 wheat was expected to lose nearly 20% of its value.

A large negative component to spreads becomes even more prevalent than already observed if capital costs, warehouse fees, insurance, and similar known and unavoidable costs of carrying wheat are accounted for. Far more often than not, spreads are less than full carrying charges. For example, referring to the December-March spread in wheat as of October 1980, the value of 6.3¢ per bushel per month is one of the larger positive values in Table 1.2. A spread of that magnitude is equivalent to a 15% annual increase on an investment in wheat of about $5.00 a bushel. If in order to make this

---

[28] October was chosen so that several of the contracts would be in the next crop-year.

investment, firms borrowed on the security of wheat, they surely paid several percentage points above the riskless rate as measured by the interest rate for the federal government. Because in the fall of 1980 interest rates for government securities were 15%, the 6.3¢ did not even cover the capital costs of storing wheat. If warehousing and insurance fees, which amount to several percent per annum, are also subtracted away, what is seemingly a generous positive spread becomes negative.

Allowance for known carrying costs should be made for all the spreads listed in Table 1.2. The proper calculation is to subtract from the spreads the known warehousing fees and the array of capital costs, as represented by the term structure of interest rates at the same moment in time as the observations on the spreads. This calculation would turn most of the other positive values listed into negative numbers. Sometimes spreads are at full carrying costs, so that this calculation would leave a value of zero. Never are spreads above full carrying costs. The reason for no spreads above full carrying charges is simple: the power of arbitrage. If a more distant futures contract stood above the nearer contract by more than the known costs of carry, anyone could make a riskless profit by buying the nearby contract while selling the distant contract and arranging a loan for the necessary funds. Thus, the appropriate standard is how spreads compare to full carrying charges. Negative spreads are unambiguously below full carrying charges. On close inspection many positive spreads are also below full carrying charges. The sign of a spread is less important than the degree to which it falls below full carrying charges.

The May-July spread in wheat tends to fall the most below the standard of full carrying costs, while the December-March spread is usually closer to full carrying costs. From this comparison alone, it might appear that spreads become more negative with increasing time from the present. But the spreads are not simply a function of the time from the present. The most distant spread in Table 1.2, July-September, one in which both contracts are in the new crop-year, is generally close to full carrying costs.

Regardless of these general patterns in spreads, it is impossible to predict one spread from another. For example, the December-March spread is nearly the same in 1974, 1975, and 1976. Yet the March-May spreads are different each of these three years. Just as the December-March price is not a complete guide to the March-May spread, the March-May spread tells only a limited amount about the May-July spread. It is in fact the individuality of these spreads that prompts trading in the distinct contracts for delivery in March, May, July, September, and December.

Wheat is not singular in its pattern of backwardations. Soybeans, and their products, meal and oil, demonstrated during that same period an even stronger tendency toward spreads below full carrying charges. Table 1.3 presents those in soybean oil. The spreads were exceptionally negative in 1974. Translated back into the original prices, those negative spreads signify that the price of soybean oil for delivery that March, namely $33.80 per 100 pounds, stood at a substantial premium over the price of the January 1975 contract, which was selling for $21.20 at the same time. In effect, soybean oil for delivery ten months later was selling at a 40% discount from oil for immediate delivery.

A comparison of the spreads in soybean oil to those in wheat shows that although spreads below full carrying charges may emerge at much the same time,[29] there is sufficient independent movement among them to ensure that the spreads in one commodity cannot be deduced from those in another. The spreads in soybean oil in 1975, for instance, were more negative relative to other years than were those for the same crop-year in wheat, as registered in October of 1974.[30] Further, in some years in the early 1980s the spreads in wheat were negative while those in soybean oil were positive. Finally, in wheat the first spread in which two contracts occur in the new crop-year (i.e., the July-September spread) was almost always positive and close to full carrying charges, while in soybean oil the majority of spreads within the new crop-year (e.g., December-January) were negative. Such diversity between the arrays of prices for wheat and soybean oil is sufficient to require separate futures markets for each.

From an inspection of the spreads in soybean oil in Table 1.3, one can deduce that there is a strong seasonal component related to the cycle of the crop-year in the spreads at any one moment in time. Generally speaking, those spreads covering later periods in the crop-year, such as August-September, are farther below full carrying charges than spreads from earlier in the crop-year, such as December-January. The same seasonality in spreads can be found in wheat in Tables 1.1 and 1.2. From this pattern of seasonality in spreads, one might make the further deduction that a cycle like a crop year is necessary for the emergence of different and negative spreads.

---

[29] The years 1974, 1978, and 1979, for example.
[30] This statement is true even if the spreads are measured on the same business day, which they are not in the tables here.

Table 1.3. Spreads in soybean oil, 1974-1983 (closing prices as of the first business day in March; spreads expressed in dollars per 100 lb. per month)

Period of spread	1974	1975	1976	1977	1978	1979	1980	1981	1982	1983
March-May	-2.60	-.40	.09	.20	-.25	.10	.35	.40	.30	.20
May-July	-1.40	-.40	.11	.15	-.10	.05	.25	.40	.30	.17
July-August	-.95	-.70	.03	.05	-.25	.00	.30	.35	.25	.15
August-September	-1.00	-1.05	.12	.05	-.45	-.40	.30	.30	.20	.15
September-October[a]	-1.00	-.55	.02	-.20	-.60	-.45	.25	.30	.25	.14
October-December	-.40	-.50	.09	-.02	-.10	-.05	.20	.30	.20	.15
December-January	-.90	-.40	.10	.05	-.10	.00	.15	.30	.15	.15
Price of January contract ($)	21.20	20.25	17.60	24.45	21.35	24.60	25.10	26.70	20.95	18.20

[a]Officially, new-crop contracts begin with October.

This idea that the cycle of the crop-year is responsible for the pattern in spreads can be tested by observing a commodity with much less seasonal demand or supply, such as copper. The top half of Table 1.4 records the spreads in copper on Comex as of the first business day in January for the years 1974-1983. Compared to the spreads in wheat or soybean oil, far fewer of those in copper are negative; those that are negative all appear in 1974. In fact, the spreads in copper display full carrying charges much more frequently than those in agricultural products. The 0.50¢ spread (per month) between the January 1975 and March 1975 contracts, for instance, was just about equal, after subtraction of the warehouse and insurance fees of somewhat less than 0.1¢ per pound per month, to the expense of carrying copper at the interest rate implicit in ninety-day commercial paper. Thus, spreads in copper would seem to support the deduction that strongly seasonal demand or supply is necessary for different spreads.

But, in fact, the evidence of copper spreads is misleading. Spreads should be inspected for the extent they fall below full carrying charges, not the nominal amount. In the bottom half of Table 1.4, full carrying costs have been subtracted from the spreads.[31] By happenstance the level of full carrying charges changed over the period 1974-1983 in such a way as to make spreads in copper appear more constant than they really were. The evidence from copper actually indicates that spreads can be different and below full carrying charges without a cycle like a crop-year.

The rising interest rates over the decade made many of the spreads in copper positive when they would otherwise have been negative, thereby disguising that they were below full carrying charges. A higher interest rate adds to the carrying cost, with the result that spreads are more likely to be positive even without covering the carrying costs. In 1980, for example, whatever the maturity of a loan, the interest rate was at least 1.3% per month. With that opportunity cost to invested capital, the observed spreads should have been on the order of 1.50¢ per month for copper to have been at full carrying charges. At .10¢ to .15¢ per month they were a tiny fraction of that, however. Had the interest expenses been lower and

---

[31] The carrying charges are a reconstruction of the prevailing interest and warehousing expenses. Inevitably this exercise is not exact. Long after the fact it is not clear which interest rate, among the prime rate, the commercial paper rate, the banker's acceptance rate, and so forth, is appropriate. Also the various warehouses had slightly different fees. Of course, traders at the time would have been aware of the exact carrying charge.

Table 1.4. Spreads in copper, 1974-1983 (closing prices as of the first business day in January; spreads expressed in cents per pound per month)

Period of spread	1974	1975	1976	1977	1978	1979	1980	1981	1982	1983
January-March	-4.60	.45	.40	.40	.40	.75	1.45	1.30	.80	.60
March-May	-1.40	.55	.50	.45	.50	.75	.15	1.30	.85	.55
May-July	-1.00	.60	.45	.45	.50	.70	.10	.95	.85	.55
July-September	-.60	.60	.45	.45	.45	.55	.15	.85	.85	.60
September-December	-.60	.65	.35	.45	.45	.45	.15	.80	.80	.70
Price of December contract ($)	80.60	58.50	59.60	67.40	65.50	75.30	112.70	99.40	83.40	75.75
Spreads after removal of carrying charges										
January-March	-5.20	.00	.00	.00	-.05	.00	.00	.00	-.10	.00
March-May	-2.10	.00	.00	.00	-.05	.00	-1.30	.00	-.10	-.05
May-July	-1.65	.00	.00	.00	-.05	-.05	-1.30	-.20	-.10	-.05
July-September	-1.20	.00	.00	-.05	-.05	-.25	-1.25	-.30	-.10	-.05
September-December	-1.15	.00	-.05	-.05	-.05	-.35	-1.20	-.40	-.15	.00

the spreads been below full carrying charges by the same amount, the observed spreads would have been negative. (In fact, in early December 1979 all spreads in copper were negative.)

Interest rates have another more subtle effect in disguising the spreads in copper. Several times by coincidence the term structure of interest rates at the time made the spreads look more rather than less similar to one another. In the spreads listed in Table 1.4 for 1977, for instance, spreads were essentially all the same. But at that time, the pattern in the term structure of interest rates was one of increasing rates, the rate for 180 days and the rate for one year both being higher than the 90-day rate. Because money for a one-month loan was more expensive for periods beginning in the future, the spreads in copper should have been slightly larger, not the same, with increasing time to the maturity of the first contract in the pair. Sometimes the pattern in interest rates conspired to make even those spreads that were different look less different. In 1979 the observed array of spreads moved inversely in relation to time of delivery while the term structure of interest rates was rising slightly. Only if the term structure of interest rates was falling (as in 1981) could a pattern of declining spreads have been consistent with full carrying charges.

In nine of the ten years from 1974 through 1983 at least some of the spreads in copper failed to display full carrying charges, sometimes, as in 1974 and 1980, by a considerable margin. That any spreads in copper were less than full carrying charges is suprising in itself. Because copper is a natural resource, having little seasonality in production or demand, and large reserves of scrap, the presumption would be strong that its price should increase to cover interest and storage costs, as presumed in most models of natural resources. Thus, even the spreads in copper display the paradoxical features of the spreads in wheat and soybean oil, although not as strongly.

This discussion of spreads in copper, soybean oil, and wheat has concerned the behavior of a spread between a particular pair of contracts as observed once each year. A related issue is the movement over time of one spread during the lives of its constituent contracts. A particular spread is usually highly volatile during its life, often moving hour to hour. Such volatility is not perverse randomness. Rather it is the reaction of spreads to underlying economic facts, which change often. As an example of the frequency with which a particular spread moves, consider the time series of the spread between the September '79 and the October '79 contracts in soybean oil from the moment both were first traded in early October of 1978 through the close of trading of the September '79 contract in September 1979.[32] Although the volatility of this spread was probably higher than average, it is, nonetheless, indicative of movements in spreads. Table 1.5 gives its value, as well as the price of the September '79 contract, every ten business days. Over the course of a year the spread between the September '79 and October '79 contracts was first −$.25, fell to −$1.20, rose at one point in June to $.10, and fell again to a low of −$1.80. Some of the observed volatility in this spread comes from rounding the prices of soybean oil, which trades in "ticks" of 5¢ per 100 pounds, making spreads somewhat imprecise. Yet rounding cannot account for all of the variability in the spread.

Relative to the absolute price of soybean oil, these movements in the spread were not trivial. A spread of −$1.20 in relation to the $26.60 for the September contract represented a discount of 4.5% for the price of the October contract. Such a discount is comparable to that on a thirty-day Treasury bill, which reflects the greater value of money delivered immediately over that delivered 30 days later. If the discounts on soybean oil were expressed as annual equivalents, as are those for money, the volatility of the September '79-October '79 spread corresponded to movements in a forward thirty-day interest rate of 13% to 54% to −5% and back to 71%. Such fluctuations are indeed large given that within a year movements of even a few percent, say from 10% to 13%, in the discount rate on Treasury bills are considered extreme.

With fluctuations of such magnitude week to week, movements in storage fees cannot account for the observed volatility of spreads. Public warehouses' fees for agricultural commodities are stable year to year, let alone week to week.[33] Likewise, over the last decade, warehouse fees in copper have changed only a few times.[34] Insurance fees also are adjusted infrequently. Moreover, insurance fees are extremely small, being on the order of 0.05¢ per month for grains (Chicago Board of Trade 1982: 40). Nor are movements in interest rates, and by extension capital costs, large enough to explain

---

[32] For other examples of the volatility of spreads, see Kallard (1982), ContiCommodity (1983), and Castelino and Vora (1984).

[33] For example, as of late 1982, Continental Grain, one of the four companies running registered grain warehouses in Chicago, had not changed its storage fee in three years (conversation with Thomas Dreps, Cash Grain Department, Continental Grain).

[34] Conversation with Ronald Andresen, Director, Metal Services, Comex. Likewise, the warehouses registered with the London Metal Exchange change their rates no more often than every few years.

Table 1.5. *Movement in a spread in soybean oil (closing prices per 100 lb. every ten business days)*

Date	September '79 contract($)	Spread between September '79 and October '79 contracts ($)
2 October '78	23.80	−.25
17 October	24.25	−.45
31 October	24.90	−.25
15 November	23.55	−.05
30 November	23.85	−.20
14 December	24.20	−.25
29 December	24.00	−.35
15 January '79	24.45	−.60
29 January	24.40	−.50
12 February	26.10	−.95
27 February	26.60	−1.20
13 March	25.95	−.75
27 March	27.00	−.95
10 April	26.05	−.55
25 April	26.30	−.45
9 May	26.05	−.25
23 May	26.40	−.25
7 June	26.15	.00
21 June	28.35	.00
6 July	28.05	−.20
20 July	29.20	−.50
3 August	26.70	−.30
17 August	27.85	−.90
31 August	29.35	−1.40
17 September	30.45	−.60

the magnitude of movements in spreads, just as the term structure of interest rates is almost never as pronounced as the pattern of spreads in an array of futures prices.

As a first approximation, therefore, a theory of futures markets can ignore interest expenses and physical storage costs like warehouse fees. They are trivial and essentially constant components of spreads. (That is not to say, however, that storage behavior is unimportant to futures prices.) Because futures markets would not exist without variable spreads, the remaining negative component of a spread is crucial to the existence of futures markets. Consequently, a study of futures markets reduces to a study of the negative component of spreads. And the fundamental question about futures markets becomes,

"What makes spreads fall below full carrying charges?" Because spreads are the return to storing a commodity over a particular period of time, the question may be restated as, "Why do firms so frequently store commodities seemingly at a loss?"

1.6.   Spreads and storage

Higinbotham (1976), for one, suggests that the paradoxes of spreads are the misleading result of averaging what will happen in the future. Recognizing that there might be times in the future when firms store nothing because the prevailing spot price is high, Higinbotham points out that averaging those periods of no storage with those of storage at full carrying charges would result in the average spread being less than the full carrying charge. If such circumstances were the case, Higinbotham concludes that the paradoxical implications of spreads below full carrying charges would be an illusion, because firms would actually be storing only at full carrying charges at the times they store.

Higinbotham's argument is consistent with rational, competitive storage, as long as marginal storage costs are not negative. When the marginal cost of storage is greater than or equal to zero, as it would be if the only cost of storage were physical costs like warehouse fees, competitive storers will occasionally find it unprofitable to store anything.[35] Such behavior is desirable from society's perspective because when the marginal cost of storage is greater than or equal to zero it is not optimal to store so much that supplies will never be short, despite the discomfort of a small harvest. The prospect of some periods with no storage makes spreads in the current array average out to be less than full carrying charges. Picture what happens in those periods when out of current availability it is optimal that there be no storage, say because of a poor harvest. Current plantings, which will not be harvested until the next period, cannot alleviate the current shortage. Thus, the current price could rise to any level while the price for delivery next period remains low.

---

[35] Theoretically, a competitive, profit-maximizing storer stores up to the point where the cost of what he puts into store plus his marginal cost of storage equals the expected price. The collective implications of such behavior on the part of many storers is difficult to derive in practice because the price expected in a future period is a function of what storers will be doing in the those periods. In other words, it is not possible to know how much will be stored for a given level of current availability until that behavior has been derived. This complicated problem in dynamic programming has been examined by several authors, first by Gustafson (1958), and most recently and more generally by Wright and Williams (1982).

Under such circumstances the spread between the price for immediate delivery and that for delivery next period will be negative. A poor harvest, by causing the immediate consumption of all available supplies, whether from the current harvest or from previous storage, will set off a pattern of futures prices in which each price decreases with length of time to delivery. With nothing being stored for the next period, total availability, in expectation, will be lower next period than is the long-run average, and hence the chances of running short next period are higher than average. In addition, if the next harvest is large rather than small, there will be pressure to rebuild stocks to a more normal level. These two effects will combine to make the expected price next period higher than that for the period following. Further, the latter will be higher than the prices expected for still more distant periods as of the present. Yet any storage that actually occurs is undertaken only at full carrying charges.

Higinbotham's argument requires that observed storage sometimes be zero. As it happens, for all commodities stocks never fall to zero. This is even more a regularity in the world than spreads below full carrying charges. Never in the more than one hundred years that the Chicago Board of Trade has compiled the statistics has the visible supply of wheat, corn, and oats fallen to zero. Similarly, all available statistics on other commodities, from plywood to copper, support the observation that stocks never reach zero. They are often low compared to their average levels, but they never fall to zero. Hence, there is always some connection between the present price and the future. By implication, spreads below full carrying charges are not an artifact resulting from periods of no storage.

Thus, despite its intuitive and theoretical appeal, Higinbotham's explanation of spreads is inappropriate.[36] The mystery of spreads below full carrying charges remains, compounded by the persistence of storage in the face of such spreads. This is not to say that storers are behaving irrationally. Rather, some important motivation for storage has been ignored. The effective marginal cost of storage must include something more than warehousing fees and capital costs, or more properly, there must be some element subtracted from these known costs. Even if the readily observed costs of storage like warehousing fees are immaterial, an analysis of futures markets

---

[36] What is still valid about Higinbotham's argument is that any spread not including the contract for immediate delivery is a forward spread. As such it is an expectation of the spread that will actually prevail and need not be one of the actual values.

must center on storage behavior. Articles that examine models of the formation of futures prices for unstorable commodities, like Feiger (1978), Danthine (1978), or Kawai (1983b), offer few insights into the reasons for the existence of futures markets.

A skeptic might question on three counts the assertion that there is always something in store. First, one might wonder how there can always be something in store for commodities that are not storable, such as live hogs, or that are not yet in existence, such as ninety-day Treasury bills for delivery one year from the present. Although storage behavior is one step removed in the array of futures prices for live hogs or T-bills, the observed spreads are still intimately connected with storage. There is some flexibility in when hogs are brought to slaughter and how quickly they are fed, feed being a storable commodity. Live hogs being marketed continuously, these adjustments become the equivalent of storage. Meanwhile, T-bills involve money, which is preeminently a storable commodity. Treasury bills can be re-created by taking the money they return upon maturity, holding it, and buying another T-bill when desired.

Second, a skeptic might argue that the statistics on known nationwide visible supply are misleading, due to the difficulty in measuring stocks, as, for example, if the reporting units do not carefully distinguish between old-crop and new-crop stocks. But this suspicion is unfounded because negative spreads emerge during periods earlier than those in which a new crop could possibly be harvested.

As a third possible reservation, one might argue that strictly speaking the spreads in futures prices apply only to the specific places where delivery takes place on the futures contracts. The stocks measured in visible supply might be too far away from the delivery points for it to be profitable to ship them there quickly despite the higher price of early delivery over late delivery at the delivery point. Under such circumstances, at the delivery point there might be no stocks, while where the stocks actually remain, the carrying charges might well be full. There are two rejoinders to this third criticism. The first is that negative spreads are not a temporary aberration in futures prices. They often appear months in advance of the times of delivery. Surely that is sufficient notice to induce a slightly faster flow of produce from interior points to the distributional centers. The second and more important rejoinder is that the certified stocks in registered warehouses, precisely those stocks that are eligible for delivery on futures contracts, never fall to zero. There has always been at least some wheat in store in the elevators in

Table 1.6. *Soybeans in store in Chicago (1,000 bushels in registered warehouses)*

Friday in September	1972	1973	1974	1975	1976
First	8,036	3,423	5,017	1,283	7,197
Second	7,949	3,154	4,939	1,234	6,108
Third	7,082	3,049	4,952	1,147	5,055
Fourth	6,164	3,508	5,013	1,404	4,973

Chicago since the figures were first kept in the 1860s.[37] This is true even of soybeans, which throughout the 1970s often displayed extremely negative spreads between old-crop and new-crop futures.[38] If stocks of any commodity were ever to have hit zero in registered warehouses, soybeans in the period 1972 through 1975 were a likely candidate. Yet, as is visible in Table 1.6, the smallest amount of soybeans recorded in the 1970s in Chicago was 1,147,000 bushels on September 19, 1975. This amount was on the order of two weeks' normal consumption or shipment from Chicago.

It is precisely the persistence of stocks like those of soybeans in Chicago in 1975 that is so perplexing. There was seemingly plenty of inducement to dispose of those stocks, since, judging from the spread between the August and September '75 futures contracts, soybeans were expected to lose 16¢ per bushel, 2.5% of their total value, over the month from late August to late September, which for the more than 1 million bushels in store during September amounts to some $200,000. In 1973, the cost of keeping the more than 3 million bushels in store in Chicago was more than $2.1 million. This expense was even larger nationwide. The total stock of old-crop soybeans as of 1 September 1973 was 60 million bushels, the smallest carryover of the decade (although it was still some 4% of the crop being then harvested). As of 1 August 1973, the spread between the spot price and the August futures contract, on which deliveries were eligible until the end of the month, was −$1.30 per bushel. This suggests that the holders of those 60 million bushels paid on the

---

[37] It might be argued further that such measured stocks are minuscule amounts left in the bottoms of elevator bins. Although oil pipelines must contain an irreducible minimum to keep operating, nothing prevents a grain elevator from being emptied. (Conversation with Thomas Dreps, Cash Grain Department, Continental Grain.)

[38] Also see Duddy (1931) for statistics about storage in Chicago in the 1920s.

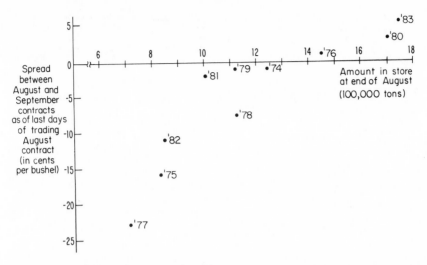

Figure 1.1. Spreads and soybeans stored in oil mills, 1974–1983

order of $78 million, quite apart from physical storage costs, for the privilege of keeping them in store that one extra month.

Although holders of soybeans will pay dearly for the privilege of keeping soybeans in store, they do adjust the amount they keep in store to the cost. Whenever the loss on storage is high, storage is low, and vice versa. This pattern of responsiveness to the extent spreads fall below full carrying charges is so strong that it emerges in even the crudest plots. Figure 1.1 plots the amount of soybeans held at oil mills, which are the major processors of soybeans, on the last day of August against the representative spread, as of mid-August, between the August and September contracts on the Chicago Board of Trade, for the years 1974 through 1983. Even without the refinement of adjustments to the spreads for warehouse fees and capital expenses and without the refinement of adjustments for increases in mill capacity, a strong relationship stands out. The relationship between spreads and storage appears to be slightly nonlinear. Plots with the amount in warehouses in Chicago or the amount of the national carryover would show the same shape.

This strong relationship between the extent spreads fall below full carrying charges and the amount in store is true of all primary commodities and all periods. Working (1934) was the first to observe this pattern, in his case for wheat over the period 1885 through 1933. Such relationships held throughout the crop-year, not just for

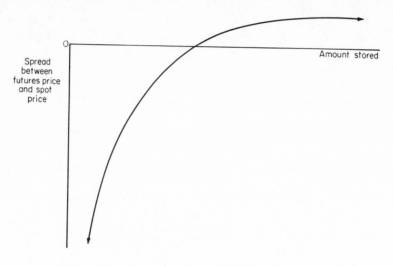

Figure 1.2. The supply of storage

the carryover between crop-years. Telser (1958) and Gray and Peck (1981) have found the pattern in wheat continuing to hold. Howell (1956) and Telser (1958) found the same configuration for cotton, Weymar (1974) for cocoa. For the interwar years, Brennan (1958) found extremely strong patterns for commodities as diverse as shell eggs, cheese, butter, and oats.

Working (1949) generalized this common pattern into what he called the supply-of-storage curve. His supply-of-storage curve is illustrated in Figure 1.2. Clearly it captures well the relationship between soybeans at oil mills and the spread in soybean futures. When stocks are large, spreads are positive, if not at the extreme of full carrying charges. Once at full carrying charges, stocks can be increased considerably without an accompanying change in spreads; as noted in section 1.5, the cost of physical storage is effectively constant over broad ranges of amounts stored. Yet what really determines the shape of the supply-of-storage curve is the mysterious negative component to spreads.

1.7.   An outline of the remaining chapters

In sum, two facts about commodity markets emerge persistently. First, spreads between futures prices rarely cover the known carrying costs of storing commodities. Second, firms that handle commodities always, taken together, keep some in store, adjusting the quantity to the extent spreads fall below full carrying charges. Together, these two facts pose the central question about the pattern of prices found in futures markets. Why do supposedly rational, profit-seeking firms regularly hold stocks when it is expensive for them to do so?

The answer advanced in this book is that firms hold stocks of physical commodities for much the same reasons they hold money. Because of the great difficulty and expense in moving commodities like wheat or copper quickly to where they are needed, firms will hold commodities despite spreads below full carrying charges. To keep their processing plants running smoothly in the face of the uncertain timing of the arrivals of their orders and supplies, they will pay to hold inventory. Therefore, the negative component to spreads is what firms pay for keeping inventories on hand and, thus, is equivalent to the expense of holding cash, measured as foregone interest.

The parallel between money and commodities like soybean oil and copper may be extended even further to encompass economic function, that of a futures market being similar to that of a money market. The sale of a futures contract in conjunction with the purchase of wheat in the spot market allows a firm to borrow wheat.[39] Because these loans of wheat are implicit in double transactions, it is not immediately apparent that they are loans when each transaction is analyzed separately. Nevertheless, the whole array of contracts, from immediate delivery to the most distant delivery, allows a flourishing loan market to function for a particular commodity. The spreads between the contracts, after subtraction of warehousing fees and the capital expense of holding inventory, are the charge for borrowing a commodity. These differences in the spreads between different pairs of futures contracts represent a much more pronounced term structure to the interest rates on wheat and copper than to the interest rates on money. Futures markets are active when there is a strong need to borrow and lend commodities and when the rates on these loans of commodities are different for different periods of the year. Just as a loan market for money helps put funds into the hands of people whose need is greatest at that moment, futures markets allocate the amount and location of inventories, serving to see that stocks are always in the hands of dealers whose need is most immediate.

The notion that futures markets are closely related to money mar-

---

[39] Paul (1966) has also observed this about hedging operations.

kets is contrary to the dominant view today, which sees futures markets as markets for insurance. The view advanced here is, however, similar to the one that Working put forth in his papers on the supply of storage (1948, 1949, 1953a, 1953b). Although many people today recognize these papers as classics in the literature on futures markets, they do not recognize that Working's theory is incompatible with the prevailing portfolio theory of hedging. This book is basically an attempt to place Working's theory again at the center of the understanding of futures markets. It is hoped that here Working's insights are supported with new evidence and more illuminating theory, specifically those theories developed recently about the demand for money and about the role of financial intermediation. Yet if readers take away only a renewed appreciation for Working, the purpose of this book will be fulfilled.

Chapter 3 in particular will seek to discredit the prevailing view of futures markets as closely related to insurance markets. That chapter will reexamine the presumed behavior of a risk-averse dealer in commodities, and in the process it will demonstrate that a more reasonable effect of risk aversion than conventionally assumed is that more risk aversion leads dealers to use futures markets less. But before this discussion, Chapter 2 will seek to establish the view of futures markets as loan markets by demonstrating that the double transaction of buying a spot and selling a futures contract (i.e., what has been defined here as a hedging operation) is equivalent to borrowing the commodity. The introduction of the concept of an implicit market as well as an investigation of actual loan markets in commodities will be essential to this line of argument. These concepts will be used repeatedly in disproving the theories based on risk aversion, as well as the more important task, which will be begun in Chapter 4, of establishing the theoretical foundations for the view of futures markets as similar to markets for money. Chapter 4 will focus on the motivation behind a firm's desire to borrow commodities, establishing that risk-neutral dealers have sufficient reason to use futures markets. Thus, it will become clear that risk aversion is neither a necessary nor a sufficient reason for futures markets. Chapter 5 will explore in more detail the connection between physical commodities and money, as well as that between futures markets and money markets, and will address the question of why, out of all the possible ways of arranging loans of commodities, futures markets have emerged as the dominant institution. Finally, Chapter 6 will use the parallels with money markets to answer a perennial question: Why do so few futures markets exist? A short conclusion will follow as Chapter 7.

CHAPTER 2

Equivalent ways to borrow and lend commodities

Often it is possible to construct a position in a good implicitly from an appropriate combination of positions in other goods. Speculators and dealers in commodities frequently do just that. Speculators often construct spreads in two futures contracts between two different delivery months or between a raw material and a final product. Dealers, by definition, combine their positions in futures contracts with positions in a physical commodity. The view argued in this chapter is that these spreads and hedging operations are prime examples of two simultaneous transactions meant to accomplish implicitly something fundamentally different from either of the component transactions alone. Spreads and hedging operations are implicit positions in the borrowing and lending of commodities.

Because of the possibility of constructing positions implicitly, a wide variety of ways exist to trade many goods and services, although often the equivalence of particular methods of trading goes unnoticed. In general, one system of trading may well be far easier to examine and to understand than its equivalent systems, with the fortunate result that the analysis and insights extend to the equivalent systems. As it happens there are several systems of trading equivalent to that of spot markets and futures markets, specifically those involving loan markets for commodities. By recognizing the equivalence of these ways to trade, it can be established that hedging operations and spreads involve loans of commodities.

The salient feature of futures markets is precisely the frequency with which positions in futures contracts are combined with other positions. Generally speaking, at least one-half and probably three-fourths of the open interest in all active futures markets is part of a combined operation. Table 2.1 shows the proportion of futures contracts combined with other positions for eight representative markets, as reported monthly by the Commodity Futures Trading Commission (CFTC). Based on traders who hold positions above some specified number of contracts, say 50 or 100 depending on the size of the market, the reports distinguish among long hedging, short hedging, long speculation, short speculation, and speculative spread-

41

ing. Three of these five categories, namely long hedging, short hedging, and speculative spreading, represent futures contracts held in combination with other positions. The proportion of reported long and short positions in these three categories is usually above 85%. That proportion does, however, overstate the extent to which futures are part of combined transactions because hedgers are disproportionately represented among traders large enough to file the positions with the CFTC. On the other hand, these three categories as a proportion of total open interest long and short (the second column) understates the percentage of combined positions because small hedgers and small spreaders are not included. Thus, an estimate of the importance of combined operations has an upper bound near 85% and a lower bound typically near 50%.

The extent of combined operations is perhaps most surprising among those classified as speculators, that is, among those who are not dealers in commodities. In all eight markets shown in Table 2.1, speculative spreading as a fraction of reported speculation is above 40%; in the soybean and soybean oil markets the fraction is above 70%. In several markets, reported speculative spreading, especially that of soybeans, is above 15% of total open interest. As can be seen in the last column of Table 2.1, many speculators report these spread positions.

By any measure, therefore, the implicit positions resulting from speculative spreading, short hedging operations, and long hedging operations are the vital part of futures markets. Thus, understanding the purpose of these combined operations is tantamount to understanding the purpose of futures markets themselves. The course of this chapter is first to develop the concepts of implicit markets and equivalent ways to trade and then to apply them to these combined positions so important to futures markets.

2.1.   Implicit markets

In the rarefied world of general equilibrium theory, markets exist for every imaginable good and service. In the real world, however, the substantial costs of operating markets keep their number to the necessary minimum. Tremendous pressure exists for one institution to do the work of two, or for two explicit markets to provide in addition the trading opportunities of a third. For instance, in the textile industry the price of spinning is implicit in the difference between the price of yarn and the price of cotton. A trader who owns cotton can implicitly purchase the spinning service by selling

Table 2.1. Extent of spreading in futures markets (average of end-of-month reports for 1979 and 1980, with standard deviations in parentheses)

Commodity	As a % of 2 × open interest				Number of reporting speculators		
	Reported positions long and short	Reported hedging and speculative spreading	Reported speculative spreading	Speculative spreading as a % of reported speculation	Long	Short	Spreads
Corn[a]	67.0 (3.8)	62.0 (4.4)	6.8 (1.5)	60.2 (9.2)	63	24	61
Soybeans[a]	64.0 (3.1)	58.5 (3.2)	20.7 (2.3)	78.8 (4.0)	55	41	112
Soybean oil	73.8 (2.6)	66.7 (3.7)	17.2 (3.0)	71.0 (5.7)	34	15	39
Live hogs	41.5 (2.7)	22.7 (3.2)	15.9 (3.0)	45.7 (7.0)	39	40	40
Bellies[a]	40.4 (5.2)	20.7 (4.1)	14.9 (4.1)	42.8 (9.9)	41	64	52
Sugar[b]	62.4 (2.9)	52.9 (3.4)	8.7 (2.3)	48.2 (10.2)	40	12	28
Cotton	61.8 (3.4)	53.2 (4.2)	10.2 (2.4)	54.2 (6.2)	46	13	32
Platinum	38.6 (4.4)	27.8 (4.0)	9.3 (3.5)	45.8 (12.8)	13	7	11

[a]Including the tiny Mid-America Exchange.
[b]The little-traded No. 12 contract added to that for No. 11.
Source: Various issues of CFTC monthly report, Positions of Traders.

his cotton and buying yarn, making an organized, explicit market in spinning redundant. Even though a purchase of spinning through the double transaction of selling cotton and buying yarn incurs the costs of two transactions, the sum of those two transactions costs may well be smaller than the single cost of using an organized market for spinning directly. Of course, this argument about relative transactions costs applies equally well to an explicit market for cotton or an explicit market for yarn. One of those two organized markets could be redundant instead of the market for spinning. In general, when two prices must bear a direct relationship to a third as a condition for equilibrium, an organized market supplying the third price may be superfluous.

Regardless of whether a price is implicit or explicit, it performs the same economic function. Spinners, for example, respond in the same manner to an explicit price for spinning as to an implicit price for their service. More important, simply because a good has no formal, organized market there is no reason why people cannot buy or sell that good. A combination of trades in explicit markets enables individuals to construct a position in that good. For instance, if Liverpool were without a cotton market, someone wanting to buy cotton there could do so implicitly by combining the transactions of an explicit purchase of cotton in New Orleans and explicit purchase of freight to Liverpool. Any number of combinations of explicit trades might yield the desired result. In short, although a good may not have a formal, organized market, it can have an implicit market. The price may be nowhere quoted directly, yet it is revealed in simple mathematical manipulations of other prices. And although no written agreement alludes to the quantities and qualities of that particular good, combinations of agreements written about other explicit goods provide, in their effect, the same position. For all practical purposes, an implicit market is the same as an explicit market.

Whether a market is implicit or explicit, the powerful force of arbitrage keeps prices in line. In the case of three explicit markets in which two prices add to a third, arbitrage can work overtly. Traders are always alert for occasions when the price in the market for spinning service moves away from the price implicit in the difference between cotton and yarn.[1] By buying spinning with the cheaper combination of trades and selling spinning where it is more expensive,

---

[1] In the case of foreign exchange markets this would be the same as asserting that interest rate parity holds for all practical purposes. See Frenkel and Levich (1975 and 1977) and Phaup (1981) for recent defenses of the theory of interest rate parity, which is really an assertion about the power of arbitrage.

traders can make money at no risk. Such two-way arbitrage is profitable until the price of spinning is the same when computed in the
two ways, and it continues until prices are restored to their correct
relationship. By definition two-way arbitrage is possible only if all
the markets involved are explicit.

Even if a particular market is implicit, a type of arbitrage known
as one-way arbitrage will keep the implicit price close to the price
that would be explicitly recorded. Unlike conventional two-way arbitrage, however, one-way arbitrage does the work covertly. In the
case of two-way arbitrage, a speculator enters who would not otherwise be making a transaction in any of the markets. With one-way
arbitrage, some party who would as a natural course of business be
making a particular transaction, say the purchase of yarn, has the
option to buy yarn either explicitly or implicitly through transactions
in other markets. If a large discrepancy exists between the return to
constructing a trade directly and constructing the trade through
several transactions, that party would naturally choose the method
with the higher return. These options for the method of achieving a
position desired in any case keep prices in line just as well as professional arbitragers would.

Consequently, an equilibrium without a particular market being
explicit can exist without any apparent arbitrage.[2] That there are no
explicit trades in that particular market is, in fact, the strongest
evidence that the implicit price is close to what the explicit price
would be. Because those who must trade in any case have a choice of
the way they accomplish their trades, they will alter their method
whenever prices are such that they can do better trading implicitly
rather than explicitly, or vice versa.

Just as in a set of three markets in which two prices must add to a
third one can be implicit, in a set of four markets in which three
prices must add to a fourth, one of the four can be implicit. The
important point to remember is that in a set of markets in which P_1
+ P_2 + $\cdots$ + P_{N-1} = P_N there will often be an implicit market.[3] Only
if transactions costs in a set of markets are roughly comparable are
all markets likely to be explicit.

[2] Deardorff (1979) and Callier (1981) have shown that the force of one-way arbitrage
is so strong that one would never expect to observe two-way arbitrage even if all
markets were explicit.
[3] Vertical integration, a firm internalizing its customers or its suppliers, also makes a
number of important markets and their prices implicit. The point made here is not
the same issue as vertical integration. The issue here is whether a firm charges
implicitly or explicitly for its service, whatever is the range of activities encompassed
in that single price.

Within a set of markets, the choice of which market is implicit depends upon small differences in brokerage fees, trading rules, computational convenience, legal precepts, and so forth. As these fluctuate the implicit market may shift. If, for example, transactions in one of the explicit markets become more expensive or become controversial before the law, what was the implicit market could take its place as an explicit market, while that previously explicit market could become implicit. While currently, in textiles, the market for spinning is implicit, at one time the market for yarn was implicit. Under the "putting out" system, a merchant bought cotton and contracted with individual spinners who sold their service at an explicit price.

The classification of markets as implicit or explicit need not be sharp. At times traders may quote an explicit price for a good while actually exchanging a combination of other goods instead of the good itself. This mixture of explicit price and implicit positions might be termed a semiexplicit market. Another class includes those markets that function only infrequently. As long as there are enough explicit markets from which all prices can be derived and all desired positions constructed, the sporadic functioning of the other markets changes nothing. Rather, it emphasizes just how well an implicit market performs the functions of an organized market. Regardless of whether a market is explicit in the sense of being a formal, organized exchange, or semiexplicit, or fully explicit only for occasional transactions, or always implicit, the market has the same economic significance.

Related to this notion of implicit markets is the idea of integrating several prices into one quotation. Services, freight in particular, often encompass several prices. For example, the movement of wheat to Chicago first involves the cost of transferring the grain from a local elevator to a rail car. Then there is a charge for the actual transport of wheat to Chicago. In Chicago there might well be a switching fee to get the car out of the central rail depot, and there will certainly be fees for inspecting the wheat and putting it into a Chicago elevator. If someone wanting to sell wheat for immediate delivery in Chicago had paid all these fees through the elevator's charge, he could demand a higher price. On the other hand, the quoted price for immediate delivery in Chicago may presume that the buyer pays for the inspection and elevator fees, in which case the quoted price is lower. Quoted prices often include either more or fewer of these incidental charges, depending on whether the seller or buyer is responsible for them.[4] Clearly, the particular arrangement for the payment of these incidental fees, being solely a matter of commercial convenience, makes no difference economically. Further, that some of the fees can be in one party's favor while others be against him makes no difference economically. As an example of this point, imagine that in cleaning wheat a valuable by-product is created. On the one hand there is the cost of cleaning and on the other the benefit of the by-product. If the by-product is returned along with the cleaned wheat, the cleaning establishment will quote the full price of cleaning. If instead the cleaning establishment keeps the by-product, it will decrease its listed price of cleaning accordingly. It is even possible that the value of the by-product outweighs the expense of cleaning, rendering the net price of cleaning negative. That is to say, the cleaning establishment, to obtain the by-product, must pay people to clean their wheat. Clearly, whether the firm lists on its bill the price it charges for cleaning separately from that which it pays for the by-product or combines them into one net price makes no difference economically.

The effectiveness of implicit markets and the commercial convenience of combining incidental fees together make a wide range of complicated trading arrangements both possible and probable. Many seemingly different trading arrangements have the same economic effect. Several simultaneous transactions with unfathomable complexity could well reduce to a simple transaction were that transaction performed explicitly.

Consequently, it is imperative to consider as one single trade all the many transactions in explicit markets that a trader makes at the same time. Because his net position is what matters, to examine separately each part of the composite trade would give a most misleading impression of the reasons for the transactions. A safer analytical approach is to treat the implicit position as if it had taken place in an explicit market with an explicit price.

A similar point concerns the economic analysis of the markets involved. Because any one market in a set of markets could be implicit, there could be many different systems of trading, although

---

[4] This distinction over who pays which incidental fees is exactly the difference between a "to arrive" contract (also known as a CIF contract) and one for future delivery. Under the terms of a "to arrive" contract, the seller is only responsible for getting the commodity into the railyard (or harbor) with "cost, insurance, and freight" paid. If the contract were for future delivery, the seller would also pay the delivery charges of getting the commodity into a warehouse.

rarely would all of them operate for the same commodity. Each of these possible systems would be characterized by its own institutions, terminologies, legal procedures, and personalities of traders. They might be thought unrelated because their methods were so dissimilar. Economists might even attempt to explain each system with a different theory. Yet the systems of trading would be equivalent economically, and for that reason, the economic analysis of them should be consistent.

The standard economic analysis of futures markets ignores these important lessons about equivalent systems of trading, and as such it is a perfect example of the misunderstanding that results whenever the possibility of implicit markets is overlooked. A short hedging operation is a purchase in the spot market coupled with the simultaneous sale of a futures contract. Being a combination of two simultaneous trades in two explicit markets, a short hedging operation is a deal in an implicit market. Specifically, a short hedging operation is a method of borrowing in an implicit loan market for the commodity. What would be said about hedging if futures markets were implicit while this loan market was explicit? Such a system of trading is a common method of dealing in goods other than primary commodities, although in fact at various times commodities now with futures markets have had explicit loan markets. In these settings, however, economists are accustomed to explaining the motivations of traders in terms that contradict their usual explanation of hedging. It is the conventional explanation of hedging and futures markets that is wrong.

2.2.   The equilibrium relationship for loan markets

Although the concepts of implicit markets and equivalent ways to trade apply in general, the remainder of this chapter will be spent applying them to a particular type of market, loan markets. Loan markets derive from an equilibrium relationship involving five prices. The price for immediate delivery plus warehouse fees plus capital expenses minus a use charge for the commodity equals the price for future delivery,

$$P_{ID} + P_{WF} + P_{CE} - P_{UC} = P_{FD}$$

The warehouse fees and the capital expenses together are the cost of physical storage, otherwise known as full carrying charges.

These five prices are registered in different units. The price for immediate delivery is quoted in terms of dollars today per unit of the commodity. Since the price for future delivery of the commodity is paid at the time of delivery, the futures price is in terms of dollars at the time of delivery. As a result, the equilibrium relationship must contain the fee for capital tied up. This capital expense equals the price of the commodity for immediate delivery times the interest rate. The interest rate (otherwise known as the time value of money) is the use charge on money, quoted as a proportion. Whether the warehouse fees or the use charge for the commodity are quoted in terms of dollars today, dollars tomorrow, or even in units of the commodity need not matter. The ratio of dollars today per unit of the commodity and the use charge on money make it possible to translate those prices into any terms desired.

Just as does using money, storing a substance involves time. Storage is like the service of freight or processing except that it transforms a substance from being available for immediate delivery into the same substance being available for delivery in the future. A loan of the commodity involves time just as much as does storage. Someone wants to borrow a substance so that he can use it for a period of time. Storage over a period and use of the commodity over a period are two distinct services. Yet both transpire simultaneously. In effect, the service of storage creates a valuable by-product, the use of the substance over the same period. As time passes, storage adds value. Use, in contrast, dissipates value. Or more accurately, if the commodity is not used, an opportunity is lost. If a chair is put into storage and the employees of the warehouse are not allowed to sit on it, the service provided by the chair is wasted.

Consequently, in the equilibrium relationship, from the perspective of a storer who is allowed to use the commodity, the price of physical storage enters positively and the use charge (or rental fee) enters negatively. These can be kept separate or combined, as a matter of commercial convenience. If they are combined, the net charge from the perspective of the person who wants to have use of the commodity, say designated P_L for commodity loan, is

$$P_L = P_{UC} - P_{WF} - P_{CE}$$

This net charge could be either positive or negative, depending on the relative magnitudes of the three components. Just like the cleaner of wheat, a storer might have to pay others for the privilege of storing their commodities because the control of the commodity he obtains thereby is more expensive than the price of physical storage. With P_L combining the use charge on the commodity, the use

Table 2.2. *Systems of trading involving loan markets*

System A	System B	System C
Explicit spot market	Implicit spot market	Explicit spot market
Explicit loan market	Explicit loan market	Implicit loan market
Implicit futures market	Explicit futures market	Explicit futures market

charge on money, and the warehousing fee, the equilibrium relationship reduces to three prices from five,

$$P_{ID} - P_L = P_{FD}$$

This relationship could also be expressed in terms of the goods and services involved:

$$ID - L = FD$$

Thus, P_L is the spread between spot and futures prices. Whenever the use charge for the commodity is positive, spreads will be below full carrying charges.

What is interesting is the large number of equivalent systems of trading based on this set of markets. Depending on which of the three main markets is implicit, there are three broad systems. These three are listed in Table 2.2. Under System A, the futures market is implicit; under System B, the spot market is implicit; while under System C, the loan market is implicit. In practice there are more varieties than these three, depending on how warehouse fees and capital expenses are combined with the use charge on the commodity. In all systems, a sufficient number of explicit markets exist to permit full positions in all the goods and services involved in carrying substances over time.

2.3.   Methods of lending shares of stock

The various stock exchanges serve as a useful introduction to the equivalence of apparently different systems of trading because they clearly trade similar substances and ones that are storable. Since the mid-nineteenth century highly advanced stock markets have operated both in London and in New York but with substantially different methods of trading. Despite the differences in trading techniques, both exchanges have traded a number of issues in common, mainly American issues, at essentially equal prices. After all, communication between the markets about prices is nearly instantaneous, and arbitragers could ship stock certificates across the Atlantic in a matter of days even in the era of sailing vessels.

Even though a discussion of the systems of trading on the stock exchanges of London and New York may seem far afield from the subject of futures markets, actually the discussion establishes several important points. The stock exchanges can demonstrate not only that different systems of trading can achieve the same economic results but also that markets can be implicit and yet be meaningful. On both exchanges traders regularly make two simultaneous transactions. The two simultaneous transactions are obviously the same as a single transaction in another setting, and this confirms that simultaneous transactions should be analyzed as a single one. Equally important, the systems of trading on the two exchanges both include a loan market for stocks, thus introducing the workings of loan markets for substances other than for the familiar substance money. In fact, from the perspective of implicit and explicit loan markets, it will emerge that stock exchanges have many similarities with futures markets not previously recognized.

In New York two markets function explicitly: a spot market for shares and a loan market for shares. This does not, however, preclude trading for future delivery, which can be done implicitly. New York operates under what in Table 2.2 was System A. Someone desiring to sell shares short sells stock for regular delivery while asking his broker to borrow stock for him in order to make the delivery. These two transactions leave him implicitly with the obligation to return stock in the future, a position he would achieve had he directly sold stock for future delivery. From the perspective of someone wanting to sell for future delivery, the fundamental equilibrium relationship involving immediate delivery, loan, and future delivery becomes

$$-FD = -ID + L$$

A sale for future delivery can thus be achieved by a sale for immediate delivery plus borrowing. Correspondingly, a person who wants to buy stock for future delivery can also combine two transactions to achieve that result implicitly. He can buy shares for immediate delivery, and simultaneously lend them out for a period of time, because $FD = ID - L$. His net position entitles him to receive the stock at some point in the future, exactly as would have happened had he directly bought stock for future delivery. In this way, the system of trading on the New York Stock Exchange contains an implicit market for future delivery.

Someone buying stock often borrows money in order to pay the seller. If he lends his just-purchased stock, he can obtain in return a loan of money approximating the market value of the stock lent. For example, if Party A lends 100 shares of General Motors when GM sells at $60 per share, Party B must at the same time lend Party A $6,000. The stock is more than collateral for the loan of money. Just as Party A is free to do anything he desires with the money, Party B is free to do anything with the stock. Neither the exact dollars nor the exact certificates need be returned. Thus, the borrowing of money to buy stock "on margin" includes a counterbalancing loan of stock. Likewise, the borrowing of stock as part of a short-selling operation is really a double loan, borrowing stock while lending money.

In the past the New York Stock Exchange maintained a market for such double borrowing and lending at a "money desk" on the exchange floor. Into this "loan crowd" came those members who desired either to lend stock while borrowing money or to borrow stock while lending money. Although these double loans were for a single day, in practice most were renewed for a number of days. In effect, the interest rate for the loan and the amount of money lent was reset each day. Because of the regulations restricting short selling introduced in the 1930s, this centralized market for lending securities has decayed. Now most brokerage firms find the stock to lend to a short seller from the accounts of their other customers (Teweles and Bradley 1982: Chapter 9).

Whether arranged on the floor of the exchange or not, in these counterbalancing loans Party A has Party B's money and B has A's stock. Yet the stock nominally still belongs to A and the money to B. Consequently, all dividends go to A. For the same reason, A must pay B for the use of his money. This payment is closely subject to the supply of and demand not only for money but for the borrowed stock. The payment in fact combines the use charge on money, registered against Party A, and the use charge on the stock, registered against Party B. (Warehouse fees for shares are negligible.) If the stock is scarce and difficult to borrow, its lender may insist that he obtain the counter loan of money at a low rate of interest. If the stock is still harder to borrow, he may pay no interest at all. Sometimes when there is immediate need for the stock, the lender of stock not only can get the money free of charge but can extract a premium.[5]

---

[5] In this case the implicit price for future delivery of shares is below the price for immediate delivery.

Such rates are usually different for each and every stock, creating, in effect, a separate loan market for every stock.

In London, the method of clearing employed on the stock exchange determines the way trading is done there. The London exchange uses System B, the one with the spot market implicit. The London exchange, instead of clearing daily, as do modern futures exchanges, clears every fortnight, because more trades cancel out the longer the time between clearings.[6] A trader does not have to honor his commitments until the next settlement period. Consequently, each trade is effectively a contract for future delivery at the next balancing of accounts.

As in New York, in London there is a double loan market for shares and money. When the next account period arrives each party must be prepared to meet his obligations. But he can meet his obligations in several ways. A party who has contracted to buy, besides producing the funds to pay for the shares, can arrange with the seller to postpone delivery. That is, he can arrange to have the shares "carried over" the one fortnight until the next balancing of accounts. This arrangement for postponing delivery might also be advantageous for the seller of the shares, if, for example, he does not actually have the shares to deliver. This carryover market can involve others in addition to the original buyer and seller. For example, someone may lend the original buyer the funds he needs. In return the buyer hands over his new shares as collateral. The shares are more than collateral, however. The one who has lent the money and has been given the shares can do anything he wants with them. In effect, the person waiting longer to get stock is lending his stock for two weeks, and the person postponing delivery is borrowing it. At the same time the person waiting to get his stock is borrowing money while the nominal seller of the shares is lending money.

In London as in New York, the quoted fee in this double loan market combines two use charges, one for money and one for the shares. The name of the net fee depends on which of the two use charges dominates. Whenever the net fee is such that the buyer of the stock pays for the extension of the delivery date, the amount paid is called a "contango." If there is no pressure to have the shares at the current account, the use charge on the shares is zero. In that

---

[6] See Gibson (1888: 41-45) for the origins of the clearing process, which in the nineteenth century was an elaborate three-day ritual because of the huge number of transactions accumulated over a fortnight. The exchanges in Paris and Milan follow the method of trading in London, except that they clear monthly instead of fortnightly (Stonham 1982).

case the contango payment exactly covers the other person's opportunity cost of the investment over those two weeks, namely the prevailing interest rate on a two-week loan of money. But because there is sometimes pressure to have the stock immediately, the person permitting delivery to be postponed often needs to pay much less, and he sometimes even receives payment himself whenever the seller finds it extremely difficult to procure certificates for delivery. The sum paid by a seller to defer delivery is called a "backwardation." Naturally the lender of shares most prefers backwardation payments, but a backwardation is relatively rare for stocks. The backwardation or contango payment is different for each stock. The use charge for money being the same for all stocks, the differences among the various contango and backwardation payments reflect the differences among the use charges for the various stocks.

This carryover market leading to contango and backwardation payments operates only in conjunction with the fortnightly clearings because that is the only time such a double loan market is needed. A true spot market in the sense of explicit trades for immediate delivery never operates, however. How then can traders buy and sell for immediate delivery? They can do so implicitly by combining trades in the forward market and the carryover market. For example, if someone wants to sell for immediate delivery, he can manipulate the equilibrium relationship from $ID - L = FD$ to $-ID = -FD - L$. In practice the trader sells stock for delivery at the next account, and meanwhile carries someone else's obligation in the current clearing, lending the stock while borrowing money. That person is then obliged to deliver stock to the trader at the next clearing, and the trader in turn fulfills his own obligation to deliver. In effect a seller of stock for immediate delivery would receive payment in two installments, first as a backwardation or contango payment and second as the contract price for the next account.[7] In total these payments would match exactly what he would have received if he had taken an explicit position in the spot market.

In summary, the New York and London stock exchanges operate quite differently. The Stock Exchange of London deals in forward contracts calling for delivery at one of the periodic clearings, while in America securities are sold in spot markets. While the London exchange developed periodic contango and backwardation payments

[7] If the carryover payment is a contango, the person selling in two steps must pay it. He then gets more at the next clearing. A backwardation, in contrast, comes to him, and he receives correspondingly less at the next clearing.

to postpone obligations, the New York Stock Exchange created a continuously active loan market in both money and stocks.

Despite these operational differences, the economic consequences of trading on the London and American exchanges obviously are similar. And what differences remain are more apparent than real. Backwardation and contango payments are simply the English terminology for the rate of interest an individual must pay in America on the money he borrows while he is lending his stock. Both exchanges have decided to combine into a single fee the use charge on the shares with the storage (or carrying) charge. Likewise, under both the American system and the English system, which party actually pays the brokerage fees, recording fees, or receives the dividends accruing during the course of the loan matters little, these charges being nearly constant and hence being easily accounted for in the observed loan charge. Thus, both English and American stock exchanges have an explicit loan market for shares. Although there is no explicit futures market in individual securities in the U. S.,[8] an individual can construct an implicit futures position from transactions in the spot and loan markets. Similarly, an Englishman can construct a spot transaction by combining positions in the futures market and the carryover market. On both exchanges, therefore, two simultaneous transactions are regularly initiated to accomplish implicitly some single but different transaction. American and English exchanges simply have a different implicit market, in one case futures and in the other spot. The American exchange uses System A and the English one System B. From this it follows that implicit markets have all the economic significance of explicit markets. From this it also follows that a system of trading stock with explicit loan and forward markets is equivalent to a system of trading with explicit spot and loan markets. Not surprisingly, and as will be shown in sections 2.5 and 2.6, the third possible system, System C, in which the loan market is implicit while the spot and futures markets are explicit, is equivalent to the other two.

2.4. Loan markets for commodities

Transactions in the double loan market of the New York Stock Exchange are often difficult to follow. This is in part because the terminology of borrowing and lending is applied to a commodity other than money. Yet stocks, too, are lent, and something akin to interest

---

[8] Actually, early in its history, the New York Stock Exchange dealt mainly in futures contracts in the English manner, not in loans of securities (Armstrong 1848).

is charged for that service. Also unsettling about these double loan transactions is a lack of any obvious reason why anyone would want to borrow anything other than money. Actually people have reason to borrow shares and commodities for much the same reason they borrow money. They temporarily need the commodity in their own possession. The reasons for borrowing commodities will be explored at length in Chapter 4; here the purpose is to comprehend the possibility of functioning loan markets in substances other than money.

What makes loans of shares possible is that stock certificates, like money, are fungible. The person who borrows 100 shares of GM need not replace it with the exact same certificate for 100 shares, just as a person borrowing $100 need not return the identical banknotes.

Other substances besides stock certificates and money, having become fungible, have developed a loan market. An early example is the loan market for warehouse receipts for Scottish pig iron. In the second half of the nineteenth century several warehouses in Glasgow issued receipts for standardized grades of pig iron in round lots of 500 tons. These receipts, which circulated extensively, were sometimes lent. That is not to say that they served as collateral for loans of money (which they often did). Rather, the warehouse receipts themselves were lent for a fee (Hecht 1884: 29-32). A more modern example of a loan market for a commodity is the swap market for electricity, electricity being fungible. One utility will provide electricity to another utility in return for electricity at a later date.

Uranium is another fungible commodity with a loan market. Over the last fifteen years, utilities with nuclear reactors have regularly borrowed and lent uranium, otherwise known as "yellow cake." Sometimes a utility finds itself needing to replace its fuel rods earlier than expected. If it buys uranium for its immediate needs, it will have extra uranium on hand when its regular supplies under long-term contracts arrive some months hence. Therefore, the simple solution is to borrow yellow cake from another utility or producer that has more than enough for its current needs. Similarly, a producer of uranium may hear of an inquiry for immediate delivery that appears to be a particularly attractive deal. If the firm makes the deal, however, it will not have sufficient quantity available for many months. Again the answer is to arrange a loan of uranium. After the negotiations are completed, the loan itself is easy to consummate.[9] A utility's uranium

[9] The contractual terms ensuring repayment of the uranium loan are quite varied. Sometimes the borrower posts a letter of credit sufficient to repurchase a like amount of uranium. In that case a money instrument serves as collateral for the loan of uranium, the reverse of the more familiar arrangement.

is stored not on its own premises but in a depository together with the yellow cake of other utilities. The lender simply instructs the depository to make a book transfer to the credit of the borrower's account. When the borrower repays the loan, another book transfer is made.

Sufficient interest exists in uranium loans for a brokerage firm, the Nuclear Exchange Corporation (NUEXCO), to specialize in arranging such deals. In NUEXCO's monthly *Report to the Nuclear Industry,* inquiries into and actual loans of uranium are usually a large fraction of the business for outright purchase. Some loans are written to run for as long as several years, while others are forward loans, that is, loans arranged months or years in advance. NUEXCO tracks the charge for loans, what it calls the "use charge" (the source of the terminology used in this chapter), expressing it as an annual percentage rate to be applied to the prevailing spot price of uranium. It is a separate quotation, which does not contain the offsetting warehouse fees and capital expenses. This percentage use charge moves with the supply and demand of loanable uranium. Since there are generally more lenders in the market than borrowers, the use charge has rarely covered the lender's interest expense on its original purchase of uranium.[10] But if the utility did not lend its surplus inventory, it would recover none of its interest expense. It is at least conceivable that some day utilities and other borrowers might be so pressed for immediate supplies that they will offer a substantial premium to lenders.[11]

The loan market in uranium is similar to the practice during the 1860s in Chicago of lending warehouse receipts in wheat, corn, and oats. These loans of grain are extremely instructive, being loans of the commodities most often considered in conventional studies of hedging and futures markets. Unfortunately, little documentation has survived about the loan market for grain, although it is clear that there was an explicit price similar to the use charge for uranium. The most detailed account is the following letter to the *Chicago Tribune* from 13 April 1861.

The loaning and issuing of warehouse receipts

Messrs Editors: I wish to call attention to some matters of considerable importance to all grain dealers, both city and country operators – especially

---

[10] In the terminology of Chapter 1, the array of uranium prices has often been below full carrying charges but has not yet been in backwardation.

[11] Mr. George White, Jr., Vice-President of NUEXCO, kindly described the loan market in uranium.

those who obtain money upon Warehouse Receipts. It is the practice that has grown up of loaning Warehouse Receipts, as an indispensable adjunct of short selling.

Commission men and Warehouse Receipt Bankers of small means advance on a large amount of grain to country dealers and city operators; and to obtain the necessary means, reloan the receipts to short-sellers, receiving therefore the price of the grain as security against loss – charging their customers interests and commissions, and also receiving use of the money, and in some cases a commission from short-sellers.

Under this system, the dealer who in good faith has obtained advances on his grain, holding for an advance [in price], has his property used by short-sellers to depreciate its value.

It is estimated that a large per cent of the grain in store has been borrowed of the receivers and the above class of bankers by short-sellers, and resold on our market. It is evidently the interest of the legitimate dealer that this practice should be checked, and it is within his power by only patronizing the commission merchant and banker who refuses to loan to short-sellers, considering it a fraud and damage to his interests.

Commission merchants in Chicago in the 1860s attracted consignments from farmers by offering advances on the produce sent to them, normally two-thirds or three-quarters of the current value. Clearly, a commission merchant earns commissions in proportion to his consignments, which are limited by the amount of money he has for making advances. Thus, if someone is willing to lend him money in return for the counter loan of the warehouse receipts in his care, the commission merchant will take the opportunity to obtain the money in the manner the author of this letter deplores. The commission merchant instead could increase his funds by borrowing from a banker, using the warehouse receipts for grain already received on consignments as security. Of course, a banker who receives warehouse receipts as collateral is in the same position as the commission merchant, being under pressure to lend the warehouse receipts in his care in order to raise more money to lend himself.

One might wonder who wanted to borrow these warehouse receipts from commission merchants or bankers while making the counter loan of money. A possible candidate was a shipper who wanted to be sure he had warehouse receipts at hand in the event he received a rush order. More commonly, at least according to the writer of the letter, the borrower was a short seller. Such a speculator would borrow a warehouse receipt and immediately sell it in the spot market, hoping that when the loan came due he could reenter the market and buy back another warehouse receipt at a price lower than that at which he had sold the original receipt. As security for return of the receipt, the speculator would offer an amount of cash equal to a large part of the value of the grain, exactly what the commission merchant needed for attracting more consignments. The commission merchant would also receive "in some cases a commission from short-sellers."

This small aside in the letter to the *Chicago Tribune*, "in some cases [receiving] a commission from short-sellers," is revealing in that this commission is what the borrower paid for having possession of the warehouse receipt over the term of the loan. Under this system of trading, the loan charge did not include the cost of physical storage. The owner of the grain on consignment, whose warehouse receipt his commission merchant had lent, paid the warehouse fees when his grain was finally shipped. The owner also paid the capital costs of holding the grain, through the interest on the advance, which the commission merchant paid in turn to the borrower of the receipt whose money he had as a counter loan. The borrower, however, paid a use charge to borrow the warehouse receipt.

Of course, the system of lending warehouse receipts is predicated not only on their widespread acceptance but also on the premise that receipts are fungible. Improvements in warehouses during the 1840s and 1850s had made it possible to store grain in bulk. Once there were many warehouse receipts in circulation for a broad grade of wheat, short selling became possible; before then a short seller was vulnerable to opportunism if he had to return one particular lot.

In view of the similarities among loan markets for goods as diverse as pig iron, uranium, and stock certificates, it is interesting to note a further parallel between the double loan market in grain and that in shares of stock. Both loan markets came under considerable criticism. Although the system of lending stock had been in use for many years, it and many other practices of the New York Stock Exchange were attacked in the 1930s. The principal objections paralleled those made earlier against loans of warehouse receipts in grain. Many claimed "it is unfair to lend a long customer's stock to a broker wishing to deliver on a short sale, since this use of the long customer's stock is contrary to his interest," because the additional selling pressure from the short sale would seem to depress the price of the stock (Meeker 1932: 90). Recall that with loans of grain, it was similarly believed that "the dealer who in good faith has obtained advances [of money] on his grain, holding for an advance [in price], has his property used by short-sellers to depreciate its value." There is no record of the response of grain merchants to this criticism, but stockbrokers argued that if the lending of a long's stock to fill a short sale hurts him, it must be equally true that the loan of money advanced against the stock loan, money belonging to the short, harms the short because it enables the long to maintain his position, effectively adding to the demand for the stock (Meeker 1932: 91). Although the long facilitates short selling by lending his shares, he does so only to the extent that the short makes the carrying of a long position possible.

2.5.   Repurchase agreements, straddles, and spreads

In the loan markets for grain receipts, uranium, and stock certificates, the parties involved actually write a compact in the terminology of borrowing and lending. Stripped to its bare essentials, such a loan agreement reads: Today I will lend you X units of the commodity in return for a loan of Y dollars. In addition, I will pay you interest on the Y dollars at the annual rate of $r\%$, while you pay me a use charge equal to $s\%$ of the current value of my commodity. (These rates on money and the commodity vary of course with the pressure in the market.) When you return my commodity or its equivalent Z months from now, I will return the equivalent of your money.

Viewed in isolation, both the initial dual loan and the subsequent mutual return appear to be an exchange of a commodity for money, or in other words, an outright purchase. Indeed, if the amount of money to be lent equals the current value of the commodity, as is commonly the case, the exchange will be exactly at the market price. Moreover, because possession is proof of title for negotiable instruments such as money, stock certificates, and warehouse receipts, title to both the money and the commodity actually pass to the new holders, just as if there had been an outright purchase.

In fact, nothing of substance would change if the double loan transaction were written in the terminology of an outright purchase: I will sell you today X units of the commodity for Y dollars. Z months from now, I in turn will buy X units for Y dollars from you. Meanwhile, I will pay you at the equivalent of an annual rate of $(r - s)\%$ on the Y dollars. (If the use charge on the commodity, namely s, is larger than the use charge on money, you will pay me at the equivalent of an annual rate of $(s - r)\%$ on the value of my commodity.) Regardless of the specific terminology, this contract still provides me with the use of your money for Z months, during which time you have my commodity for your own use. Through this purchase and repurchase of the commodity, or what is more commonly referred to as a sale-repurchase agreement or just a repurchase agreement, a double loan is achieved, a transaction much more extensive than an outright purchase. A repurchase agreement is a variety of System C from Table 2.2.

From a strict legal perspective a sale-repurchase agreement is not a loan. Traders are not indifferent between a double loan drawn up as a formal loan and a double loan drawn up as a repurchase agreement. Among other reasons, the actual legal form affects their standing in bankruptcy court. Nevertheless, it is not an abuse of the term "loan" to call a repurchase agreement a loan. That is its economic effect. It is interesting to consider why the economic effect of a loan is accomplished as a formal legal loan or as a repurchase agreement. That is in fact the purpose of Chapter 5. Yet what is more important is to recognize that a number of seemingly unrelated legal forms have the same economic effect.

Repurchase agreements, termed "repos" for short, have become common in the market for U.S. government securities. Extremely intricate, they were the preserve of bond dealers until 1982 when the debacles involving Drysdale Government Securities and Lombard-Wall, Inc., made such transactions front-page news.[12] Most interesting for current purposes, regardless of the specific terms of the contract, the bond dealers, government officials, and newspaper reporters referred to Drysdale's repurchase agreements as double loans of money and bonds and to the market as the loan market for government securities.[13]

All sale-repurchase agreements are, for all intents and purposes, double loans. When accomplished through a repurchase agreement, a double loan requires two transactions made simultaneously with the same party, one transaction being the purchase of a commodity and the other its sale for delivery on a different date. Nothing requires that the two parties to a repurchase agreement be present at the redelivery. Each could transfer his obligation to another person. In fact one could simply be a broker who routinely places his obligation under the repurchase part of the agreement into other hands. For that matter it is not essential to the concept of a repurchase agreement that one party deal with only one other party even in the initial stages. He could for example negotiate the purchase part of the agreement with one person and the repurchase part with another. What is essential to a repurchase agreement is that the two

[12] Drysdale had lent cash and borrowed securities, a deal called a reverse repo.
[13] See for example the *Wall Street Journal*, 19 and 20 May 1982.

components, one to buy and the other to sell at a different date, be arranged simultaneously. Examined separately, neither transaction appears to have any connection to a loan. Yet it is the net effect of the two explicit transactions that matters. By extension, those transactions and combinations of transactions that resemble repurchase agreements are loans in substance, whatever their actual terminology.

A repurchase agreement is yet another permutation on the fundamental equilibrium relationship $ID - L = FD$. The New York Stock Exchange manipulated this relationship to provide positions in future delivery of a commodity. The London Stock Exchange manipulated the equation to provide implicit positions in immediate delivery. Instead of solving for FD or ID, solving for L yields an implicit method of borrowing the commodity (or securities) while lending money,

$$L = ID - FD$$

A purchase for immediate delivery and a simultaneous sale for delivery sometime in the future leave the commodity in the hands of the purchaser over that interval of time while leaving money temporarily in the hands of the one who sells. From the original seller's perspective an implicit method of lending the commodity while borrowing money is

$$-L = -ID + FD$$

The price P_L of this double loan, from the perspective of the borrower of the commodity and lender of the money, is

$$P_L = P_{ID} - P_{FD}$$

If this price P_L is negative, the use charge he must pay for the commodity is larger than the interest he receives lending the money.

Trades resembling repurchase agreements occur frequently on American futures markets, especially as contracts near their expiration dates. Normally, if a person who has sold a contract reaching maturity wants to postpone delivery, he simply buys a futures contract for that month and sells one for the next delivery month. If, as is often the case, the same trader is party to both of these transactions, then the person who is buying now will be selling the commodity back to the party from whom he bought it, exactly the conditions making for a repurchase agreement. Being a repurchase agreement, these transactions on futures exchanges must amount to a double loan of the commodity and money. The party wanting to postpone a delivery he has contracted for in effect meets his obligation to de-

liver in the current period by borrowing the commodity from someone else.

The bargaining is not in terms of the two futures contracts themselves, but rather in terms of the price of postponing delivery, or in
the jargon of the trade, "rolling the contracts over" to another delivery month. The charges for rolling over contracts are equivalent to
contango and backwardation payments on the London Stock Exchange. (Indeed, this similarity explains why commodity markets
have taken up the terms "contango" and "backwardation.") The
charge is the net result of combining physical storage costs, capital
costs, and the use charge on the commodity, which explains why it is
sometimes positive and sometimes negative. When warehouse fees
and interest expenses outweigh the use charge on the commodity, the
net charge is in favor of the party postponing delivery, who receives
the equivalent of a contango payment. When the use charge outweighs the carrying charges, he must pay a backwardation payment.

Although rollovers ordinarily take place just as a contract is about
to expire, similar deals occur far in advance in the more active futures markets such as soybeans and corn. Thus, within what appears
to be a futures market is also a well organized and active market for
forward double loans, of the commodity and money. In these futures markets, highly specialized traders on the floor of the exchange, by quoting the price of a spread explicitly, alleviate the need
for other traders to perform subtraction between two futures prices.
(Recall that a spread is the difference in the price of two futures
contracts.) The quoted price is the difference between the use
charge for the commodity and physical storage costs including capital expenses. These traders quoting spreads are offering to buy a
near-term futures contract while selling a more distant contract.
Having taken a position in two different contracts, the trader is said
to have "straddled" them. This term is descriptive both literally and
figuratively, for the traders specializing in a particular spread actually stand in the trading pit straddling the areas in which the two
component contracts are traded. The two contracts are referred to
as the "legs" of the straddle, completing the metaphor.[14] Basically

---

[14] When it was still common in commodity markets to sell for future delivery either at
the buyer's option as to time of delivery or the seller's option, some traders would
sell a contract at buyer's option and buy a contract for delivery in the same month
at seller's option. Generally speaking, the contract at buyer's option sold for more
and was usually exercised first. In effect, the double transaction amounted to a
commitment to make a loan, but of uncertain timing and duration. Such a straddle
was aptly called a "spread eagle."

market makers, these specialists in straddles are also prepared to make the opposite deal, sell a near-term contract and buy a more distant one, both from the same party, if the price is right. In either case, the double transaction arranges a repurchase agreement in advance. Although the bargain is based solely on the quoted price for a spread,[15] the exchange officially records the repurchase agreement as two transactions in futures, as does the Commodity Futures Trading Commission in its reports on the positions of large traders. Yet the exchange is aware that a straddle is not really two positions in futures: Lower original margin is required. This practice of candidly quoting explicit prices for spreads and straddles while recording the resulting position as two positions in futures contracts is a good example of a semiexplicit market.

The system of explicitly quoting the price of straddles is organized most formally on the Commodity Exchange in New York, the principal American market in metals. On Comex deals in straddles constitute as much as 75% of the volume of trading.[16] Until recently, there was sufficient interest in straddles to conduct a separate session after the close of Comex in which straddles alone were exchanged.[17] The extensive straddle market allows Comex to keep operating even with the large swings in price that would have suspended trading on other futures exchanges. On most futures markets, the maximum movement on any one day of the price of a contract, with the exception of the expiring contract, is limited. Consequently, when true prices move more than this limit, most futures markets shut down, because either buyers or sellers find the official price unrealistic. On Comex, however, a trader who wants to buy a distant contract can avoid the constraints of limit moves by combining two transactions, one of which will be a straddle. First he can buy one of the expiring

---

[15] Explicit quoting of the price of a spread is hardly a modern invention. It has been part of futures markets since the inception of those institutions. Throughout the 1880s, the *Chicago Tribune* presented the spreads between months in a separate table, referring to them as premiums or discounts and discussing them extensively. For example, on 26 June 1886, the paper observed that "Some parties on 'Change are apprehensive about the market for July wheat. They fear it has been oversold. It was widely expected that the August premium would rise about 2¢, and a very large quantity was 'straddled' on this theory. Now it has all to be changed back and one party has as much to say as the other as to the ruling difference at which the market shall be equalized."

[16] Until objections by the Internal Revenue Service and changes in the tax laws, trades for tax purposes provided much of the depth of the straddle market. "Butterfly spreads," which combine two straddles, one being a a bull spread and the other a bear spread, were a popular device for minimizing taxes.

[17] These straddles in particular were entered into as a way of postponing taxes.

contracts, in which there is always a free market. Then he can sell a straddle between the spot contract and the distant contract he desires. The sale of that straddle comprises a sale of a spot contract and the purchase of a distant contract. The trader has made both a purchase and sale of the expiring contract, which offset each other, leaving him with his objective, the purchase of a distant contract. Although these permutations could be arranged on any futures market, they are rarely done without a reasonably active straddle market such as the one on Comex.

Considering the number of futures contracts traded on Comex that are actually straddles, one might wonder why Comex does not arrange to trade straddles explicitly. Because what is bargained over is the single price for a straddle, the market is already semiexplicit. Yet the straddle market could be even more formal. The exchange could record a single repurchase agreement, rather than the double transaction of one sale of a futures contract and the purchase of another. The sole difference between this repurchase agreement and more familiar ones involving government securities would be that the agreement would be arranged in advance. How far would depend on the month of the near leg of the straddle.

Of course, the exchange could also rewrite straddles into the terminology of a double loan, and nothing of substance would be different. Therefore, it is fair to say that straddles, so much a feature of futures markets, are nothing but forward loans of the particular commodity in return for forward loans of money. When a trader initiates a bull straddle, in which the near leg is the long position and the far leg is the short, he is implicitly arranging in advance to borrow the commodity in return for providing a counter loan of money. When a trader initiates a bear straddle, in which the near leg is the short position and the far leg the long, he is implicitly arranging in advance to lend the commodity in return for borrowing money.

2.6.   Hedging

Like straddles, a hedging operation is essentially a repurchase agreement. Because a repurchase agreement amounts to a loan, a hedging operation must be an implicit method of borrowing commodities in return for a counter loan of money. A short hedging operation in particular is none other than a combination of trades undertaken to create an implicit position in another good entirely. To view a hedger's sale of a futures contract in isolation is to misrepresent his transaction completely.

To see the economic effect of a hedging operation, consider a specific short hedging operation where a miller buys wheat in the cash market for immediate delivery and sells wheat for future delivery on a futures exchange. In essence, he is pledging to buy and then sell back – in other words, he is enacting a repurchase agreement. The components of a repurchase agreement are especially obvious if the wheat bought in the cash market is for delivery at the same location as where the redelivery is to be made. Through this repurchase agreement the miller borrows the the commodity and lends money.

A short hedging operation is not a pristine repurchase agreement because the hedger does not make the agreement with one single party. Rather he buys for immediate delivery from some person in his local market and sells for future delivery on an organized futures exchange to some completely different party, often a speculator. But this complication makes no difference to the hedger. From his perspective the simultaneous transactions in the spot and futures markets amount to a repurchase agreement. Imagine that he had in fact made a formal repurchase agreement with one single trader. Suppose that trader had sold the rights to buy back the commodity to someone else. That trader selling the repurchase rights would naturally instruct the person responsible for returning the commodity to him to deliver instead to the substitute, because that would save on handling and rehandling the commodity. Under these circumstances the original purchaser would end up dealing with two different parties, one for his original purchase and another when he fulfills his obligation to resell the commodity. This setup involving a repurchase agreement is different from a hedging operation only in that a conventional short hedger deals with two parties from the outset. He buys while promising to resell at a later date. His opposite party can in some sense be thought of as the whole market.[18] One trader out of the whole market makes the original sale; another steps in to make the repurchase.

Spot and futures markets together provide an ingenious method for a party to assemble repurchase agreements without having to negotiate with one single opposite party. The substance of such pairs of transactions is apparent from the lexicon applied to them on the London Metal Exchange. On the LME, traders frequently seek to

[18] In this context it is worth noting that in the abstraction of economic theory, the economic actor is postulated as lending or borrowing from the impersonal market rather than from individuals.

postpone previously promised deliveries, particularly when supplies for immediate delivery are tight. They purchase tin, copper, lead, and so forth for immediate delivery and simultaneously sell for later delivery. (These two transactions, of course, are identical to a short hedging operation.) A trader scheduled to make a delivery but who arranges to postpone delivery with the double transaction of buying spot and selling forward is said "to borrow from the market." Sometimes traders institute the opposite double transactions, selling for immediate delivery while buying for later delivery. A person who agrees to accept delivery later than originally scheduled is said "to lend to the market."

Perhaps it is difficult to envision a hedging operation as a repurchase agreement because every short hedger in corn, for instance, uses the same futures market. Some are buying for immediate delivery in Peoria, and others for delivery in Des Moines, Galveston, or New Orleans. Further, each is purchasing a different grade and type. Yet at the heart of all these complex operations is a simple repurchase agreement. If all corn were of the contract grade for futures contracts and were in Chicago (or could be sent there instantly), it would be clearer that a corn contract for immediate delivery would be only one of a whole spectrum of contracts for delivery dates stretching from the present to the most distant date. Under these circumstances a short hedging operation is clearly a repurchase agreement because the identical corn is first purchased and then resold. The complexities of actual short hedging operations are little different. They involve two implicit positions at once rather than the one implicit position in a pure repurchase agreement. For example, if corn bought on the spot were No. 3 rather than the No. 2 of the contract grade, the hedger would have an implicit obligation for cleaning No. 3 (i.e., a short position in cleaning), and a repurchase agreement for No. 2. Likewise, a hedging operation involving No. 2 corn in St. Louis comprises an implicit position in the freight rate between St. Louis and Chicago, and a hedging operation in Chicago. All actual short hedging operations can be broken down into spreads involving location, cleaning, and storage plus use over time. All these spreads could be, and should be, thought of as explicit positions with explicit prices. All short hedging operations include a repurchase agreement involving storage plus use over time, and hence a double loan of money and the commodity.

Confusion also arises in interpreting a short hedging operation as a single transaction because the effective fee paid for the double loan is sometimes positive and sometimes negative. Yet as has been stressed in section 2.1, this is simply the result of combining prices, two in favor of the short hedger and one against him. Generally speaking, a short hedger holds the commodity on his own premises. Responsible for the interest expense and warehousing costs, he can expect to recover them. But this storage service renders a valuable by-product – the control of the commodity for a period of time – for which a short hedger is willing to pay a rental fee. Naturally, only the net price is quoted, since it makes little or no difference economically whether the expense of physical storage is expressed separately or combined with the use charge. In a short hedging operation, the net price for the double loan is implicit in the difference between the spot and futures prices. There is no difference economically, and there should be no difference analytically, between a system of markets in which the loan market is explicit and the prices of storage and use of the commodity are distinguished and one in which the loan market is implicit through short hedging operations and the storage costs and use charge for the commodity are combined together into the spread between spot and futures prices.

What does this perspective on a short hedging operation as an implicit method of borrowing a commodity imply about a long hedging operation? Since a long hedging operation involves the exact opposite action on a futures market as a short hedging operation, they would seem unrelated. Quite the contrary, long and short hedging operations are closely connected. While the short position in the futures market as part of a short hedging operation is the repurchase part of a repurchase agreement, the long position in futures constituting half of a long hedging operation is the purchase part of a repurchase agreement.

Once again confusion arises from a failure to treat the long position in the futures market as part of a complex set of transactions. The purpose of a long position in May wheat when entered into simultaneously with a sale of May flour is obvious. The transaction in the futures market is one of two trades implicitly making for the forward sale of milling. Likewise, a long position in a copper futures contract and a forward sale of fabricated products for delivery far enough ahead to allow for processing time amount to a position in forward fabricating despite there being no such explicit market. The appropriate combination of a long position in soybeans and short positions in meal and oil, taken either in futures contracts or in the cash market, amounts to the forward sale of the service of crushing soybeans. This combination of three simultaneous trades is known specifically as "putting on the crush." The combination of a long position in corn and a long position in feeder cattle plus a short position in live cattle is implicitly the sale of the fattening service. A long position in the Chicago corn futures market and a contract to deliver corn in Rotterdam is the implicit sale of corn freight.

But many long hedges implicitly involve more than just processing margins. Even so, their result is to establish another implicit position in addition to the implicit position in processing. Like typical short hedging operations, actual long hedging operations involve several implicit positions all at once.

A common position in addition to the processing margin is a re-purchase agreement for the raw material. Many of the long positions in futures contracts as part of long hedging operations are in con-tract months somewhat earlier than required by the forward sale of finished products, often to cushion any delays in delivery or in pro-cessing. For example, a sale of flour for delivery in May will often be hedged in a March contract despite the relative speed in making flour. This long hedge in March wheat of May flour can be broken down into a March-May straddle in wheat (i.e., a long March and a short May position in wheat futures) and a May milling spread (a long May wheat position and a short position in May flour). The May positions in wheat, long and short, because they cancel out, are invisible in practice. Yet a repurchase agreement made in advance is clearly present in this long hedging operation, even if it is implicit, because of the extra time between delivery of the wheat and delivery of the flour.

The combination of an implicit position in forward crushing with an implicit provision to borrow soybeans also results from a typical long hedging operation in soybeans. Because it involves three com-modities, not two, it is hard to follow, however. For example, as of January a soybean processor has committed himself in separate transactions in the cash market to deliver meal in May and oil in May. He is observed to buy simultaneously a futures contract for March delivery for the necessary number of soybeans. This long position in soybean futures makes the processor a long hedger. Be-cause soybean processing takes a few weeks at most, these three trades together can be thought of as the yet more complex set. Suppose April to May represents the normal time for crushing the quantity of soybeans involved. The set of trades can then be refor-mulated by adding a short position in April beans along with a long position in April beans. The positions in April beans, long and short, are invisible in practice because they cancel out. The set of trades then becomes a long position in March beans paired with a short position in April beans and then a long position in April beans paired with a short position in May meal and a short position in May oil. As of January, the long April beans paired with short May meal and oil is an implicit forward position in crushing soybeans over the period April to May. The pair of long March beans and short April beans amounts to a forward repurchase agreement. Thus, the original three trades involve a forward commitment to processing and a forward commitment to borrow soybeans while lending money. These three explicit trades in beans, meal, and oil could also be interpreted as the implicit forward sale of crushing over the period of March to April and then the implicit forward borrowing of both meal and oil over the period April through May, since nothing indicates when the crushing will take place. Regardless of the exact interpretation, several implicit positions, all recognizable as plausible transactions if accomplished explicitly, are the result of the three trades in soybeans, meal, and oil. By any interpretation of the precise implicit positions involved, the analysis of the long position in soybeans in isolation from the short positions in meal and oil misconstrues the purpose of the position in soybeans. The same will be true for any long position in futures held by a dealer or processor in combination with other positions. Almost always the net effect of the positions taken together will implicitly be some very different, yet economically meaningful, position.

In conclusion, a long hedging operation often contains a forward repurchase agreement. A short hedging operation, on the other hand, is typically a repurchase agreement instituted immediately. What both long and short hedging operations have in common is that they are repurchase agreements permitting the hedgers to borrow commodities in return for counter loans of money.

2.7.   Basis trading

Crucial to this interpretation of a hedging operation as a double transaction amounting to a repurchase agreement is evidence that the two transactions are done in concert. In descriptions of their operations, hedgers, both long and short, invariably imply that their position in the futures market is taken on simultaneously with the one in the cash market.[19] Such simultaneity is a consistent theme in

---

[19] Occasionally, elevators and processors take a position in futures in advance of cash transactions, because the closing of the exchange forces them to anticipate their dealings later in the afternoon or early the next morning.

the talks by dealers and processors about their hedging practices as compiled in Peck (1978).[20]

Not only do dealers and processors initiate two positions simultaneously, but they also regularly terminate their positions in futures in concert with some other transaction in yet some other market. When a short hedger offsets his short position in the futures market with the purchase of a long contract, "lifting the hedge" in the language of the trade, his move is not accidentally timed. Rather it coincides with the sale of inventory or the sale of another forward commitment. The same simultaneity is a feature of even more complex methods of closing out positions in futures contracts. Often when a short hedger sells his grain or cotton, he knows that the other party with whom he is dealing will also be wanting to close out his position in some futures contract. Provided the contracts are in the same month, with the simultaneous sale of the grain the two swap and cancel their futures contracts "ex pit," which is to say, the trade is done away from the trading pits on the floor of the exchange.[21]

Clearly, these operators called short hedgers do not buy a commodity in the cash market, and then, after contemplating the riskiness of their situation, decide on a position in the futures market. Nor do they end their position in futures without some simultaneous transaction in the cash market. They conceive and execute two transactions, one of which happens to involve a futures contract, from the standpoint of a single implicit trade with a desired result different from either explicit component.

Even more convincing evidence of the simultaneity of dealers' trades of futures contracts with other transactions, and hence even more convincing evidence of the interpretation of positions in futures contracts as components in an implicit position in some other

---

[20] In this volume, see in particular Virgil A. Wiese, "A Case History of Hedging," p. 19; M. D. Guild, "The Use Made of Commodity Markets by Terminal Elevators," pp. 108, 110-111; Richard O. Westley, "Commodity Markets and the Terminal Elevator," pp. 116-117; Ben Raskin, "The Dynamics of Terminal Elevator Management," p. 125; Ellis D. English, "The Use of the Commodity Exchange by Millers," pp. 145-146; Fred W. Lake, "The Miller's Use of the Commodity Exchange," p. 156; Richard Williams, "How a Soybean Processor Makes Use of Futures Markets," pp. 173-175; and W. C. Miller, "A Processor and Futures Markets," p. 187.

[21] For a description of this practice, see Richard O. Westley, "Commodity Markets and the Terminal Elevator," in Peck (1978: 118). In metals markets, where this procedure is common, it is called an "exchange for physicals," while in some other markets the term is "exchange for product" (Paul, Kahl, and Tomek 1981: 112-113). The clearinghouse of the futures exchange is notified within a day or two and removes these contracts from its books.

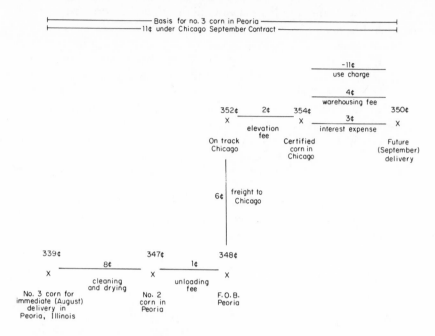

Figure 2.1. Components of the basis

good or service, is the practice known as "basis trading." In most local commodity markets, the spot market is implicit. The haggling is not about the local spot price but about the discount under or premium over a specified futures contract in a major market. This discount or premium is referred to as the "basis." Basis trading is a variety of System B, in the nomenclature of Table 2.2.

The basis combines several fees into one price. The basis on a commodity for sale locally is the net spread comprising four implicit prices: (1) the price of cleaning the local grade into a grade deliverable on a futures contract (or the premium for a superior grade); (2) the price of transportation to or from, as the case may be, the delivery point on the futures contract; (3) the physical cost of storage including insurance and capital costs; and (4) the use charge for the commodity. Effectively the four fees, plus several other incidental ones, aggregate to the price of transforming a commodity into one deliverable later at another place. Figure 2.1 exhibits the components behind the basis for a hypothetical structure of prices for No. 3 corn for immediate delivery in Peoria compared to future delivery of No. 2 corn in Chicago. Here the use charge alone is in favor of the owner of the Peoria corn. Consequently, the Peoria corn is "under" the Chicago price.

Even though comprising several fees, the basis is still an explicit price. Basis trading is an example of a semiexplicit market, in which the price for a good or service is quoted explicitly even though the good or service itself is constructed from other positions. Rather than a single certificate entitling the holder to the service of transforming a current local commodity into a commodity at the main market at a later date, a certificate for the local commodity and a futures contract are used together.

An early market report for spring wheat in Buffalo on 4 May 1900, illustrates the mechanics and origins of basis trading:[22]

Closing prices based on 73-1/4¢, New York July were:

No. 1 hard spot, 74-3/4¢; 1-1/2¢ over.
No. 1 northern spot, 72-3/4¢; 1/2¢ under.
No. 2 northern spot, 70-3/4¢; 2-1/2¢ under.
No. 1 northern c.i.f., 71-3/4¢; 1-1/2¢ under.
No. 2 northern c.i.f., 69-3/4¢; 3-1/2¢ under.

On this date in May in Buffalo local prices were "based on" the New York futures contract for July delivery; hence the origin of the term "basis." The futures contract used as the point of reference is further ahead than the length of time it took to transport wheat from Buffalo to New York City. Not only the spot price but the price of wheat to arrive was based on the New York futures's price. "C.i.f." (or "CIF") is an abbreviation for the expression "to arrive with cost, insurance, and freight paid," and refers not to wheat already in Buffalo but to that expected to arrive some time later, probably within a week or two.

Although the market report recorded explicit spot prices, 74-3/4¢ for No. 1 hard spot for instance, the actual bargaining on the Buffalo exchange was solely in terms of the second column of numbers, the amounts "under" or "over." An observer in the Buffalo market would never have heard a spot price mentioned, only the New York futures price and the basis. The newspaper computed the spot prices, which were otherwise implicit, as a service to its readers. (Modern newspapers do the same, since rarely is there an explicit spot price.)

Almost everyone trading wheat in Buffalo would have simultaneously been taking on or ending a position in the New York futures

---

[22] *Buffalo Commercial Advertiser*, 4 May 1900.

market, most commonly the July contract. The effect of such simultaneous transactions was implicit positions in freight to New York or in differentials in grades measured against the grade deliverable on the futures contract in New York. Because the traders cared solely about the implicit positions in freight to New York or in grade differentials, it was convenient for them to bargain over those prices directly.

One can conclude, therefore, that whenever there is basis trading, as there now is for most if not all commodities with futures markets, the traders are using futures contracts to construct implicit positions in entirely different goods or services. Otherwise, traders would not continue to quote prices in terms of the basis, if all that concerned them was an explicit trade for immediate delivery or an explicit trade for future delivery.

2.8.   Futures markets as implicit loan markets

To reiterate the principal conclusion of this chapter: A short hedging operation, the spot purchase of a commodity and its simultaneous sale for future delivery, amounts to borrowing a commodity over an interval of time while lending money. Likewise, a typical long hedging operation is often in part an implicit forward loan of a commodity. Since long and short hedging operations along with straddles constitute the majority of positions on futures markets, it follows that a futures market for a commodity is primarily part of an implicit loan market for that commodity.

Recall the several steps by which this conclusion was reached. First, it is common to borrow and lend fungible commodities such as uranium, pig iron, and grain. Second, a repurchase agreement is just like a loan in its results. Third, a hedging operation is in effect a repurchase agreement. Hence, the two transactions constituting a hedging operation have the economic effect of borrowing a commodity while lending money.

The same conclusion can be reached from the perspective of designing an implicit market in commodity loans. Suppose one wanted to borrow or lend commodities with a counterbalancing loan of money. Although not as obvious as the service of spinning, a loan of a commodity provides the service of having the commodity over a period of time. Likewise, the costs of warehouses, insurance, forgone capital, and spoilage are the consequences of the service of physical storage. Thus, someone designing a loan market begins with this identity: The commodity today minus the use of the commodity over time plus the storage of the commodity over time equals the commodity as of some date in the future. In terms of prices, the price for immediate delivery minus the use charge for the commodity plus the two prices for physical storage (warehouse fees and capital expenses) equals the price for future delivery, or symbolically,

$$P_{ID} - P_{UC} + P_{WF} + P_{CE} = P_{FD}$$

Among the three prices in this relationship representing time value, the use charge on the commodity is more important by far than the warehousing fee and use charge for money. Because the same party who is storing the commodity is normally the one who has use of it, it is commercially convenient to subtract the storage charges from the use charge for the commodity, combining them into one price, say the price of a loan, P_L, as measured from the perspective of the borrower, which will be sometimes negative and sometimes positive depending on the relative size of the use charge and the costs of physical storage. Thus, the fundamental equilibrium condition is that

$$P_{ID} - P_L = P_{FD}$$

By a now familiar argument, in this set of markets one of the three is redundant. All necessary trades for future delivery could be achieved implicitly through the appropriate combination of transactions in the explicit loan market and the explicit market for immediate delivery. Likewise, the market for immediate delivery could be implicit in combinations of the other two. Most interesting is the third permutation, in which the markets for immediate and future delivery are explicit while the market for double loans is implicit. If some dealer or processor wanted to borrow the commodity in return for providing storage services and a counter loan of money, he could manipulate the identity to

$$P_L = P_{ID} - P_{FD}$$

In other words, he could accomplish the double loan implicitly by purchasing the commodity for immediate delivery and simultaneously selling it for future delivery. This pair of simultaneous transactions is precisely that pair common to all futures markets and best called a short hedging operation.

The so-called hedges of processors and dealers are one of a pair of transactions that amounts to an arrangement to borrow commodities in return for lending money. Because processors and dealers are observed to make the other transaction in the pair, the conclusion is inescapable that they intend their positions in futures contracts to be part of an indirect method of borrowing commodities. Consequently, the proper question to ask about dealers and processors is not why they hedge, but why they want to borrow commodities. Why are they in the loan market for commodities? Answering this question will be the objective of Chapters 4 and 5. But first, the concept of implicit markets can be used in Chapter 3 to expose inconsistencies in the accepted explanations of futures markets, namely those based on risk aversion.

Futures markets and risk aversion

Now that the notions of equivalent ways to trade and implicit markets have been established, it is time to apply those perspectives to the theories of why futures markets exist. The purpose of the subsequent chapter is to develop a new theory of futures markets based on the conclusion that a hedging operation amounts to a loan. But before proceeding to that task, it is necessary to discredit the principal existing theories of futures markets.

The majority of scholars have examined futures markets from the perspective of aversion to risk. This perspective has led to two distinct, although closely connected, theories: The older theory is that of normal backwardation; the now dominant theory is best called the portfolio theory of hedging. Both these theories depict the primary function of futures markets as the transferal of risk from handlers of the commodity to those who are more willing to bear it and, in the extreme, have described futures markets as no more than markets for insurance against fluctuating prices. Depending on a processor's or dealer's aversion to risk, he "hedges" his positions in the physical commodity with positions in futures contracts.

These two theories based on risk aversion both err in their fundamental assumption of futures markets as isolated, explicit markets. Although the two theories acknowledge that the positions in futures contracts are taken in reference to positions in the physical commodity, they present the decision to use futures contracts as an afterthought rather than an integral part of the decision to take the position in the physical commodity.

Because of their schooling, especially training in modern finance theory, economists quite naturally have examined the behavior of handlers of commodities from the perspective of risk aversion. A variety of positions, such as owning shares of Ford in addition to GM, is advantageous to any investor averse to risk. Manifestly, the typical handler of commodities who hedges holds several positions, one in the physical commodity, and another in a futures contract. Thus, economists follow their training: A variety of positions indicates an attempt at portfolio diversification; the desire for diversification stems from risk aversion; hence handlers of commodities who sell futures contracts do so because they are risk averse.

Yet even the strongest believer in the concept of portfolio diversification must admit it poorly describes some combinations of positions in the stock market. Yes, an investor observed to own 100 shares of Ford and 100 shares of GM is almost surely attempting to diversify. But what if that investor is observed instead to have sold the 100 shares of Ford short, rather than to have purchased them? Rather than describe the position in Ford as a response to the risk of holding GM alone, it is much more insightful to describe the positions in Ford and GM together as a method of speculating on the performance of GM relative to Ford.

At the very least, combinations of positions should not automatically be presumed to be responses to risk aversion. For one, the typical hedging operation, comprising a long position in the physical commodity and a short position in futures, looks more like the second example of long one stock and short another, rather than long both stocks. As with the combination of long GM and short Ford, one suspects that risk aversion and portfolio diversification do not capture the motives for a hedging operation.

Given that positions in several assets may arise either as a response to risk aversion or as a means of constructing implicitly yet some other single position, how can one recognize the purpose of a combination of positions? One reasonable standard is whether or not the positions are conceived of simultaneously and executed simultaneously. If there is a pattern of executing certain trades together, then it is likely they should be viewed as one. In contrast, portfolio diversification will show transactions made at different times. Of course, this standard is not failsafe. A widow, seeking diversification, might buy shares in GM and in Ford on the same day. A second and more stringent standard is whether the combination of positions itself has any economic content. The purchase of 100 shares of Ford along with 100 shares of GM can be described in no other way. But the short sale of 100 shares of Ford simultaneously with the purchase of 100 shares of GM can be described as a position in the performance of GM relative to Ford. Hence, the purpose of those two positions is not diversification.

By these two standards, the perspective of risk aversion and portfolio diversification is inappropriate for analyzing the combination of positions taken by handlers of commodities. Dealers and processors are commonly observed to execute their transactions in futures contracts simultaneously with transactions in the physical commodity. More important, the combination of positions constituting a

hedging operation has an economic content. A short hedging operation amounts to borrowing the commodity immediately. A long
hedging operation amounts to the forward sale of processing services, and sometimes in addition, an arrangement made in advance
to borrow a commodity.[1]

Proof that a hedging operation has a recognizable economic content should stop all discussion that one of its component transactions, namely the position in the futures market, is motivated by risk
aversion. Unfortunately, the association of futures markets with risk
aversion is too firmly entrenched, even though Working in 1962
characterized that association as disproved (1962: Table 1). Fortunately, it is also possible to dismiss the theory of normal backwardation and the portfolio theory of hedging on their own merits. That is
the purpose of this chapter.

Circumscribed as they are by the notion of risk aversion, both the
theory of normal backwardation and the portfolio theory of hedging
provide inadequate explanations of the salient features of the
spreads in futures prices as outlined in Chapter 1. Moreover, they
are both internally inconsistent as logical arguments. The theory of
normal backwardation examines only one trade out of a simultaneous set of trades, and consequently the effect of that trade is misrep-
resented entirely. For its part, the portfolio theory of hedging misrepresents the return to hedging operations because it fails to see
them as implicit positions. If the return to hedging is represented
correctly, the theory itself shows that a dealer's decision to use futures markets depends on his desire to speculate, far from his presumed desire to avoid risk. More important, the portfolio theory of
hedging begins the analysis at an inappropriate predetermined position. If the correct starting point were chosen instead, the exact
opposite prediction from the initial presumption of the theory
would be deduced, because in fact more risk aversion induces
dealers in commodities to use futures contracts less rather than
more. This is true even if so-called basis risk is included.

3.1. The dominance of the perspective of risk aversion

In the scholarly literature on futures markets, two strands may be
discerned in which risk aversion is the starting point of the analysis.

---

[1] By these standards, Schrock's (1971) explanation, based on portfolio diversification,
of the straddles typical of positions of speculators in futures markets is off the mark.
Peterson (1977) in his criticism of Schrock also misses the point that straddles have
an economic content sufficient to explain why traders take positions in them.

The much older approach is associated with the name of Keynes, although many others have advanced variants of his theory.[2] Keynes's theory of normal backwardation explains the prevalence of negative spreads as an insurance premium handlers of a commodity pay to speculators to protect themselves from the risk of the fluctuating value of their inventories. When people buy life or fire insurance they base their actions on their own utility functions. Because most of them have diminishing marginal utility for any particular good, they prefer a certain amount of that good to a variable amount with the same average. That is, the risk aversion displayed in their utility functions encourages them to buy insurance because insurance provides certainty.

The second strand of literature is based on portfolio theory. Just as investors in stocks select a mixture of securities to reduce the variance in the rate of return of their whole portfolio, handlers of commodities are posited to use futures markets to achieve the best combination of the variability in and the average of rates of return. How much a firm uses futures markets depends on its owners' or managers' preferences toward risk. The portfolio theory of hedging maintains that the more averse to risk a firm is, the more it uses futures markets.

Scholarly discussions of risk, such as the theory of normal backwardation and the portfolio theory of hedging, distinguish sharply between risk and risk aversion, much more so than common usage. "Risk" is the inherent and inevitable randomness in the world. "Risk aversion" refers to the attitude toward such risk embodied in a firm's or trader's preferences. Risk aversion corresponds to a nonlinear utility function, such that the firm or trader prefers a certain outcome to a variable outcome with the same average. Although all may agree on the extent of risk in a given situation, the degree of risk aversion depends on the individual. While some people are risk neutral in that they are indifferent between a certain outcome and a variable outcome with the same average, and others who love a gamble prefer risk, most people are risk averse. The attitude of aversion to risk encourages such people, including managers and owners of firms, to buy insurance, restrict their assets, and so forth, in an attempt to make their circumstances more certain.

The pervasiveness of theories like that of normal backwardation and the portfolio theory have advanced the association of risk aver-

---

[2] Hicks (1946: 137-140), for one, restated and expanded Keynes's theory, and so the theory is also associated with his name.

sion and futures markets beyond the sphere of scholarly preoccupation. In part this is because laymen have a different definition of risk aversion than the scholarly one. To laymen risk aversion commonly means avoidance of downside risk exclusively while to scholars it means avoidance of swings, both up and down. The lay definition may accord with reasons dealers use futures markets even though the scholarly definition does not, and as a result practitioners may not contradict theorists. But for whatever reason, the popular literature in the trade reflects a reliance on some notion of risk aversion. For instance, when a handler of commodities buys or sells a futures contract, his transaction is called a "hedge" in the idiom of risk. Meanwhile, the Chicago Board of Trade maintains in its promotional literature (1972: 3) that "the objective of hedging is to protect the value of existing inventory and to earn a storage return if possible." Finally, Congress, when establishing the Commodity Futures Trading Commission in 1974, believed that handlers of commodities use futures markets "as a means of hedging themselves against possible loss through fluctuations in price."[3]

3.2.   The theory of normal backwardation

The scholarly association of futures markets with risk aversion is long-lived: A professor of insurance solicited the first collection of papers on futures markets, published in 1911.[4] In those early papers, and as popularized in modern economic textbooks as well, futures markets are portrayed as providing simple insurance against movements in the value of inventory.[5] Firms using futures were thought to sell a futures contract against their spot purchases in order to achieve a capital gain that would counterbalance a decline in the value of their inventory. The roughly parallel movement in spot and futures prices was thought to make this "insurance" possible. A typical representation is that of a miller who having bought wheat at $3.00 a bushel, sells a futures contract for $3.00. Through a fall in the futures price to $2.50, he would earn back on his profitable short position what he lost on the simultaneous drop in the spot price. Likewise, a gain of $1.00 on spot wheat would be eliminated

---

[3] *United States Code* Title 7, Chap. 1, Sec. 5, Resolution Declaring Dangerous Tendency of Dealings in Commodity Futures.
[4] *Annals of the Academy of Political and Social Sciences* (1911).
[5] See, for example, Charles W. Baird, *Prices and Markets: Intermediate Microeconomics* 2nd ed. (St. Paul, Minnesota: West Publishing, 1982), which devotes an entire chapter to futures markets.

by a simultaneous loss of $1.00 per bushel in the futures market. Naively viewed, futures contracts counterbalance the "price risk" of holding inventories.

In the 1930s and early 1940s several British economists, among them Keynes (1930), Kaldor (1939), Dow (1940), and Blau (1944), focused upon this simple description of futures markets as insurance markets for price risk. Blau (p. 10) succinctly stated their position:

The system of futures trading is based on the fact that cash and futures prices move together. Clearly, the effectiveness of hedging (i.e. the effectiveness of neutralising price risks in the cash market by assuming opposite risks in the futures market) must be impaired to the extent to which the movements of cash and futures prices diverge.

Although maintaining that futures markets resemble markets for insurance, Blau recognized that futures markets could not operate like standard insurance markets. By pooling the independent risks of many individuals to fire, theft, or death, an insurance company can closely anticipate the number who actually suffer a loss, and thereby substantially reduce its own risk. Unlike with fire or theft, all firms gain or lose together on their inventories, because the value of inventory is determined by a marketwide price. Pooling their risk will not reduce it. How can futures markets operate as insurance markets if the risks of holding inventories cannot be pooled? According to Blau, they do so by transferring the risk of owning the commodity from a party who wants to avoid the risk to someone else (p. 1):

Commodity futures exchanges are market organizations specially developed for facilitating the shifting of risks due to unknown future changes in commodity prices; i.e. risks which are of such a nature that they cannot be covered by ordinary insurance.

The theory of normal backwardation, and the portfolio theory of hedging as well, presume that handlers of commodities use futures contracts because they, being risk averse, wish to transfer the risk of holding inventories to others. In conjunction with their inventories many dealers sell a futures contract. Other dealers, especially exporters and processors, make deals with their customers several months in advance. These dealers often buy a futures contract, usually in their input. Regardless of whether they are short or long in the futures market, hedgers, by definition, are combining a position in futures with some other position, commonly referred to as a position in the "cash" market or in "actuals."

Sometimes the buyer of the short hedger's sale of a futures con-

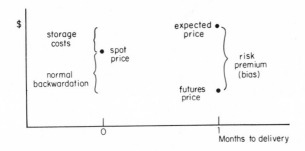

Figure 3.1. The theory of normal backwardation

tract will be another dealer in the commodity, that is, a long hedger. Yet the amount of short hedging usually outweighs long hedging.[6] If more hedgers want to sell rather than buy futures contracts, someone has to buy the excess. According to the theory of normal backwardation, speculators who are willing to take on risk buy the excess. Generally speaking, speculators are traders in futures who are not in a business associated with the physical commodity and hence could avoid risk by circumventing futures markets altogether.

What induces speculators to take on the risk of a position in futures? The answer to this question is central to the theory of normal backwardation first formulated by Keynes. Keynes (1930: 143) argued, when stocks are of average size,

> the spot price must exceed the forward price by the amount which the producer is ready to sacrifice in order to "hedge" himself, i.e. to avoid the risk of price fluctuations during his production period. Thus in normal conditions the spot price exceeds the forward price, i.e. there is a backwardation.

The speculator earns a premium for bearing risk because futures prices are biased downward as estimates of the spot prices that will rule in the future. These relationships are shown in Figure 3.1.

At the crux of the theory of normal backwardation is the observation that hedgers are net short as a group. From this fact comes both the belief that hedgers are seeking insurance and the prediction that speculators must be paid a risk premium to provide it. It is the apparent selling pressure from short hedgers that causes the supposed bias in the futures price; the subsequent buying pressure

---

[5] In recent years, long hedging has come to equal or dominate short hedging in several markets, for example, the corn market, because of increased long hedging by exporters.

whenever the hedgers offset their positions bids the price back up, with speculators profiting from the advance. If a speculator maintains a long position consistently, which speculators as a group do inasmuch as hedgers are net short as a group, he will earn a profit on average from the general tendency of futures prices to rise as the contracts mature. (They become less biased as their expiration approaches, and at the end they must equal the spot price.) Sometimes of course the long will lose money, when there is a general decline in price, for instance; at other times he will make more than the risk premium. Because a short hedge placed in a more distant contract provides insurance over a longer period of time, a short hedger must offer a larger inducement to speculators, increasing the bias with the distance of the contract to the present.

The crucial prediction of the theory of normal backwardation is that futures prices are biased. This bias is precisely what gives rise to the mysterious negative component of spreads. According to Keynes, the risk premium under normal conditions is large enough for futures prices to be biased to the extent of being in a backwardation. If the true expected prices were visible, they would be much more likely to display full carrying charges in their spreads.

3.3.   A critique of the theory of normal backwardation

A critical examination of the theory of normal backwardation reveals a number of problems. Not only does its major prediction, that of bias in prices, fail, but the theory is extremely limited in its explanatory power since it cannot fully account for the diversity and volatility so significant to the spreads in futures markets. Most important, the theory suffers from inconsistencies in logic.

To begin, one can question the empirical validity of the prediction of the theory of normal backwardation that futures prices are biased downward. A test for bias concerns whether as time passes futures prices rise to meet spot prices or whether spot prices fall to meet futures prices (they must of course be equal when the futures contract expires). The test must necessarily be imprecise because prices, both spot and futures, move considerably even as they converge. Yet to support the theory of normal backwardation, futures prices should rise on average to an extent equal to the average degree to which futures prices are below full carrying charges.

If any consensus has emerged, it is that no significant bias exists in futures prices. They show no systematic tendency to rise as the futures contract approaches expiration. The subject of bias in futures prices is still controversial, in part because it is so difficult to account for the upward trend in prices with the unanticipated inflation of the last decades. Telser (1958 and 1960) studied the wheat and cotton markets and claimed to have found no bias, although Cootner (1960), in reworking Telser's data, concluded that some bias was present. Gray (1960 and 1961), attempting to balance the two, concluded that there was effectively no bias in large markets like corn, although smaller, relatively inactive futures markets might be biased. Rockwell's work (1967) covered a greater number of commodities, and while some appeared biased downward, just as many appeared biased upward. He concluded (p. 127) that the "theory clearly does not have general applicability for all futures markets and it is questionable whether an analysis of variance performed over the 25 markets would indicate a single market with a positive return significantly greater than zero."

All of these studies searched for bias by considering what a trader with a hypothetical position in futures would have earned given the actual series of spot and futures prices. They varied, however, in their choice of sample and of the appropriate hypothetical position, specifically in whether it should vary in size with the extent of hedging in the market. Dusak (1973) avoided these problems by approaching the question of bias and risk premiums from a different perspective, that of what a speculator would have to earn to induce him into the futures market. She concluded that a speculator does not need to be enticed with a risk premium. Her point of departure is the observation embraced by modern finance theorists: Speculators need be compensated only for what is called systematic risk, because all other risk can be diversified away. Systematic risk is best defined by an example. If the price of stock in General Motors moved randomly in relation to other stocks, the risk of owning GM could be pooled with the other stocks with the result that GM would add little risk to the whole portfolio. Consequently, there would be no risk premium in the price of GM for such diversifiable risk. But if the price of GM moved systematically with the portfolio of other stocks, say as represented by a broad index like Standard and Poor's 500, then the risk of owning shares in GM could not be diversified away. A holder of stock in GM would demand compensation in the form of a premium for this systematic risk. Because of this risk premium, the rate of return on GM stock would be higher. In the setting of futures markets, a speculator would need to be compensated for bearing risk only to the extent that the risk was systematic. Thus, the amount of bias expected in futures prices equals the extent to which futures prices move systematically with a broad portfolio of assets in the economy. Dusak determined that there is no systematic relationship between movements in futures prices and movements in a broad market portfolio.[7] Thus, there is no reason to expect futures prices to include a risk premium; that is to say, there is no reason to expect futures prices to be biased.[8]

There may always be some doubt about the search for a bias in futures markets. Yet, if any bias exists, the difficulty in spotting it suggests that it must be small. But anything other than a large and easily discernible bias controverts Keynes's theory of normal backwardation. Keynes was explicit that in times of average stocks, the gap between the observed spread and the known carrying charges of interest and warehousing is solely attributable to the risk premium. That is why the theory carries the name "normal backwardation." He (1930: 144) estimated this typical risk premium to be on the order of 10 percent per annum, due to the considerable risk speculators must take on. Surely a bias as large as 10 percent per annum would be easily discernible in futures prices if it existed.[9]

If one looks in detail at the actual pattern of spreads found in futures prices, several more disquieting facts emerge, at least disquieting for the theory of normal backwardation. First of all, the theory cannot explain those periods when spreads are at full carrying charges. Keynes argued that speculators should receive the largest risk premiums when stocks are above normal levels because periods of large stocks are riskiest for them. Moreover, if his theory of normal backwardation is correct, there should never be periods of full carrying charges unless short hedging just balances long hedging. His predictions are exactly opposite the facts. In all futures markets there are times when spreads are unambiguously at full carrying

---

[7] Her estimates of the "beta" for corn, wheat, and soybeans were all on the order of .05 (1973: Table 3). GM in contrast has a beta around .60 and the market portfolio by construction one of 1.0. Carter, Rausser, and Schmitz (1983) questioned whether Dusak had constructed the broad market portfolio properly, with the inadvertent result that she understated the systematic risk of positions in futures markets. Marcus (1984) in turn has argued that Carter, Rausser, and Schmitz erred in favor of finding systematic risk when they constructed their broad market portfolio. If Marcus's results can be taken as the final word, commodities have little systematic risk.

[8] A related argument is that speculators, if they truly sought only to earn a risk premium, would hold long positions in many futures markets, since that would reduce their exposure to the vagaries of a single market. On the contrary, the largest speculators tend to specialize in a particular market.

[9] All those after Keynes who have investigated empirically the bias in futures accepted that the bias would be small. Consequently, all conceded that bias, even if it existed, cannot on its own explain the pattern of backwardation found in arrays of commodity prices.

charges, that is, when a hedger can be certain of covering all his expenses for storing the commodity. But these periods of full carrying charges, which occur most often early in the crop-year while large stocks are in store, are the periods when short hedging is highest, both absolutely and relative to long hedging (Houthakker 1968: Table 3). With short and long hedging so out of balance, it should be precisely these periods in which the largest risk premium would have to be paid to attract the additional long speculation.[10] Keynes attempted to explain away this contradiction by arguing that in times of full carrying charges the futures price and the current spot price are both biased downward (i.e., so they appear as full carrying charges). Keynes's explanation is inadequate. If the spot price itself is biased downward, what happens to the supposition that futures prices are biased predictors of the spot price? Furthermore, what determines the periods in which the current spot price is no longer biased downward? Clearly, a major inconsistency in the theory arises from the presence of full carrying charges simultaneously with long and short hedging being out of balance.

In addition, Keynes's emphasis on bias, even if it were justified, is not sufficient to explain the volatility in spreads and hence is seriously incomplete as an explanation of their behavior. Sometimes with the passage of a week or two, spreads will move up or down the equivalent of several percent of the spot value of the commodity, as the behavior of the September '79-October '79 spread in soybeans illustrated. Keynes would have attributed such volatility to changes in the risk premium. But changes in the risk premium alone cannot be large enough to cause such fluctuations. First of all, from the supposed demand side for insurance, the imbalance of short hedging over long hedging does not move so radically as it would need to do to cause such swings in spreads, even if the supply of speculators is relatively inelastic, which it almost surely is not. Second, speculators, the supposed suppliers of insurance, do not revise, in a week's time, their estimates of the riskiness of their long positions to the extent that they double or halve the risk premium that they require.

For the same reasons the theory has trouble explaining why spreads in the same commodity move differently. Sometimes the spread between two nearby delivery months moves closer to full carrying charges, which would be interpreted as the risk premium

---

[10] A related point concerns those markets in which long hedgers dominate. These markets are not prone to full carrying charges, which they should be without short hedgers' downward pressure on futures prices. Rather, these markets too display spreads below full carrying charges.

becoming smaller, while the spread between two distant contracts moves in the opposite direction. It seems implausible that over the course of a few hours or a few days the demand for insurance over one period shrinks while it expands for a later period. Nor does it seem plausible that the behavior of the supply of insurance could explain such changes.

Yet the volatility of spreads is damaging to the theory of normal backwardation for a more important reason. According to the school represented by Keynes and Blau, volatile spreads should impair futures markets. The system of futures trading as price insurance rests on the parallel movement of spot and futures prices; the more nearly parallel the movement, the better is the insurance and the more dealers want to short hedge. By definition volatile spreads imply that spot and future prices do not move in parallel. Far from being inactive when spreads are volatile and price insurance poor, that is precisely when futures markets are robust.

Although the theory of normal backwardation receives little empirical support, researchers who have tested it, including those skeptical of the theory, have persisted in viewing the theory's validity as an empirical issue. They have never questioned its underlying logic. The starting point of the whole theory is questionable, however. Slight alterations in the method of transacting between hedger and speculator that do not change the effect of the transactions do radically change the theory's perspective on the motives for the transactions.

At the center of the theory of normal backwardation is the relationship between a short hedger and a long speculator. A typical short hedging operation begins when a miller, for example, buys wheat from a farmer on the spot market. The miller in turn sells a futures contract to a speculator, supposedly to avoid the risk from the fluctuating value of his inventory. To persuade the speculator to take on this risk, the miller must, according to the theory, offer the futures contract at a discount.

But the same line of reasoning applied to the relation between the miller and speculator would be untenable if the trades were conducted in a slightly different manner to achieve the same economic effect. Imagine that instead of buying the wheat outright, the miller makes a repurchase agreement with the farmer. The effect of this repurchase agreement is that the miller has the use of the farmer's wheat over the period of the agreement, just as if he had received it on loan, while the farmer has the use of the miller's money, just as if he had received it on loan. Once the initial step of the repurchase agreement has passed, the miller now holding the wheat and the farmer the money, it will appear that the farmer has an obligation to buy wheat from the miller while the miller has the obligation to sell wheat to the farmer. Despite these appearances, the repurchase part of the agreement exists to return the wheat and money to their original owners. Suppose, however, that the farmer decides that he no longer wants to own his wheat. He could wait until it is returned to him to sell it outright, or he could sell it in advance of its return by selling a contract for future delivery, say to a speculator. But he already owns a contract on which he will be receiving wheat, as the result of his repurchase agreement with the miller. Rather than receive wheat from the miller and deliver it in turn to the speculator, would it not be much easier for the farmer to instruct the miller to deliver the wheat directly to the speculator? The miller, of course, will want his money back, so the farmer and speculator must agree upon how to return the miller's money. Regardless of the particulars of the deal between the farmer and the speculator, the speculator will assume the farmer's obligation with the miller, and consequently it will look as if the miller has sold the speculator a contract for future delivery. This appearance will be especially pronounced if the farmer sells his repurchase contract quickly.

The effect of a miller's purchase of wheat from a farmer and simultaneous sale of a futures contract to a speculator is equivalent to that of the miller entering into a repurchase agreement with the farmer and the farmer independently selling a contract for future delivery to a speculator. The miller and speculator need have nothing to do with one another; their only contact is an effort to reduce the handling costs of delivering wheat back to the farmer and then his redelivery to the speculator. The transaction at the heart of the theory of normal backwardation, namely the miller's short sale to a speculative long, disappears. Because nothing of substance has changed with this reformulation, the theory cannot have captured the motivation for that transaction.

The confusion in interpreting a hedging operation arises from looking at only half of the whole repurchase agreement. In isolation it would seem that a miller's decision to sell wheat short would depress the price of wheat for future delivery, that the firm has also bought wheat for immediate delivery, and that purchase should raise the price of wheat. Taken together, it is not at all clear what effect the two transactions have on the level of prices, because spot and futures prices are not unaffected by the other. All that is evident from this double transaction is that the hedging operation should affect the price of the spread between immediate and future delivery. It is possible that the hedging operation has an effect on the forward price of wheat, but the direction of the effect is far from obvious. It could well be that the expressed demand to borrow wheat, if that demand is presumed to be sustained, boosts its price for future delivery, even as it changes the spread.[11] That is to say, a hedging operation may raise both spot and futures prices even as it raises the spot price relative to the futures price. In any case, it is far from clear that a hedging operation, with both of its constituent transactions taken together, biases futures prices downward as estimates of the spot prices that will prevail rather than simply changing both futures prices and expected spot prices.

The tendency to view in isolation the part of the repurchase agreement that involves the futures market is natural because the center of interest is the use of futures contracts. But the origin of the wheat against which the short sale is made must not be ignored. If the miller obtained the wheat by standing for delivery on a futures contract he bought while simultaneously selling a contract in a more distant month, it would be clear that his two transactions would have to be examined as a pair. The same approach is appropriate even if he bought on the spot market because the spot transaction is really just another contract in the whole range of contracts with delivery dates stretching from the immediate to the distant future.

3.4.   The portfolio theory of hedging

The other major theory presuming a role for risk aversion, the portfolio theory of hedging, contains internal inconsistencies as well. The problem is not with portfolio theory itself but with its application to hedging. The major postulate of portfolio analysis, not disputed here, is that among assets with the same average return, people prefer those whose returns are least risky. Of course, a higher expected return might induce people to hold a riskier asset. The tradeoff between risk and return induces people to combine several assets into a portfolio, because generally speaking a mixture of assets will be less risky than any one single asset.

After the formulation of portfolio theory in the 1950s, one of its first applications was to the question of hedging by dealers in commodities. Johnson (1960) and then Stein (1961) contended that firms

---

[11] To put the problem another way, what does a French firm's decision to borrow francs for three months do to the ninety-day forward rate between the franc and the dollar?

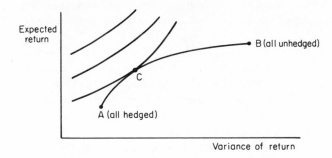

Figure 3.2. The choice of the extent of hedging

in the commodity business consider a blend of two assets, hedged inventory, which earns a low but relatively steady rate of return and unhedged inventory, which has a higher but riskier return.[12] Depending on his preference toward risk, a dealer or processor hedges some proportion of his inventory with the sale of a futures contract. The fundamental conclusion of the portfolio theory of hedging is that a greater degree of risk aversion induces a processor or dealer to use futures markets more.

In its simplest form, the portfolio theory of hedging begins with the assumption that hedged and unhedged inventory are two separate assets that a dealer in commodities could combine into a portfolio based on the riskiness of their returns. Unhedged inventory is simply a commodity in store while hedged inventory is actually a package of two assets, a commodity in store and a short position in a futures market. Since the asset hedged inventory embodies the sale of a futures contract, the number of futures contracts sold depends on the proportion of hedged inventory in the portfolio. Stein (1961: 1015), for example, portrays the choice of the amount of inventory to hedge graphically, as shown in Figure 3.2.[13] At point *A*, all the resources in the portfolio are hedged, which is to say, futures contracts for all of the inventory have been sold. At *B*, all resources are in unhedged inventory, which is to say, no futures contracts have been sold. The curve connecting these two extremes represents the

---

[12] Telser (1955) made the choice of hedging depend on the riskiness of positions, although not in the analytical framework of portfolio theory, which was just then emerging. Also see Ward and Fletcher (1971).

[13] The choice could also be presented algebraically as in, for example, Anderson and Danthine (1981), but what is wrong with the portfolio theory of hedging is most easily seen graphically.

expected return and the variance of the return of various combinations of hedged and unhedged inventory. A point halfway along the curve corresponds to 50% hedged. The shape of that curve depends upon the correlation between the returns to the two assets; the more negative is the correlation, the more the curve is bowed up to the left. If the indifference curves corresponding to a firm's preferences toward risk were superimposed on the figure, the portfolio that particular firm would select would correspond to point *C*, and by extension, the firm's use of a futures market could be calculated. (It is about 70% hedged as drawn.) Each and every dealer would chose to hedge more or less depending on his own preferences toward risk. If a dealer were neutral toward risk, he would select the asset with the highest expected return, ignoring entirely the asset's variance. With the choices as drawn, he would hold all his inventories unhedged. Therefore, since risk aversion would seem to induce dealers to use futures markets more, portfolio analysis would seem to buttress the belief that the vitality of futures markets depends crucially on the risk aversion of dealers and processors.

This representation of hedging as the selection of an optimal portfolio, in which aversion to risk is fundamental, has come to dominate research on futures markets. Rutledge (1972: 239), in examining soybean processors' demand for futures contracts, employed a model "in which both risk and expected return are used as decision-making variables." Peck (1975) used the portfolio theory in an article on egg producers, Leuthold and Mokler (1979) in one on cattle feeding, and Rolfo (1980) in one on cocoa producers. Ederington (1979) applied the portfolio perspective to the new futures markets in financial instruments. Anderson and Danthine (1980 and 1981) have applied the portfolio perspective to the problem of a firm whose output, sorghum for example, is not exactly the commodity traded in the futures markets, while Batlin (1983) considered the effect of imperfect timing. Others on the strategy of a single firm include Baesel and Grant (1982) and Benninga, Eldor, and Zilcha (1984). Stein (1979), Stoll (1979), Anderson and Danthine (1983a and 1983b), and Britto (1984) have worked to extend these models of a single firm to the equilibrium resulting from the combined actions of many such firms. The portfolio theory of hedging has been a spectacular growth industry.

3.5.   Misconceptions in the portfolio theory of hedging

Despite its popularity, the portfolio theory of hedging examines inappropriate assets and misrepresents the risks associated with positions in commodity markets. After the risks of positions have been properly stated, one can use the precepts of portfolio analysis itself to cast considerable doubt on the validity of the fundamental prediction of the portfolio theory of hedging. The theory presumes that the more dealers are averse to risk, the more likely they are to use futures markets. A more careful analysis of the risks facing a miller, soybean crusher, or exporter suggests that exactly the opposite behavior may be the most common. If the risks of owning processing facilities, not inventory, are taken as the starting point, which seems reasonable given their greater importance to the firm, portfolio theory implies that dealers who are most risk averse use futures markets least.

The portfolio theory of hedging is unduly sensitive to a slight change in perspective or starting position. How would the results differ if the firm's processing facilities, the returns to which are risky, were included in the analysis? What would be given as the motives of a new owner of a processor who is observed to be going long in the futures market? What would be the results if the inventory involved were deliverable on a futures contract? With any of these slight changes, the portfolio theory of hedging breaks down.

Because of the sensitivity of the results to the starting point, it seems best to begin with the simplest case possible. Imagine a miller in Chicago whose inventory of wheat is of the grade deliverable on futures contracts. Suppose further that whenever this miller sells a futures contract against part of his inventory, he makes delivery on that contract. Think of the miller as being in the storage business, owning an elevator. In later sections of this chapter, the complications of the miller not having a deliverable grade, called "basis risk," and of him routinely "lifting his hedge" rather than make delivery will be considered. The standard version of the portfolio theory of hedging begins with these complications. Instead of leading to broader results, however, starting with these complications hides several misconceptions in the analysis.

The simple starting point of a dealer with deliverable inventory uncovers four problems with the portfolio theory of hedging. First, there is no risk to a hedging operation involving a deliverable grade.[14] The apparent fluctuations of the spot price relative to the futures price are actually the inevitable convergence of the two prices. Second, the portfolio theory of hedging actually rests on the discredited proposition of the theory of normal backwardation,

[14] There could be a risk, however, if the firm cannot deliver its own inventory on its short position in futures, as will be discussed later in sections 3.7 and 3.8.

namely that futures prices are biased downward. Third, the decision
about the extent of hedging could well be the result of the desire to
speculate, rather than because of risk aversion. Fourth, and ultimately most important, if the hedger's processing facilities are included in the analysis, portfolio theory itself implies that the dealers
and processors who are most risk averse will use futures markets the
least, rather than the most.

The first three of these misconceptions are best exposed by reference to the diagram of the choice of the extent of hedging, Figure
3.2. That is not to suggest this diagram properly represents a processor's possible portfolios. (Quite the contrary is true.) Rather, there
are problems with the diagram even granting the suppositions behind it – the choice being only between the two assets hedged inventory or unhedged inventory and the unhedged position earning a
higher mean return.

First of all, contrary to the presentation in Figure 3.2, the variance
of the return to hedged wheat should be zero, as long as the wheat
in question is deliverable on the futures contract. A simple example
indicates the source of the confusion. Suppose today, 1 January, the
hedge is placed in March wheat (delivery will be late in March).
Imagine that the price of wheat for immediate delivery is 12¢ per
bushel below the price of the March futures contract. Quite clearly
on the day of delivery in late March, the spread between spot and
futures prices must be 0¢, since on that date both represent contracts for the immediate delivery of the same variety of wheat. All
the movement in the spread was the convergence of the spot and
futures prices. The portfolio theory of hedging mistakenly assigns
the movement resulting from this inevitable convergence as a risk to
hedging operations. It is not a risk, being fully predictable.

Gray (1984) has made this point emphatically in his criticism of
the portfolio theory of hedging and his defense of Working's alter-
nate explanation. Yet Working himself, contrary to his intention, has
furthered the impression of hedged inventory being an asset with an
uncertain return rather than one with a certain return. He states
(1953b: 547), "The effectiveness of hedging . . . depends upon *in-
equalities* between the movements of spot and futures prices and on
reasonable predictability of such movements" (emphasis in original).
Contrary to the impression given by Working's statement, however,
the movement is not a movement in relative price but the convergence of spot and futures price as the contract matures, which must
occur if they truly refer to the same grade and location. Working
intended to emphasize this convergence of spot and futures prices

and how closely they are tied together, but he chose a way that left exactly the opposite impression. Given the possibility of such misunderstandings, the main point bears repeating. The price of wheat of the contract grade for immediate delivery in Chicago must converge with the price of the futures contract in which the hedge is placed, because the futures contract when it expires will be for immediate delivery of that type of wheat. As a result, the return to hedging wheat of the contract grade in Chicago is certain.[15]

Often a perfect hedge is claimed, as by Blau, for the period of time during which the spot and futures prices track each other with a perfect correlation of +1.0. But because the spot price and the futures price must converge, they cannot track one another perfectly. Consider the case where the futures price does not move from $3.00 a bushel. The spot price, whatever it began at some months before, say $2.80, is ultimately $3.00. The correlation between spot and futures is 0.0, yet there is no risk to the hedging operation.

The certainty of the return to hedged inventory of the deliverable grade is true even if the spot price does not steadily converge on the price of the futures contract. After the hedge is put on, say at the rate that would return 1¢ per bushel per week for the twelve weeks of the hedge, a sudden shortage of supplies in Chicago might drive the return for holding wheat, if set at the new rate, much lower. Even so, the original hedger can always persevere, deliver as arranged, and still earn the 1¢ per bushel per week. If the return on a hedging operation suddenly rises, say because of a sudden glut of wheat in Chicago, the dealer can still do no better than the return he previously contracted for. To sell his storage service at a higher price, he must buy back his previous commitment at exactly that price.

The next two misconceptions are exposed with the aid of a simple manipulation of the definition of a hedging operation. Although the normal perspective is to view a hedging operation as a package of assets, namely as the addition to unhedged inventory of a short position in futures, it is just as legitimate to view unhedged inventory as a package, as the addition to hedged inventory of a long position in futures. After all, one need only imagine a palpable certificate,

[15] One might object to this assertion because even if the monetary return is certain its purchasing power is not. This is the same question as whether Treasury bills have a riskless return. Yet this issue is not relevant here. Implicitly this complication adds other assets to the two portrayed in the portfolio theory of hedging. If the theory has any validity, it should not need to rely on such a deus ex machina.

denominated in units of hedged inventory and representing a single item rather than a package. In that case, the asset called unhedged wheat, rather than a single item, would be the combination of the single financial instrument representing hedged wheat and the financial instrument representing a long position in a wheat futures contract. Thus, both hedged and unhedged inventory can be viewed either as a solitary instrument or as a package of assets. Consequently, wherever unhedged inventory is mentioned, it can be replaced by the sum of hedged inventory and a long position in futures.

This perspective of unhedged inventory as itself the package of hedged inventory plus a long position in futures changes the emphasis in the analysis of futures markets from one of asking why firms sell short to one of asking why they take on a long position in futures. Of course, they are not actually observed to buy a futures contract, that position being implicitly the result of their decision to hedge less than all of their inventory. Surely, the firms should have the same motive for taking on a long position whether they do so implicitly or explicitly. Consequently, it is reasonable to ask why they take on a long position.

How is it that the question about dealers' and processors' use of futures contracts has been recast into a question about their holding long positions when, in fact, they are observed to be short? All this is not mere sleight of hand. Every combination of assets creates a net position. The portfolio theory of hedging imagines firms beginning with all their holdings in the asset unhedged inventory and then achieving their desired portfolio with the sale of futures contracts. Yet the same final blend of hedged and unhedged inventory can be reached just as easily from the starting point of all inventory being hedged. In that case, the firm achieves its final blend by buying futures contracts. Perhaps the nature of the argument can best be understood by imagining a new owner taking over a commodity processor. Because he has different preferences toward risk than the previous owner, he wants to adjust the inherited portfolio of hedged and unhedged inventory. If the existing portfolio is too weighted toward unhedged inventory for his taste, he sells futures contracts. If the existing portfolio is too weighted toward hedged inventory, he goes long (in effect canceling some of the outstanding short positions). In the extreme, the inherited (i.e., initial) position could be either a position of all hedged or a position of all unhedged. For the portfolio theory of hedging to have any validity, it must explain the decision of the new owner from any existing position. Thus, a question about dealers' use of futures markets in going long is entirely reasonable.

Unfortunately for the portfolio theory of hedging, which provides a seemingly convincing explanation of the decision to sell short when the starting point of the analysis is an unhedged position, the plausible reasons to go long, which arise when the starting point is a position of entirely hedged inventory, are dramatically opposed to the presumptions of the theory. It is instructive to consider what could be put forth as reasons for a dealer taking on a long position in futures contracts, whether hypothetically as an explicit position or in practice as an implicit position. Broadly speaking, there are two plausible reasons for a dealer to take on a long position in futures. These are for the purposes of speculation or of avoidance of risk. Although these two purposes are at odds with each other, both are antithetical to the idea that a firm goes short in futures, that is, hedges, in order to avoid risk. If a firm is speculating, clearly it is not avoiding risk. Or if a firm is going long to avoid risk, it cannot be going short to do the same. Thus, either the demonstration that a dealer is speculating or the demonstration that he is avoiding risk by not hedging suffices to discredit the portfolio theory of hedging.

To begin these demonstrations, the recognition of unhedged inventory as a combination of positions confronts the issue of the difference between the expected rates of return on hedged as opposed to unhedged inventory. One might well ask why hedged and unhedged inventories are drawn in Figure 3.2 with their particular combination of variances and expected rates of return. Why does unhedged inventory enjoy a higher expected rate of return? It does only if futures prices are biased downward. Implicitly the portfolio theory of hedging is relying on the theory of normal backwardation, which is a shaky foundation indeed. Because unhedged inventory equals hedged inventory plus a long position in futures, the two rates of return differ by the expected return on a long position in the futures market. In opposition to the theory of normal backwardation, my empirical and logical analysis of holding a long position in futures contracts concluded in section 3.3 that the expected return is zero. In that case, the expected returns on hedged and unhedged wheat are the same, and points A and B in Figure 3.2 should be drawn at the same level, rather than with point B higher than point A.

Because the return to hedged inventory has no variance when the inventory is of the deliverable grade, the diagram of expected return and the variance of the return should be redrawn to look something

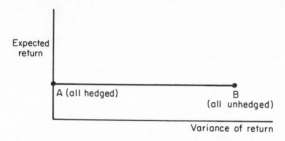

Figure 3.3. The choice of the extent of hedging for the deliverable grade

like Figure 3.3. First, because hedged wheat has an assured return, the point for it is now on the axis. Its height depends on the spread between the spot and futures prices at the time that the hedge was placed. (As pictured here, the hedging operation earns a positive return, indicating that initially the spot price was below the futures price.) Second, the expected return to unhedged wheat is the same as the return to hedged wheat, because the long position implicit in unhedged wheat only earns something above zero on average if there is a downward bias in futures prices. Given this reformulation of the possible portfolios ranging from all hedged to all unhedged, according to the portfolio model itself, any firm the least bit risk averse will choose always to be hedged completely. It would gain no extra return by taking on the additional risk of an unhedged position.

Even if there is an extra return to be gained from a long position in futures, any motive special to being a dealer is immaterial to the firm's decision to hedge a quantity of the deliverable grade. This conclusion is even more damaging to the portfolio theory of hedging than the realization that it rests on the theory of normal backwardation. This conclusion negates the initial assumption of the portfolio theory of hedging that a dealer's motives are special because he is a dealer. By not hedging fully, a dealer is taking on a speculative long position and making decisions like any long speculator, decisions that do not depend at all on being a dealer. How a dealer can be acting as a speculator can be seen by considering once again the definition of hedged and unhedged inventory. Although the portfolio theory of hedging is supposedly comparing two assets, hedged wheat and unhedged wheat, one asset, hedged wheat of the deliverable grade, whose return is fixed, is included in the package representing the other asset, unhedged wheat. Hence, the asset hedged wheat could be dropped from the analysis entirely, leaving the firm to consider how large a long position in futures to take on.[16] But without any effect from the size of inventories, that decision no longer involves attributes or circumstances special to a dealer in the commodity. Although the firm's attitude toward risk surely influences the size of its long position in futures contracts, this is true of any speculator's position.

Perhaps the issue at hand can be made clearer with an example of portfolio theory applied to assets other than commodities. Imagine an investor considering the proportion of two possible investments: riskless Treasury bills or shares in a mutual fund. According to the standard perspective of portfolio theory, the investor is best advised to construct the locus of expected returns and variance of returns achieved through different combinations of T-bills and mutual fund shares. The combination he selects depends on both the performance of T-bills and the performance of the mutual fund. But suppose on closer inspection the investor discovers that the mutual fund itself invests heavily in T-bills, its other asset being shares of GM. Whether he buys shares of the mutual fund or T-bills directly, he buys T-bills. Therefore, the only decision left to him is how many shares of GM he wants to buy. The performance of T-bills is immaterial to that decision, since T-bills are riskless. Likewise, the two assets open to a dealer in commodities, as portrayed by the portfolio theory of hedging, overlap. The asset unhedged wheat is actually a mutual fund itself containing the two assets hedged wheat and a long position in wheat futures. There is, in fact, no portfolio choice at all, only the single decision about the extent of a long position in wheat. Moreover, because it is the asset hedged wheat that is special to a dealer, nothing remains in the problem that is at all connected to a dealer.

Thus, at the heart of the portfolio theory of hedging there can be speculative behavior that in no way depends on firms being handlers of the commodity, although the theory intends to explain behavior special to dealers. Worse yet, such speculative behavior on the part of the firm is opposite from that which the portfolio theory presumes. According to the portfolio theory of hedging, a dealer differs from a speculator because a dealer acts to minimize exposure to risk, while a speculator seeks risk. The dealer, however, is behaving like a speculator when he refrains from hedging.

---

[16] The point can be approached from another direction: If one of the assets is riskless, the portfolio frontier will be a straight line.

Firms with inventories of the deliverable grade who choose to hedge less than completely are taking on risks that they, like speculators, could avoid entirely. This argument is related to that of Holthausen (1979) and Feder, Just, and Schmitz (1980). They demonstrate that a firm with no uncertainty in its output, such as a copper mine, should base its production decisions solely on the futures price, that is, that it should act as if it has sold all its output forward. Any speculation based on expectations concerning price is a separate decision.[17] Such producers may begin with a large short position because of their level of production, but any decision to go long implicitly by reducing the size of the short position they make just like any speculator.

There can be no dispute that a final portfolio of hedged and unhedged wheat can be approached analytically from the starting point of either all hedged or all unhedged. The existing presentation of the portfolio theory of hedging always begins with the initial position of all inventory unhedged. In an analysis emphasizing risk aversion, a starting position of complete hedging of inventory would seem more natural, given that a hedged position involving the deliverable grade provides a riskless return. At the very least, it is damaging to the portfolio theory of hedging that the descriptions of a dealer's actions can be reformulated to make that dealer appear risk seeking rather than risk averse. Indeed, the weakness of portfolio theory in general, and of the portfolio theory of hedging in particular, is its extreme sensitivity to what is taken as the predetermined position.

3.6.   Not hedging as a response to risk aversion

Due to the sensitivity of portfolio analysis to a firm's predetermined position, surely a proper analysis of the reasons dealers use futures contracts should start with the asset that is fundamental to the firm. Rather than its inventory, a firm's processing facility is its fundamental asset. Holdings of inventories can be used or supplemented quickly. In contrast, a flour mill is far more long-lived and inflexible in size than Johnson (1960), Stein (1961), and others who take inventories as the predetermined position assume. More important, because milling and other merchandising profits are actually variable, as when a breakdown or strike reduces output or as when fluctua-

---

[17] Marcus and Modest (1984) show that even with uncertainty in production, for all practical purposes the two decisions can be made separately.

tions in the size or quality of the harvest affect the demand for milling, Johnson and Stein have excluded the important risky asset from their analysis.

This exclusion of risky processing and merchandising facilities is the fourth and in many ways most important misconception in the portfolio theory of hedging. On its face omission of processing and merchandising facilities would seem reasonable enough since the purpose of the analysis is to investigate the hedging of inventory. After all, the simplicity of a model involving two assets is an advantage compared to a model involving three assets. Yet such simplicity is appropriate only if the main conclusion remains intact. As it happens, beginning the analysis with merchandising facilities reverses the standard prediction of the portfolio model of hedging. In other words, the prediction of portfolio theory when applied to the proper initial assets is: More risk aversion implies less use of futures markets. This reversal occurs not because of something inherent in portfolios of three assets but because of the particular relationship between returns on processing facilities and returns on positions in futures contracts.

An investigation of risk aversion and commodity markets properly begins by taking a firm's position in milling, spinning, or exporting facilities as given. By owning a flour mill, a miller can be said to begin with a long position in milling. Because the return on his long position in milling fluctuates, the miller wants to know what other assets he could hold whose returns in combination with those to milling would give a better blend of expected return and variability of return than holding milling capacity alone, just as in any application of the principle of portfolio diversification.[18] Possible candidates closely related to milling are positions in forward wheat and forward freight. If it can be established that a position in these assets has a return negatively correlated with the return on milling, these are positions a risk-averse miller would reasonably include in his portfolio.[19]

The return on forward wheat, for one, does seem to be negatively correlated with the return on milling. The calculation of the correlation between assets such as milling and a long position in wheat futures is complicated by the difficulty of defining the returns on

[18] The following examples could be constructed to apply to spinners, exporters, and merchandisers as well.
[19] The emphasis on correlations places a restriction on the utility function of the miller (that it be quadratic), but relaxing this restriction would not change the analysis except to make it more complex.

such capital assets. Because the objective here is only to discover the sign rather than the exact value of the correlation, to define returns precisely, as by taking into account capital gains and losses on milling, is unnecessary. The relationship between a change in the price of milling and a change in the price of wheat closely approximates the relationship between the returns to the two assets over a relatively short period.

All available evidence points to a negative correlation between processing margins and prices of inputs. Empirical evidence is difficult to find, mainly because the prices of goods like flour are sporadically quoted, making computation of processing margins subject to considerable error. In Chicago from 1884 through 1892, the correlation between the price of milling and the price of wheat was −0.30 (Williams 1980: 305-306). Rutledge (1972: Table 2) calculated the correlation between changes in the price of soybeans and the processing margin in thirteen crop-years in the 1950s and 1960s. Eleven of the thirteen years had negative correlations; more than half were below −0.5. Paul and Wesson (1966: Figure 5) made similar calculations for soybeans for much the same period comparing crop-years rather than the behavior within one crop-year, and they found an unmistakable negative relationship between the price of soybeans and the processing margin. They concluded (p. 950) that in general "processors' margins move in the opposite direction from farm prices." Their conclusion is perfectly reasonable. After all, a large crop depresses the farm price even as it strains the capacity of processors, dealers, and shippers. A miners' strike raises the price of copper while lowering the fabricating margin. Yet there are possible exceptions. A surge in the demand for finished copper products raises both the fabricating margin and the price for copper. Thus, most generally, when the surge is in demand downstream, prices and margins move together; when it comes in supply upstream they move oppositely (Gardner 1975). In the agricultural sector of the U.S., the world's dominant producer, surges in supply must predominate. Consequently, the return on a long position in milling will be negatively correlated, although not perfectly negatively correlated, with the return on a long position in wheat.

Because of the negative correlation between the price of wheat and the price of milling, a risk-averse miller will rationally add a long position in wheat to his existing long position in milling. Even if the miller never held an inventory of wheat in the regular course of his business, he would want to add a long position in wheat. This conclusion upsets the whole portfolio theory of hedging. Its damage is not immediately obvious, however, because a miller does in fact hold an inventory of wheat in the regular course of his business. Suppose the risk-averse miller's mill is in Chicago, and as a part of his business, quite apart from any consideration of risk aversion, he holds deliverable stocks. Being deliverable, if this wheat were hedged it would have a certain return, as has been argued in section 3.5. Consequently, the size of his position in hedged inventory cannot directly influence the miller's reaction to risk. The position in hedged inventory can, however, affect the appearance of the miller's final position. To add a long position in wheat futures, he buys back some of his short contracts, which are part of his riskless short hedging operations. Or he could achieve the same result by not fully hedging any new inventory he buys. In either case, his risk aversion affects his final use of futures markets: The more risk averse is the miller, the less he uses futures contracts because of a greater desire for implicit long positions in wheat futures. This decision to go unhedged is a response to risk aversion. If the miller were neutral toward risk, he would be fully hedged, and his use of futures markets would be greater.

A careful analysis of the portfolio problem of dealers in commodities, taking their positions in processing facilities as given, implies that risk aversion inhibits their use of futures markets, since returns to processing facilities are likely to be negatively correlated with returns to long positions in the raw material. In section 3.5, it was argued that a firm's decision to go unhedged might be motivated by a desire to speculate. Whether a firm goes unhedged to speculate or to respond to the riskiness of its processing business, it is behaving exactly opposite from the presumption of the portfolio theory of hedging, namely that risk aversion induces firms to use futures contracts. One must conclude therefore that (1) futures markets are not analogous with markets for insurance, and (2) the portfolio theory of hedging does not explain why firms use futures markets.

3.7. The risk of lifting a hedge

Of course, these doubts about the portfolio theory of hedging rest upon the proposition that the return on a hedging operation is certain. But firms who actually hedge testify repeatedly to the risks of hedging. The risklessness of a hedging operation came from the assumptions that (1) the inventory involved was deliverable on the futures contract and (2) any inventory sold short was actually delivered. Whenever the actual commodity is not deliverable, whether because it is not in Chicago or because it is a different grade, a firm incurs "basis risk," as it is known in the trade. Whenever the contract to deliver is offset ahead of time, there is a risk to "lifting the hedge." Yet neither of these risks, although both are aspects of any actual hedging operation, substantiates the portfolio theory of hedging.

Although the risk of lifting a hedge may be classified as one form of basis risk, each type of risk requires a different emphasis in the analysis. Nevertheless, the discussions of both basis risk and the risk of lifting a hedge draw on three principles established in the analysis of deliverable stocks in section 3.5. The first principle is that a hedging operation involving deliverable stocks is riskless. Any other type of stock can always be thought of as deliverable stock plus some difference in grade or location. It is this difference that has the risk, and hence it should be examined explicitly. The second principle is that speculative positions may be intertwined in dealers' complex positions. This speculation itself, however, does not depend on the dealer being a dealer. Consequently, an objective of the analysis should be to disentangle a dealer's speculative positions from those that do depend on his being a dealer. The third principle, established in section 3.6, is that positions in futures relating to inventory may arise as a response to the risk of more fundamental assets like processing facilities.

With these principles in mind, the risk of lifting a hedge will be the first complication considered. The risk associated with lifting a hedge comes from the common practice of firms that short hedge, choosing not to deliver on their contracts but rather to cancel them by offset before they come due. This practice arises from necessity for those firms that hedge wheat other than the contract grade in Chicago because they have no wheat of the standard grade. Yet it is not unheard of for firms with deliverable wheat to buy back their short position at some point before the futures contract matures.

Rather than hedging itself, it is the practice of lifting a hedge early that gives the appearance of risk. If a firm has hedged wheat of the contract grade stored in a Chicago elevator, nothing compels the firm to lift the hedge early. If it does so, it must be presumed to have acted rationally and profitably. Acting on an unexpected opportunity should not be classified as a risk to hedging.

Yet some presentations of the portfolio theory suggest that one reason for holding hedged inventory is precisely to be in a position to profit from fluctuations in the return to lifting a hedge before its expiration date. But this is an improper definition of the returns to a hedging operation. It combines a riskless hedging operation with a speculative position in a forward spread. In precisely such a case the second principle should apply. The analysis should disengage the speculation from the positions special to a dealer, rather than combine them. If that is done, the risk of lifting a hedge is revealed to be speculation pure and simple.

As an example of the speculation implicit in the risk of lifting a hedge, imagine a firm that finds it advantageous to hold deliverable wheat hedged from January through March. It buys the package of a purchase of wheat for immediate delivery and a short sale for March delivery. Suppose the same firm believes the March-May spread is likely to fall before March. To speculate on its expectations, it should buy a March contract and sell a May contract, conceiving of those two positions as a package through which it buys a March-May spread. Once it examines its two packages, it discovers that for one operation it is buying a March contract and for the other selling a March contract. To avoid this duplication, the firm buys one grand package of assets, placing the short position in the May contract rather than the March. Although this grand package appears to outsiders to be a single hedging operation covering January through May, it is really the combination of a hedging operation yielding a fixed return and a speculation in a forward spread. When March arrives, the firm can unwind its combined operations by buying back a May contract and selling the wheat for immediate delivery. In effect, the firm is selling its speculative spread. The difference in the price of this spread compared to its value in January is the profit or loss on holding a position in the forward spread. The firm would record this profit or loss in its books as part of its return on hedging. More properly, the firm should separate its accounts so that its speculation in a forward spread is distinguished from its pure hedging operation. In that case, it is clear that the return on the hedging operation itself is not variable.[20]

Much of the confusion in interpreting actual hedging operations comes from the frequent combination of speculation with pure hedging operations. What appears to be a risk to hedging is actually a speculative position willingly taken, the speculation being in forward spreads. Although a dealer is free to combine a speculative position in spreads with a pure hedging operation, he could avoid the riskiness of a forward spread altogether by not extending his

---

[20] Of course, the return on a three-month hedging operation put on in January 1976 differs from that on a three-month hedging operation put on in May 1982. What is not variable is the return on a particular hedge of deliverable stocks.

hedge into a more distant month. To study those dealers who refrain from hedging or extend their hedge into a more distant month from the perspective that because of their risk aversion they behave oppositely from speculators is to misrepresent them completely, since under these conditions they are behaving just like speculators.

The issues concerning the risks and rewards of lifting a hedge can be seen more clearly with the help of an example from outside futures markets. Suppose an oil firm has rented a drilling rig for six months at a rate of $50,000 per month. After a month has elapsed, the market rental rate has risen to $75,000 per month. Now that the rental rate has risen, the firm might recalculate that its own use can no longer cover the opportunity cost of $75,000, and if so it will sublet the rig to others. It will enjoy a windfall gain of $25,000 per month on the remaining five months of the contract. In this setting, the firm's motive for renting the rig in the first place was not to speculate on forward rental fees. Rather, the firm made a rational calculation based on a fixed rental rate of $50,000 a month. The fee of $50,000 is certain. In contrast, had the oil firm planned to use the rig for three months but rented it for six, the rerental after six months would have been clearly speculation. Is it no less clear that the period of the first three months involves no risk, even if the rents fluctuate? When making its plans the firm considered its first three months as set.

The appearance of speculation and risk arises with any asset yielding a service over time. The forward rates of the service change. In the case of an oil drilling rig, someone who wants to speculate on the forward rental rate might have to rent the rig beginning immediately because of imperfections in the forward contract market for oil rigs. But such restrictions are not the case for commodities traded on futures markets. Anyone can speculate in a forward spread without being a dealer. Hence, the seeming profits from being able to lift a hedge early are immaterial to a true hedging operation. A hedger of deliverable stocks can take the return on hedging as fixed, even if he may reevaluate his positions as time passes. Much of the apparent risk in hedging comes from a firm's own decision to combine risky speculative positions in spreads with riskless pure hedging operations.

3.8.   Basis risk

Basis risk arises from implicit positions in transportation or grade differentials. To effect delivery, a firm must buy back its futures contract and sell its wheat for immediate delivery in its local market, say downstate Illinois. If the freight rate has fallen in the meantime, the downstate hedger makes more than he expected because wheat in his local market has appreciated relative to wheat in Chicago. On the other hand, if the freight rate has risen in the meantime, the hedger makes less than he anticipated.[21] The portfolio theory of hedging views basis risk as undesirable. In contrast, dealers may well arrange to take on basis risk as a means of counterbalancing the more important risks derived from the processing and merchandising facilities.

One must be careful in analyzing basis risk. As explained in Chapter 2, the "basis" is measured as the difference between a local spot price and the next expiring futures contract. Hence, some of the movement in the basis is actually the convergence of the spot price with the futures price. Being predictable, that part of the movement in the basis should not be classified as a risk of hedging. True basis risk is the movement in the basis not attributable to the convergence of spot and futures prices. True basis risk arises from changing freight rates or changing premiums or discounts for different grades.[22] If the spot price in the local market always bore the same relationship to the spot price in Chicago as when the hedge was put on, as would be the case if the freight rate remained constant, the return on hedging undeliverable stocks would be fixed, just as is the return on deliverable stocks.

A hedge of undeliverable wheat is a combination of positions. In the case of a hedge of an inferior grade of wheat held in Chicago, a commitment to clean wheat is implicit because the inferior grade, once cleaned, is the contract grade. Thus, a hedging operation with inferior wheat in Chicago can be thought of as a package of two positions: a hedging operation with deliverable wheat and an implicit short position in cleaning. Similarly, a hedging operation with wheat of the contract grade outside of Chicago is implicitly the combination of a short position in freight to Chicago and a hedging operation with deliverable wheat. It is as if the firm sold freight by buying downstate and selling in Chicago and then undertook a hedging operation, buying wheat in Chicago and selling it for future delivery. Because the spot purchase and sale in Chicago cancel, it is not immediately obvious that two positions are involved. Even more

[21] For articles on basis risk, all in the tradition of the portfolio theory of hedging, see Vollink and Raikes (1977), Ward and Dasse (1977), Bobst (1979), and Hayenga and DiPietre (1982).
[22] Even some of these movements may be predictable, and hence not a risk to hedging properly speaking. But something unpredictable usually remains.

complex hedging operations can (and should) be broken down into such a combination of positions.

Common to all these complex deals is a hedging operation involving deliverable wheat. Such a hedging operation is itself a riskless position. What is relevant to basis risk are the remaining implicit positions in services like forward cleaning and forward freight. It makes sense to make these implicit positions, whether in grade differentials or freight, explicit in the analysis. The pure hedging operation involving deliverable stocks could be suppressed instead. This perspective sharply contrasts with that of the portfolio theory of hedging.

Taken on their own terms, the implicit positions in freight and cleaning and the basis risk they cause do not resuscitate the portfolio theory of hedging. Just as in the case of extending a hedge into a more distant month as a means of speculating in forward spreads, the implicit positions in cleaning and freight that give rise to basis risk could be purely speculative. As such they are not special to dealers and processors. They themselves could also be a response to the riskiness of a more fundamental position, milling for example. Thus, while risky in its own right, the acceptance of basis risk can be a rational response to risk aversion. Contrary to the formulation of the portfolio theory of hedging, dealers and processors may actually be pleased to take on basis risk, because it helps counteract the risk of their main business.

To see more clearly how this can be true, imagine a miller in Peoria, Illinois, who has hedged in inventory of wheat in a futures contract calling for delivery in Peoria. Because his hedge is in the Peoria futures market, his wheat is deliverable. Hence, his position is a pure hedging operation, which is riskless. What is risky for the miller is his return on milling. Effectively, he has a large long position in milling (unless he has sold his service forward). As a diversification motivated by risk aversion, suppose he decides to add a short position in hauling wheat from Peoria to Chicago, a long position in milling being negatively correlated with a short position in freight (processing margins, including transportation, move together [Martin, Groenewegen, and Pidgeon 1980]). No explicit market in forward freight exists, so that he must construct his short position in freight through a combination of buying wheat for future delivery in Peoria and selling it for delivery in Chicago. Since, as a part of his pure hedging operation he has sold wheat for future delivery in Peoria, the purchase and sale cancel. Thus, as a means of adding an implicit short position in forward freight, the miller transfers his hedge from the Peoria futures market to the one in Chicago.[23] The return on his implicit short position in freight depends on how prices move in Chicago relative to Peoria. However, far from being troubled by this basis risk, the miller takes it on to offset partially the risk of being in the milling business.[24]

Thus, even when the inventory against which the sale of a futures contract is contemplated is not deliverable on that contract, the proper analysis of the portfolio problem of a miller concludes that basis risk does not deter hedging operations. The conventional analysis of hedging is misleading in its implication that futures markets depend on the risk aversion of commodity dealers. Given the correlations among processing margins, input prices, and output prices, the contrary is probably true.

3.9.   Conclusion: Risk average dealers' use of futures markets

The many criticisms of the portfolio theory of hedging made in this chapter, often requiring convoluted permutations of this or that implicit position, actually rest on three straightforward propositions: First, the return to a hedging operation involving deliverable stocks is certain. Second, there is no bias in futures prices. Third, the prices of the services of processing, storage, freight, and exporting tend to be negatively correlated with the price of the commodity. The first of these axioms is indisputable. The second has long been the center of controversy, but if any empirical and theoretical consensus has emerged, it is not in favor of the theory of normal backwardation and the notion of bias in futures prices. On the last there has been little empirical work. What little there is supports the proposition. Thus, the three axioms seem reasonable.

Given that one accepts these three propositions, one must reject the portfolio theory of hedging and the prevailing idea that the function of futures markets is to transfer the risk of holding invento-

---

[23] Another asset negatively correlated with milling is a bull spread, which the miller could buy implicitly with a purchase of a nearby contract and a simultaneous sale of a contract for a more distant delivery date. Already he has sold a nearby contract, so the effect of adding a bull spread to his portfolio is to place the hedge in a more distant delivery month. What began as a short sale for delivery in Peoria becomes a short sale for delivery in Chicago for a much later delivery date.

[24] Of course, this risk-averse miller, as discussed in section 3.6, might also consider adding a long position in wheat to his portfolio, leaving some of his wheat unhedged in the Chicago futures market. The exact amount would depend on the interrelationships among all these assets. But the fact remains that the more risk averse a dealer is, the less he uses futures markets.

ries from handlers of commodities to speculators. Risk aversion among dealers and processors is neither a sufficient nor a necessary condition for the existence of futures markets. If anything, risk aversion keeps handlers of commodities from using futures markets.

CHAPTER 4

The demand to borrow commodities

At the heart of the problems of both the theory of normal backwardation and the portfolio theory of hedging is their failure to
consider why firms hold inventory in the first place. Each theory
pictures a risk-averse firm with a predetermined inventory whose
fluctuating value causes it concern. Obviously, the most effective
way of avoiding such a risk is to hold no inventory.

A more comprehensive theory begins by considering why firms
hold inventory at the apparent cost of spreads below full carrying
charges. The extent spreads fall below full carrying charges is the
use charge for the commodity, in the terminology of Chapter 2.
Thus, a more comprehensive theory investigates whether firms will
pay a use charge to have commodities under their own control. That
line of questioning immediately leads to the conclusion that risk-neutral firms have sufficient reason to use futures markets. Risk aversion is a red herring.

The theory for holding inventory presented in this chapter consciously parallels the analysis of the reasons firms hold money at the
cost of forgone interest. The reasons for holding money not only
resemble the reasons firms hold inventories but also illuminate the
existence of spreads below full carrying charges, interest, after all,
being a use charge for money expressed in percentage terms. Perhaps most significant, conventional models of the demand for
money demonstrate that even risk-neutral firms desire to hold cash.

As with money, a minimum of four reasons for holding inventory
can be discerned: pure storage to smooth out consumption, a speculative demand, a transactions demand, and a precautionary demand.
Each of these will be examined in turn. The first two prove unimportant for the analysis of spreads and futures markets. The latter
two, however, encourage a firm to borrow commodities, even when
spreads are below full carrying charges and the use charge for the
commodity is positive, because a loan of commodities provides the
firm with secure supplies of raw materials in the face of the inflexibilities of transporting and processing commodities. Thus, although
risk and uncertainty themselves matter, the behavior of dealers can

111

be explained without recourse to risk aversion. Once this point is established, the perspective of accessibility to raw materials is contrasted with Working's concept of the supply of storage. Finally, several themes are tied together in a theoretical investigation of why firms might borrow commodities rather than own them outright.

This last model, contrasting borrowing with outright purchase, is central because it alone establishes why risk-neutral firms use futures markets. The investigation of why firms hold inventory establishes that that they will borrow raw materials explicitly. It is easiest to conceive of such transactions as being similar to those in the loan market for warehouse receipts that functioned in Chicago in the 1860s. But such borrowing when accomplished implicitly through a hedging operation incurs two transactions costs. Outright purchase involves only one. A risk-neutral firm will accept the added expense of borrowing implicitly over outright ownership for reasons similar to those explaining why financial intermediaries exist. These reasons, once again, need not involve risk aversion.

The models used in this chapter intentionally present firms as price takers, as little more than automatons. Obviously, actual firms are not so passive. Commodity dealers actively watch prices, form expectations, and take speculative positions. Yet the same competitive equilibrium, the same pattern of prices, will emerge whether firms are active or passive. Or perhaps it would be more accurate to say that precisely because of the intense competition among firms, the resulting equilibrium appears as it would if firms were passive price takers. The advantage of the assumption of passive price-taking behavior, so common in microeconomic theory, comes from its analytical simplicity. One need not accomplish the hopeless task of comprehending and representing how firms form their expectations about prices or how they administratively regulate their inventories. Such activity, however much actual firms devote to it, is also a red herring when one's objective is an understanding of the resulting pattern of prices.

4.1.   Pure storage and speculative storage

Two of the reasons for holding inventories prove to be uninteresting, at least from the perspective of a study of futures markets. Pure storage to match seasonal production and demand, although constituting a large fraction of actual inventories, occurs only at full carrying charges. Consequently, pure storage cannot be part of the paradox of storage in the presence of spreads that are less than full carrying charges. For its part, speculative storage, although possible in theory, rarely occurs in commodities with futures markets. Futures contracts themselves are a superior vehicle for speculation.

Because the production of some commodities is highly seasonal, in order to spread consumption throughout the year someone must hold stocks. The costs of pure storage, which would appear in spreads, comprise the marginal cost of physical storage and the opportunity cost of invested capital. The marginal cost of physical storage is effectively constant at all levels of storage. Storage capacity for bulk goods can be increased quickly and at little additional cost, especially for goods like cotton, which can be left outside covered only with a tarpaulin. Likewise, since capital costs are simply the interest rate times the value of what is stored, marginal capital costs are also constant.

With constant marginal physical storage costs and constant marginal capital costs, spreads would be constant if pure storage alone mattered. They are not. Because pure physical storage costs and interest expenses are both positive, and because firms are observed to store when spreads are negative, they must have other reasons for holding inventories besides pure storage.

In addition, for all commodities there are many storage facilities regularly in use that are not minimum cost. If pure storage were the only reason for holding inventories, those elevators and warehouses offering the least expensive storage would hold all inventories. Hence there must be something more to storage than matching seasonal patterns in production and consumption. For example, although the storage of oil is cheapest per barrel in the salt domes of Louisiana, no private storers of oil choose to keep their reserves there. Rather, they store their oil in expensive metal tanks near their refining or distribution centers. Nor does the observed spatial distribution of storage fit that expected of pure storage. Given that a commodity must be both stored somewhere and shipped at some point in time, it is best to postpone shipment because storage costs would be higher by the interest expense on the value of the transportation after transporting the commodity.[1] But storage of oil and other commodities is far from producing centers, although storage at such locations has the lowest direct capital expenses. High-cost storage near processing and distribution centers is the norm.[2]

---

[1] Strictly speaking, this argument requires that the array of forward prices for transportation and distribution shows the same prices for performance at all periods throughout the year.

[2] Commodities such as cocoa, however, cannot be stored at producing centers because they spoil too quickly in tropical climates.

Speculation can be another reason for holding inventory besides pure storage. Sometimes "unreasonably" low offers encourage holders of commodities not to sell but to store, waiting for a rise in price. In this hope of rising prices, holders may be joined by others who have no connection with shipping or processing the commodity but have arranged for warehouse space in which to store their purely speculative purchases.

Although some firms and individuals hold stocks on speculation, a fine example being the recent craze for holding high-grade diamonds as part of investment accounts, this reason for holding inventory is rare. Any pure speculator must overcome the opportunity cost of the value some people and firms gain simply by having inventory on hand. In the case of diamonds, a person who gains intrinsic pleasure from the gem will hold it for less annual appreciation than someone who retains a diamond solely as an investment. Similarly for more mundane commodities, if other firms desire inventory apart from speculative reasons, and as a consequence are willing to pay a premium for holding stocks themselves, a speculator must expect to make at least that premium before he buys the commodity to store it.

Speculators are at a disadvantage compared to someone who can make use of the goods while in storage, whether for serving customers or displaying beautiful gems. But they can avoid this disadvantage by using speculative instruments without this burden of holding inventory idle. For example, speculation in commodities is possible through contracts for future delivery. Or the speculator could lend his stocks temporarily to someone who values them for their own sake, but in that case the speculator would no longer be storing the commodity. Likewise, there are better ways than hoarding cash for speculating that money will appreciate in value relative to goods and services. One can preserve principal and yet continue to earn interest by holding a short-term asset like a Treasury bill. Generally speaking, as long as someone else is willing to pay for the advantage received from holding grain, diamonds, and money, speculators will necessarily prefer other investments over storing the commodity itself.[3]

---

[3] That is not to say that speculators never hold the physical commodity. Some speculators may observe they can buy a commodity for immediate delivery, pay the storage and interest costs, and deliver it on a futures contract for a profit. But such storers are better referred to as arbitragers than speculators, since there is no risk in their operation.

4.2.   The transactions demand for inventories

Another reason for holding inventories more prevalent than speculative demand or pure storage is what might be called the transactions demand, after the transactions demand for cash. For present
purposes, the importance of such a motive is that in a world of
perfect certainty, where risk aversion cannot be a consideration,
firms will hold some inventory despite a backwardation in prices.
Thus, unlike the demand for pure storage, the transactions demand
is associated with a positive use charge, meaning spreads below full
carrying costs.

A simple model of farmers bringing wheat to market can establish
several important points. First, storage can be rational when spreads
are less than full carrying charges. Second, the amount stored is
sensitive to the size of the use charge, that is, the degree spreads fall
below full carrying charges. Third, the costs of transforming a commodity from one good into another or moving it from one location
to another are the source of this storage behavior.

Imagine that in a regional marketing center the posted price of
wheat for delivery at this week's market day, P_1, is higher than the
posted price for delivery next week, P_2. How these prices were determined or whether they can be sustained is not important for the
moment. Rather, the issue is whether any of the region's farmers will
wait, given that pattern, until the second week to market their wheat.
If they do, they store in the face of a backwardation.

Suppose a typical farmer has just harvested W bushels of wheat.
He must decide W's best allocation between the amount marketed
the first week, w_1, and that marketed the second week, w_2. The
amount held until the second week is what he stores. Presumably,
because the price of wheat is lower for delivery the second week and
because he could earn interest, at the rate r, on his immediate revenue, it would be best for the farmer to market all his wheat the first
week. Yet if he were restricted in some way in the amount of deliveries he could make during the first week, say by the size of his truck,
he might consider storing. More likely than the abrupt constraint of
his truck's capacity, he feels an increasing restriction on his deliveries, if for no other reason than the handling and disposition of
larger quantities keep him from ever more important tasks around
his farm. Suppose the total costs of marketing follow a relationship
such as cw^2, where c is some positive constant. With these nonlinear
total marketing costs, the farmer must balance the additional reve-

nue of an earlier sale against the higher costs that earlier sale entails. Consequently, it might well be optimal for the farmer to postpone some sales until the second week.

Formally stated, the farmer is concerned with maximizing the present value of his net revenue from sales at either P_1 or P_2. This present value is

$$P_1 w_1 - c w_1^2 + (1 + r)^{-1} [P_2 w_2 - c w_2^2]$$

subject to the constraint that $W = w_1 + w_2$. For simplicity let warehousing fees for storage itself be costless. The optimal amount marketed in week two, which is also the amount stored, is

$$w_2 = \{W + [P_2(1 + r)^{-1} - P_1]/2c\} \cdot [(1 + r)/(2 + r)]$$

In this expression, the term $[P_2(1 + r)^{-1} - P_1]$ is central, related as it is to the spread between prices for two different dates of delivery. A price in the second week higher than that in the first week in proportion to the rate of interest, given the absence of any warehousing costs, would imply a spread of full carrying charges. At full carrying charges, the term in the expression involving prices would equal zero and the optimal allocation, say with r equal to .001 (or 5.2% per annum), would be to market effectively one-half of the wheat the first week and the other half the second week. Yet, even if the spread were below full carrying charges, there would still be some storage, although less than half of the initial amount W. As long as P_2 is not so far below P_1 that $[P_1 - P_2(1 + r)^{-1}]$ is no longer less than $2cW$, there is some storage. Thus, because of the rising marginal costs of marketing the wheat quickly, it can be optimal to store even if prices are in backwardation. Moreover, the amount in store will be sensitive to the extent the spread is below full carrying charges, the larger the backwardation, the less stored.

This model's simple representation of a farmer's marketing problem applies to much of the processing and transporting of commodities, since the marginal cost curves for these activities are steep. If a backwardation were present in the price of soybean oil, crushers would still hold inventories of soybeans because they can do little to increase their output in the short run once their equipment is running continuously.[4] Likewise, exporting facilities running around the clock can increase the amount they load only slightly on short notice, no matter how much higher is the price for immediate over later

---

[4] Paul and Wesson (1966) conclude that the short-run elasticity of supply for crushing services lies between 0.13 and 0.24.

shipment. In general, the facilities of commodity dealers, from copper smelters to fuel oil distributors, are extremely inflexible over periods as long as months or years. Consequently, even if inventory loses value it often pays to hold inventory as a way of reducing the total costs of processing and transporting the commodity.

Goods in process or en route are also inventories, and if the price were right these transformations would be run not only at higher capacity but at a faster speed. A limit on practical speed also causes storage in the face of a backwardation. For example, a premium for speedy delivery of oil (such as in 1979) will almost never justify sending crude oil by air freight. Oil companies will, however, run their tankers at their highest possible speed. But because tankers can only go so fast, there will always be some oil in them in total. Large inventories of crude oil will be registered despite large backwardations. High speeds are expensive, of course. When the demand is less immediate, tankers run at a lower cruising speed, sometimes nearly drifting, making for larger inventories of oil on the seas.[5] In this situation, the amount of oil in inventory is sensitive to the degree of the spread between the prices of oil for immediate and future delivery. The real source of the relationship between oil afloat and spreads, however, is the variable and rising cost of running tankers faster. If tankers could run at any speed at the same cost, spreads in crude oil would be at full carrying charges or else oil would be shipped so quickly that nothing would be on the seas.

As the previous examples demonstrate, the decision to delay processing or delivery despite an opportunity cost depends upon the rising marginal costs of processing or transportation. Similar factors are at the heart of the transactions demand for cash. If cash could be converted back and forth into interest-earning assets costlessly, it would never make sense to hold currency; rather, one would convert an interest-earning asset into cash moments before a scheduled purchase. Once there is a cost to transforming cash into interest-earning assets and back, it will be optimal to hold some currency despite the opportunity cost of forgone interest. What makes this practice economically interesting is that the magnitude of the inventory of cash will be sensitive to the use charge on money.

The transformation costs for commodities are likely to be much greater than those associated with money. The transformation costs

---

[5] When most tankers are cruising at six knots below full speed, oil afloat nearly doubles compared to the amount when all tankers are at full speed (Exxon Corp. 1981: Figure 3).

that give rise to the transactions demand for cash are conventionally portrayed as brokerage fees, the bid-ask spread on government securities, the time spent waiting in line in banks, and so forth.[6] These transactions costs in converting interest-earning assets back and forth into currency, rather than the need for currency in order to make purchases, recommends the name "transactions" demand for cash. Perhaps a better name would have been "transformations" demand. Similar considerations about the costs of buying and selling give rise to inventories of commodities, as for example the decision to buy large quantities infrequently. In the case of commodities, however, these transactions costs associated with accumulating inventories, large as they may be on an absolute scale, are probably small in comparison to the additional costs of speedy processing and transportation.

4.3.   The precautionary demand for inventories

A demand for inventories arising from the cost of transformations occurs even in a world of perfect certainty. Another motive, analogous with the precautionary demand for cash, applies in a world of uncertainty. With a precautionary demand, once again firms will keep commodities on hand despite a backwardation, and they will do so even if risk neutral. Moreover, what they most desire is to borrow commodities rather than own them outright.

These points can be established with a model analogous to the typical representations of the precautionary demand for cash. Models of the precautionary demand for cash consider the problem of the optimal holdings of currency given uncertainty in the timing of receipts and expenditures.[7] Likewise, models of optimal asset management for banks consider the proper blend between income-producing assets and reserves of currency given the uncertain timing of withdrawals and deposits.[8] The individual's or bank's risk aversion is immaterial in these models. Instead, each seeks to minimize the expected (i.e., average) total costs of the sum of holding money balances M at an opportunity cost of the interest r plus the costs of

[6] These costs are usually presented as linear, with the expense of converting two securities into cash proportional to the expense of one. But this expense is positive regardless, and would correspond to a large step upward in the cost of marketing wheat.
[7] Among the many articles on this subject, Tsaing (1969) uses inventory control theory most formally.
[8] See Baltensperger (1980) for a survey of this literature.

converting some interest-earning asset at expense c per unit in the event that money balances do not cover the excess of expenditures over receipts. This excess of expenditures over receipts, commonly designated e, is a random variable with density function $f(e)$. Expected total costs are thus

$$EC = Mr + \int_M^\infty [(e - M)c]f(e)de$$

Optimal money balances M^* are where the marginal cost of holding money, namely r, just balances the marginal expected cost of being short of money,

$$r = c \int_{M^*}^\infty f(e)de$$

The important point of this model of the precautionary demand for cash is that currency is held despite an opportunity cost.

This well-established model describes the precautionary demand for commodities as well. Millers, spinners, shippers, and exporters are in businesses in which the time and sale of their next output is uncertain. Firms dealing directly with clients might receive an unexpected order, while those selling on an organized exchange might at any moment discover a profitable opportunity for a trade. To gain speed and flexibility or to retain the business of customers in a great rush, it would seem natural for such firms to keep supplies on hand.

Uncertainty in demand alone, however, does not prompt stockholding. Rather, stockholding stems from inflexibilities and uncertainties in production. Just as no one would ever hold currency if interest-earning assets could be converted into cash instantaneously and costlessly, a firm would never hold inventories if it could be certain of obtaining the goods it sells the moment it needed them and at no extra cost. A miller would never keep flour on hand if he could instantaneously and at no extra cost produce flour from wheat. Unfortunately, plagued with an insecure supply of wheat, machine failures, absenteeism, as well as the time for milling itself, which can only be done faster than a normal pace at extremely high additional costs, he cannot respond so quickly and confidently. The uncertainty and technologically imposed delay in a firm's own supply is sufficient reason for it to stockpile raw material and output. Uncertainties in demand can, however, compound the effects of lags in supply or of uncertainty in supply.

Picture a representative firm with a fixed capacity and one variable cost of production, that of a raw material. An example of such a firm is a lake shipper, who either operates his vessel with a full crew or not at all. Flour mills and spinning establishments also have substantial production costs relatively fixed in the short run. Such firms always try to run at full capacity as long as the price of their output is above the price of their raw material, because the net revenue covers some of their quasi-fixed costs.

The firm loses some revenue whenever scarcity of raw material keeps it from operating at full capacity. Suppose for simplicity that the market for the firm's output is large enough so that what happens to the firm does not affect the marketwide price. Lost revenue then is simply the price of the firm's service times the shortfall. Thus, a firm with fixed capacity and a constant price for its service will find its shortage cost to approximate a constant amount per unit of shortage. A miller short of wheat will produce cornmeal rather than flour, if possible, but even with such substitutions the firm would still lose a set amount for each bushel of wheat it is short, equal to the difference between the return for using corn and the return for using wheat. Suppose for the moment that this solitary firm is unable to control the amount of grain being forwarded to it, nor its time of arrival, much like a consignment merchant. The total amount arriving during a stretch of time, designated as X, is likely to follow a statistical pattern. Let $f(x)$ be the probability that a particular amount, x, arrives. The amount x is of course nonnegative. If x is less than the fixed capacity, designated as K, minus the secure amount of raw material, I, then the shortage cost the firm suffers is $(K - I - x)c$, where c is the constant loss from the shortage. If the firm is not averse to risk, so that it is not consciously avoiding extremes in shortage costs, it is concerned only with the average shortage cost over all possible outcomes of x. This expected shortage cost is,

$$\int_0^{(K-I)} [(K - I - x)c]f(x)dx$$

The problem confronting such a firm is how much inventory to keep on hand in order to avoid these shortage costs. If inventory were costless to hold, the optimal amount would be infinite. But because inventory is costly to hold, to choose the best level of inventory the firm must solve an exercise in inventory control in which shortage costs are balanced against holding costs.[9]

The proper measure of the cost of holding inventories is the ex-

---

[9] The third relevant cost, that associated with placing an order and receiving a delivery, would be an unnecessary complication here.

tent to which spreads fall below full carrying charges. The term "holding costs" itself suggests only warehouse fees, insurance, spoilage, and the opportunity cost of capital invested. Yet, if the value of the commodity appreciates over time, some of these expenses can be recovered. Likewise, if the value of the commodity depreciates, that loss should be added to the expenses of physical storage. The typical model of inventory management implicitly assumes that the price of the good to be put in inventory is the same next period as this. Hence, the extent that the spread falls below full carrying charges (i.e., the use charge) is precisely the carrying charges. Clearly, the opportunity cost of holding inventories can be something other than this while still remaining above zero.

It is not necessary for the firm itself either to own the raw material or to administer storage. Its primary concern is making sure it has immediate access to the raw material. Therefore, it would be content simply with an arrangement that ensures such access. If someone else in the area specializes in the storage business, the firm might be able to buy the right of access to raw material, avoiding the burden of overseeing the raw material. The right of access to raw material could be as formal as a contract patterned after a common banking practice, allowing a business a line of credit. This practice of credit lines arises when a business anticipates the possible need for some additional cash. If the business knew for certain that it would need the money, it would obtain the money outright. Otherwise, it would be content to negotiate a line of credit that would ensure prompt access to cash when it needed it without worry that the bank might take weeks to process its request. What is important here is that the business wants access to money, not money itself. Similarly, a miller is satisfied owning access to wheat, knowing, for instance, that he can obtain wheat at a moment's notice from his local elevator.

The important issue is how much a miller would pay for an arrangement ensuring access to raw material if someone were to charge for that service. Let I stand for the amount of raw material ensured by an arrangement similar to a line of credit, and P_A the price of that arrangement per unit of I. If the firm held the inventory itself, P_A would be its holding costs, the extent that spreads were below full carrying charges. The firm must pay IP_A regardless of whether or not it exercises its right to the raw material. The firm should select the amount of I that gives the minimum for the expected total cost, expected total cost being the sum of the certain cost of the arrangement for access plus the expected cost of shortage,

$$EC = IP_A + \int_0^{(K - I)} [(K - I - x)c]f(x)dx$$

The optimum value of I, I^*, is where,

$$\partial EC/\partial I = 0 = P_A - \int_0^{(K - I^*)} cf(x)dx$$

That is, the optimal inventory is where the price of holding the marginal unit of inventory equals the expected cost of shortage. Because the holding cost is that of an arrangement ensuring access, this solution can be interpreted as the firm's willingness to pay up to P_A for access to inventory I^*.

This willingness to pay for available and secure supplies of raw material is a crucial result. Risk-neutral firms will pay a positive use charge. Risk-neutral firms have a sufficient reason to hold inventories even when spreads are less than full carrying charges. The firms balance that opportunity cost against the shortage costs arising from uncertainty in their supply of raw material or in their production processes.

Both the standard model of the precautionary demand for cash and the similar model of the demand for inventories embrace the intuitive notion that an uncertain flow, whether of wheat or of dollars, induces firms to pay for some quantity of readily available supplies. Yet this model of precautionary demand leaves unanswered the question of why the firm suffers the irregular flow. Many firms, able to combine orders with inventory, can further reduce the uncertainty in the supply of their raw material. Flour mills and exporters, for example, are likely to be in contact with their suppliers, and order their raw material some time ahead. Likewise, utilities have begun allowing their customers to spread out their estimated fuel bills into twelve equal monthly payments. Their customers should need to hold less money on average as a consequence.

Although firms can reduce the uncertainty about their supplies through ordering in advance, it is impossible for them to eliminate uncertainty. With orders, uncertainty over whether the order will arrive on schedule persists because of weather, strikes, and shipping bottlenecks. The order may arrive too late to be of use, or too early to have a place in the warehouse.[10] Even if a firm insists on a con-

---

[10] If disposal of excess orders were free, it would be cheapest to order as much as possible without paying to hold inventory, because a shortage would never occur when the firm had ordered an enormous amount. Thus, there must be some cost for ordering too much.

tractual penalty for late delivery, it only succeeds in shifting the problem to its suppliers, much as utilities operating under a plan requiring equal monthly payments for anticipated consumption must now bear the risk of financing the fuel consumed in an unexpectedly cold January, and hold reserves of cash accordingly. Although suppliers may be better able to control or bear the uncertainty of deliveries, even they cannot do away with it entirely. Consequently, a firm must still pay to have access to a secure supply of its raw material, either paying directly by holding inventory itself at an opportunity cost or paying higher prices to a supplier willing to include penalty clauses in a contract and which itself holds inventory at an opportunity cost.

Encompassing the option of orders and negotiations with suppliers, more general models of the precautionary demand for stocks are far more complex problems of inventory control. Sometimes no explicit solution for the best amount to order and the best amount to keep on hand is possible. For example, if the lead time, which is the time between the placement of the order and delivery, is random, the possibility of crossed orders in which one shipment could be delayed so long that it arrives after a subsequent order makes the problem mathematically intractable (Kaplan 1970, Liberatore 1977).

In any event, it is possible to make one general observation about the solutions to more realistic models of inventory control: It is worthwhile to pay a premium for having goods on hand rather than on order. Although wheat is still wheat and cotton still cotton, there is one big difference between the raw material embodied in inventory and that on order. Raw material in inventory is definitely available for use while it is not at all certain how much of what is on order will arrive on schedule. Wheat on hand differs from wheat on order precisely because its availability is guaranteed.[11]

Although the notion of guaranteed availability suggests a form of insurance, it is important not to associate this issue of uncertainty with risk aversion. A firm that is risk neutral, as defined by the nature of its preferences, still holds inventories as a precaution against irregularities in its receipts, ordered materials, or sales. It does so to minimize its average costs, quite apart from any concern with the variability of those costs. Because of its precautionary demand, a risk-neutral firm arranges for secure access to some of its

[11] Carlton (1977) uses this concept of availability to explain pricing patterns in restaurants, airlines, retail stores, and similar businesses. A similar theme applied to the subject of optimal delivery lags can be found in Maccini (1973) and Carlton (1979).

raw materials just as it would arrange access to money for the same
objective.

4.4.   Market parlance and inventory control theory

Commercial terminology itself lends credence to the idea that futures markets are concerned not with risk aversion but with uncertainty and guaranteed availability. Traders and commercial reporters, needing to differentiate between goods, particularly as to
why they sold at different prices, can be expected to express the
essential nature of the transactions described. If the essential difference is between the good and the good coupled with insurance, the
distinction predicted by the theory of normal backwardation, one
would expect reporters to mention terms like insurance, premium,
and risk. On the contrary, the parlance of commodity traders distinguishes material already on hand from that on order, precisely
the distinction emphasized in inventory control theory. Alone
among the vocabulary of commodity traders, the term "hedging"
connotes risk. Moreover, it is a relatively recent adoption into what
is otherwise a remarkably coherent and precise set of commercial
terms.

The emphasis in commercial parlance is clearest in the 1840s, a
period during which the expressions describing trades were used in
settings and combinations that indicate they had not yet become the
verbal formulas they are today.[12] The correspondent for the *Buffalo
Morning Express* reported the following about the market in New
York City on 24 March 1847:

Flour and meal still, but moderate inquiry for parcels on the spot. To arrive
the demand is considerable and prices steady; sales 13 to 15,000 bbls at
$6.12 [per barrel] for delivery in May and deliverable in June at $5.87. To
arrive at the opening of the [Hudson] river, 1,500 bbls sold at $7.12.

The reporter was clearly distinguishing on the basis of price between
flour that was already on hand, that is, already on the spot in New
York City, from that expected to arrive at some date in the future.
The essential distinction made was between goods on hand and
goods on order. Thus, the traders' own terminology reveals their
concern with those problems addressed by models of optimal inventories. A good when on the spot was certainly on hand in New York,

---

[12] These old commercial reports are also interesting because of the high frequency
with which the price of the good to arrive at some uncertain date in the future was
in pronounced backwardation to the price of the same good already on hand.

but there was no telling when it might arrive if expected later. "Rye was offered 90¢ on the spot, and 80¢ to arrive some time hence."[13]

In these early market reports, the conditions attached to sales of a good "to arrive" invariably emphasized the inherent uncertainty in the time of arrival: "To arrive two or three weeks hence, $5.75 could probably be obtained" for each barrel of flour,[14] or "To arrive some time ahead, there is a demand at higher rates."[15] In Buffalo on 23 April 1847, there were sales of "10,000 bu Masillion [Ohio] wheat to arrive by the 10th of May and 7,800 bu St. Joseph [Michigan wheat] to arrive in June."[16] To arrive any time in June definitely left a large ambiguity as to the exact day of delivery. Stating only "To arrive, sales 5,000 bbls Western [flour] at $5.87-1/2 @ $6, deliverable in all May," implicitly the reporter was adding "with the seller's option as to the day of delivery."[17] To informed readers the cryptic comment "Flour, $9.20 for all the month; $9.50 on the spot"[18] sufficed to distinguish whether the good was expected at some uncertain time within the month or was immediately available.

The uncertainty in the time of arrival can be seen not only in those transactions that gave a month's leeway for delivery but also in those transactions that were tied to a particular natural event. For example, there were frequent sales in New York City of flour and grains "to arrive at the opening of the [Hudson] river."[19] The day the ice clears on the Hudson or the Great Lakes is indeed uncertain, as witnessed in 1847 when it was nearly a month later than usual, a delay that made it difficult to fulfill all contracts for flour to arrive in New York City by the end of May. In Buffalo, there was a sale of wheat deliverable twenty days after the canals opened in Ohio, as well as a sale of wheat "to arrive on the first vessels," whenever that might be.[20]

In the 1840s the term "to arrive" applied to deliveries ranging from those "near at hand" to those scheduled for many months ahead.[21] For the more distant arrivals the term "future delivery" was

---

13 *Buffalo Morning Express*, 27 January 1847, report for New York City market.
14 *Ibid.*, 7 October 1846, report for New York City market.
15 *Ibid.*, 8 October 1846, report for New York City market.
16 *Chicago Daily Journal*, 28 April 1847, report for Buffalo market.
17 *Buffalo Morning Express*, 13 March 1847.
18 *Chicago Daily Journal*, 9 June 1847, report for New York City market.
19 *Buffalo Morning Express*, 20 February 1847, report for New York City market.
20 *Ibid.*, 25 March 1847.
21 In today's usage, the term "to arrive" refers to contracts with arrival in no more than a few weeks' time and the term "future delivery" applies to contracts with arrival in distant months.

often used interchangeably.[22] It is that term, of course, that persists
in modern usage. As far as the person arranging to receive the
commodity was concerned, except for an incidental fee for placing it
in a warehouse, it made no difference whether delivery was from a
ship that had just arrived or from a warehouse that had been holding the commodity for some time. Whenever a delivery was from a
ship, it was natural to call the contract for delivery a "to arrive" sale;
when from a warehouse, the more general "contract for future delivery." Regardless of how the commodity was delivered, delivery in
the future was (and is) uncertain, particularly if the day of delivery
was at the seller's option.

Synonyms for "on the spot" also emphasized the distinction between goods on hand for certain and those whose future delivery was
uncertain. Clearly, a sale for "immediate delivery" referred to the
same transaction as "on the spot," because only those supplies already
present could be delivered immediately.[23] "Cash" was another synonym for "on the spot," because most contracts, whether for immediate
or future delivery, are "payable on delivery." Consequently, it was
natural to associate the immediate need for cash with immediate
delivery and to refer to these as "cash" sales after the manner of
payment.[24]

Although the terms "to arrive" and "for future delivery" were
applied to the same transactions, they were never interchangeable
with "on the spot," "immediate delivery," or "cash." The critical distinction for prices was whether or not the good was already on hand.
How it was delivered and how it was paid for did not matter nearly
as much. Today "on the spot" has been abbreviated to "spot" and
"contract for future delivery" to "futures," but the origins of the
terms demonstrate that the insights of models of optimal inventories
are fundamental to understanding the relationship between spot
and futures prices. Moreover, the continued use of these terms, as
abbreviated, indicates that the underlying problem for shippers of
commodities has not changed from the 1840s. As it happens, in the
spring of 1984 a late-season ice jam closed the Great Lakes to shipping, just as in 1847.

---

[22] Compare, for example, *Buffalo Morning Express,* 28 and 29 January 1847, reports
for New York City market.
[23] For example, see *ibid.,* 12 November 1846, report for New York City market.
[24] The word "cash" itself derives from the manner in which medieval money changers
conducted business, namely their habit of storing coins in a box, the medieval
Italian word for which was *cassa.*

4.5.   The demand for accessibility

For a variety of reasons, risk-neutral firms will be willing to hold
inventory at the seeming loss involved in spreads below full carrying
charges. For one, the precautionary demand for a secure supply of
raw material induces a firm to pay to hold inventory. As mentioned in
section 4.2, even when there is certainty, the steeply rising transformation costs associated with processing and moving commodities also
prompts firms to hold inventories at an opportunity cost. But because
of this opportunity cost, reflected in spreads below full carrying
charges, speculative storage is likely to be zero. For its part, pure
storage to smooth out consumption has little to do with the peculiar
patterns in observed spreads, although at times pure storage may
account for a substantial portion of total inventory. Either a precautionary motive or a transactions motive is sufficient to explain storage
at an opportunity cost. But as it happens both motives exist. Of
course, these reasons for holding inventory are not independent, the
combined demand for inventory not being a simple addition of the
so-called pure storage, precautionary, and transactions motives. More
than one motive only makes inventory behavior more interesting.

Judging from the many uncertainties in shipping and processing
commodities, the precautionary motive might well be the more important reason for holding inventories in the face of spreads below
full carrying charges. Overall, however, the problems arising from
transformation costs are the more fundamental reason for holding
inventories, the precautionary motive actually being a function of
the transformation costs. If at a moment's notice and at no extra cost
wheat could be delivered to a miller who discovered he was short,
the miller would have no reason to hold his own supply of wheat. In
other words, without marginal transformation costs there would be
no precautionary demand for inventories. In the case of money, if
brokerage commissions for selling Treasury bills were insignificant,
all assets held for emergencies would be in the form of interest-earning T-bills rather than cash. For money, there are in fact many
near-moneys, assets so easily converted into currency as to be virtually as useful as money. But in the case of commodities, the costs of
converting other assets into the desired one are substantial. A miller
in an isolated location whose regular flow of receipts is interrrupted
has few and imperfect substitutes for wheat in his own warehouse.

At the center of the predicament of the miller, or any handler of a
commodity for that matter, are the extremely nonlinear marginal

costs of processing and moving wheat, whether measured in reference to volume or to speed. The tremendous increase in costs to move wheat above the normal pace of farmers, country elevators, and railroads induces the miller to hold wheat himself. Coupled with these rigidities in transportation, the capacity of his own mill is inflexible. If he could adjust the size of his facilities easily, he would respond to interruptions or surges in receipts by adjusting production rather than by holding inventories. In turn, bakers, apprehensive about the miller's inability to adjust his capacity, become concerned about their own supply of raw material. The cumulative response, hardly surprising, is for all firms to desire access to commodities.

Thus, because of transformation costs, firms desire access to commodities. In the models of the transactions demand, whether of money or wheat, accessibility is as important to the analysis as the transformation costs explicitly considered. Because of the trouble getting money or wheat quickly, people and firms make sure they have a ready supply. In the models of precautionary demand, on the other hand, access is the center of the analysis, while transformation costs are given secondary status. Whatever the emphasis in either set of models, transformation costs and accessibility clearly go hand in hand. The demand for accessibility is large whenever transformation costs are substantial.

Despite transformation costs being the root of a demand for accessibility, in the context of explaining the patterns in the prices of goods, whether of wheat or money, it is the demand for accessibility that is most interesting. The demand for accessibility, expressed as a desire to hold inventories, affects prices directly.

In some sense, accessibility is an ordinary input like labor or machines. Its contribution to production is a reduction in expected shortage costs and transformation costs. Not surprisingly, accessibility is desired up to the point where its marginal product equals its price. And similar to other inputs, there is a well-behaved derived demand curve for accessibility. Recall the exact condition for cost minimization in the simple model of the precautionary demand for inventories,

$$0 = \int_0^{(K-I)} cf(x)dx - P_A$$

This equation implicitly defines I in terms of its price, P_A. This relationship looks like that in Figure 4.1, such that more accessibility is demanded as its price falls. A similar conclusion about the shape of the demand curve for accessibility could be made if the transac-

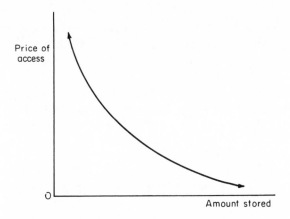

Figure 4.1. The demand for accessibility

tions demand model were used instead. In that case, however, the demand for accessibility is more properly thought of as an opportunity cost.

A firm can purchase accessibility in a number of ways. It can buy accessibility directly by arranging a line of credit in a commodity at a nearby warehouse. What the firm obtains through a line of credit is the right to purchase the commodity at the prevailing price without fear of questions, lengthy negotiations, or an empty warehouse.[25] An explicit charge for a line of credit resembles that of hook-up fees for telephone systems. A charge for joining the network, that is, access to communication by telephone, is made separately from the charge per call. A similar fee for access is contained in prices for electricity. The literature on peak-load pricing for electric utilities investigates the proper structure of prices to charge not only for actual use of electricity but also for the potential to use electricity.[26] In this problem of peak-load pricing, the crucial feature is the extreme inflexibility in short-run generating capacity, much as the inflexibilities in processing and transporting commodities give rise to a demand for access to them.

Another way to obtain access to raw material is through an explicit loan of the commodity. A loan takes a line of credit one step further. Under a loan the commodity is unambiguously in the firm's possession and accessible to it for the period of the loan. Borrowing a fungible commodity is equivalent to purchasing accessibility. If the

[25] See Campbell (1978) for models of lines of credit and revolving credit.
[26] See in particular Dansby (1978) and Saving and De Vany (1981).

firm suddenly needs raw material, it can use immediately what it has borrowed and then leisurely find the equivalent to return. If all a firm wants is access to its raw material over a period of time, it might be content to borrow the commodity rather than buy it outright.

A good on the spot may be thought of as a composite of two distinct goods: a good on order and a good called accessibility, which is not a tangible commodity but the attribute unique to a good on the spot. A good already on the spot differs from a good on order because it provides access to raw material over the intervening time. When that intervening time has passed, the goods are no longer distinguishable. When a miller or spinner buys on the spot, he is really buying two characteristics at once, the right to the good in the future and the right to have secure access over the intervening period. Thus, one way to obtain accessibility is for a firm to buy a good on the spot and sell the right to have the good sometime in the future. These are the two simultaneous transactions constituting a hedging operation.

As has been argued before, a short hedging operation, the combination of buying spot and simultaneously selling for future delivery, is the same as borrowing the commodity. Dealers in commodities can conduct hedging operations as an implicit method of buying accessibility. Such firms use futures markets not because they are risk averse but because they demand accessibility.

It is important to understand that the use of futures contracts themselves is not the purchase of accessibility. A short hedger's sale of a futures contract does not guarantee raw material. Rather, when combined with other transactions, futures contracts allow dealers in commodities to purchase access implicitly. In effect, a firm conducting a hedging operation exercises its line of credit, so to speak, by buying back its short sale, or in other words, by lifting its hedge. Lifting a hedge on a central futures exchange is easier to accomplish than finding raw material in the spot market quickly.

4.6.   The explanation of spreads

The premium for a good on the spot is the price of accessibility. That is to say, the spread between the spot price of wheat (or of any other commodity) and the futures price is primarily the amount firms are willing to pay to borrow wheat. Ignoring incidental charges like warehouse fees and capital expenses, this relationship between the spot price of wheat and the price for later delivery can be expressed mathematically as

$$P_{SPOT} = P_A + P_{FUTURE}$$

Just as spot wheat comprises two goods, forward wheat and accessibility, the price of spot wheat comprises the prices of these two goods, the price for future delivery and the price of accessibility.

Strictly speaking, this relationship holds only in normal conditions. A firm is willing to pay a premium for wheat now because it fears over some future period none will be available at any price or only at great inconvenience. Without a functioning spot market, namely the condition of nothing being immediately available at any price, one cannot properly speak of the spread between spot and futures prices. But the issue is precisely to explain the pattern of spreads during times when a spot market is functioning. A person, as he withdraws currency from his bank on Friday afternoon, can observe that because of forgone interest the currency cost him more than if he had withdrawn it Monday. On Saturday he cannot speak of the spot price for money in relation to Monday's price as of Saturday because with his bank closed he cannot obtain money at any price. It is this difficulty in obtaining money on Saturday and Sunday that leads him to withdraw money Friday, paying the premium of forgone interest in the process.

A similar relationship holds among the prices of the various dates for future delivery. One delivery date is earlier than another. Hence the difference in their prices is the premium for that earlier delivery. When one contract is for immediate delivery, the premium in the spot price is simply the premium for the earliest possible delivery. In general, the price of a near-term contract equals the price of the distant-term contract plus the price of accessibility over the intervening time:

$$P_{NT} = P_A + P_{DT}$$

The spread between two futures contracts is the price for accessibility over a period now in the future. Being a forward price, it is also the anticipated price for that period when the near-term contract becomes the spot price. Changes in spreads between futures prices are none other than movements in the forward prices for accessibility.

The significance of spreads would be much more straightforward if they were calculated by subtracting the more distant month from the nearer month $(P_{NT} - P_{DT})$, and by accounting for storage and capital costs. In contrast, the spread between the price of wheat for two different months is conventionally calculated by subtracting the price of the contract for delivery in the nearer month from that of the more distant month $(P_{DT} - P_{NT})$. This difference is negative in many cases, and always less than or equal to zero when storage fees and interest charges are accounted for. The proper perspective is not that firms lose money holding wheat, but that the sooner wheat is delivered the more it is worth because its availability helps firms reduce their shortage costs or transformation costs. Rather than comparing the price for distant delivery to that for nearby delivery, one should compare the price for nearby delivery to the price for more distant delivery. The more distant delivery would make a better base. A nearer time of delivery would be observed to command a premium over more distant months, because the commodity would be accessible over the interim. That premium is the price of accessibility over that period.

Perhaps the terminology developed in Chapter 2 can make the point clearer. The equilibrium relationship is that the price for immediate delivery plus the price for warehouse fees plus capital expenses minus the use charge for the commodity equals the price for future delivery. Among the three prices representing time value, the use charge on the commodity is the most important. As it stands, the use charge enters with a minus sign. Because it is much more natural to have positive prices, the relationship should be turned around. Moreover, warehouse fees and capital expenses should be subtracted away, being mainly nuisances. The remainder, the use charge for the commodity, is what this chapter calls the price of accessibility. It could also be called the rental fee for the commodity or the premium for early delivery. It is also what Chapter 1 referred to as the mysterious negative component in spreads. By any name, it is central to the spreads among prices for various dates of delivery.

Spreads among futures prices are confusing precisely because no effort is made to isolate the use charge from the warehouse fees and capital expenses. But such calculations are straightforward. Table 4.1 presents such adjustments for wheat prices from 6 September 1979, the array of futures prices discussed first in Chapter 1. From every entry in Table 1.1, except the one for immediate delivery, the prevailing warehouse fee of 4¢ per month and the prevailing interest expense, at a rate of 1% a month, have been subtracted. (Insurance fees were too small to matter.) This leaves, as in the first column of Table 4.1, prices in terms of current dollars rather than dollars at the time of delivery. The prices are also as if the person taking delivery must himself, in a side transaction with a warehouseman, pay the warehousing fees rather than reimburse the person making delivery for having paid them. If the original prices had

Table 4.1. *Interest rates on money and wheat as of 6 September 1979*

$10,000 Treasury bill

Date of maturity	Price in current dollars	Use charge over intervening period (dollars)	Interest rate in % per annum
6 September	10,000	—	—
27 September	9,940	60	10.49
25 October	9,861	79	10.50
27 December	9,686	175	10.56
21 February '80	9,531	155	10.69
29 April	9,341	190	10.95
24 June	9,186	155	11.08
19 August	9,049	137	11.22

1 bushel of contract wheat in Chicago

Month of delivery	Price in current dollars	Use charge over intervening period (dollars)	Interest rate in % per annum
Immediate	4.175	—	—
September	4.170	.005	2.4
December	4.005	.165	13.9
March '80	3.832	.173	16.1
May	3.705	.127	17.7
July	3.315	.390	29.4
September	3.225	.080	28.1

been at full carrying charges, the adjusted prices would all be equal. Actually, the more distant the delivery date, the lower the adjusted price. The differences among these adjusted prices, with the later delivery date subtracted from the earlier delivery date, is the use charge over the period. When someone buys wheat he pays a use charge for having it earlier than if he had arranged for a later delivery date.

Once transformed, prices for wheat look just like prices for money, as expressed in instruments like Treasury bills. Although one normally talks of the discount rate, in percent per annum, on Treasury bills, T-bills are simply a contract the government makes to deliver a commodity, namely dollars, at some time in the future. The discount rate, when adjusted for the time span, is the proportion below 1.0 a future dollar sells for in terms of a current dollar. The prices in terms of current dollars for money delivered at various times in the future, as can be seen in Table 4.1, have the same declining pattern as did the wheat prices in Table 4.1. The use charge for money over a particular period is the difference between the prices for the two different delivery dates. This use charge could be expressed as a percentage of the price of a future dollar and that percentage converted into a rate per annum. That is the interest rate on money. The same conversion of the use charge into an annual percentage rate could be made in the case of wheat by dividing the use charge by the price of wheat delivered at the end of the relevant period and adjusting for the span of time involved.[27] Such a percentage rate is the annual interest rate on wheat. These computed interest rates for wheat, as of 6 September 1979, are shown in Table 4.1.

Just beneath the surface of every array of futures prices is a term structure of interest rates for that particular commodity. These interest rates are not an interest rate on money specific to that commodity. Rather they are interest rates on the commodity itself. Such rates represent the extra wheat one would have to return if one borrowed a bushel of wheat. Substances other than money have interest rates. Futures prices express those commodity-specific interest rates.

The idea of commodity-specific interest rates within arrays of futures prices is far from novel. It dates at least to Keynes (1936: Chapter 17), who borrowed from Sraffa (1932: 49-50). But little was made of the idea. However insightful, Sraffa's observation was but a brief remark in a book review. Keynes, at pains to make money prominent in his analysis of macroeconomics, claimed that commodity-specific interest rates are uninteresting compared to the interest rate on money. But commodity-specific interest rates are most interesting, and it is regrettable that Keynes's claim inhibited further theoretical and empirical investigation. It is even more regrettable that of Keynes's two asides on commodity markets, his earlier one outlining the theory of normal backwardation has become canon in the literature on futures markets. His later comment on commodity-specific interest rates itself discredits his first, and it would have unlocked the content of futures prices if given the attention devoted to his theory of normal backwardation.

The content of an array of futures prices goes unnoticed for three reasons. First, the main action is in the spreads between futures

---

[27] Whether it is better to express the use charges for commodities as a percentage of the prices of the commodities or in dollars per unit depends on whether the amount held in inventory (or the fee willingly paid for accessibility) depends on the price of the commodity.

prices, not the futures prices themselves. Second, warehousing fees and the interest rate on money obscure those spreads. Third, the use charge on commodities is expressed in dollars per unit, while one is used to the use charge on money being expressed as a percentage. Strip these impediments to an understanding of futures markets away, and the prices become readily comprehensible with the analogy of money markets. Clearly in Table 4.1, the entries for Treasury bills and wheat are comparable.

Of course, the points about the demand for accessibility were based on the motives of an individual firm, while these pertaining to spreads apply marketwide. Each firm finds it advantageous to ensure access, by whatever arrangement, to some raw material. If it were exceptional, one firm could probably hold inventory without paying a use charge. Because many other firms follow the same logic, their combined demand yields a positive price, P_A, for that access, given that the supply of inventory is limited, as it is for goods costly to produce like agricultural commodities or metals. Similarly, because many firms and individuals want to hold or to borrow money despite the cost of interest, their combined demand, given that the supply of money is not infinite, leads to a positive interest rate on money.

Naturally, the precise demand curve for each firm depends on its particular shortage and transformation costs. It is likely that what one firm considers as too high a price for access another is willing to pay. Consequently, inventory will gravitate to those most willing to pay to hold it. For example, if there are conditions in a local market such that someone will pay for access to wheat, a farmer or anyone else with wheat will rush supplies to those persons most desirous of access. Anyone who retains inventory whose accessibility profits him not while someone else could use it needlessly forsakes the value of that accessibility.

The inverse of this argument that inventory gravitates to the place where having it on hand is most useful is that anyone who retains inventory in the face of a demand for accessibility must, himself, be demanding accessibility. For a farmer to retain wheat, even if he does so as a strategy for minimizing his total costs of transportation, is to act as if he, too, were wanting access. Regardless of reasons farmers or millers hold stocks of wheat, all of them are buying accessibility if any one of them is. Therefore, the demand for accessibility applies to everyone who owns wheat in store. The marketwide demand curve is the sum of the separate demands for access of all those who might hold inventory in the area.

The market supply of accessibility is the sum of all the inventory holdings in that area. If one dealer finds himself with extra inventory for a period of time, he can lend it to someone else who has more immediate need for it. Yet this reallocation among dealers reaches the limit of the amount of inventory they hold collectively. In a small region, the supply could be supplemented relatively quickly by shipments from surrounding areas. But ultimately the current supply of accessibility is fixed; there is only so much wheat or copper currently available worldwide. Naturally these supplies will be supplemented with the next harvest or production cycle, although the supply will not always expand to the point where it satiates the demand for accessibility even temporarily. After all, it costs something to produce extra wheat or copper. Rather than incur excessive production costs, it will be worthwhile, from the perspective of the whole market, for firms to hold inventories at a loss. Occasionally, however, an abundant supply of a commodity reduces the premuim for its accessibility to zero. These are the rare times of full carrying charges.

For a particular commodity the array of prices for different delivery dates represents a complex equilibrium. The price for immediate delivery represents both the value of withdrawing stocks for current consumption and the value of holding them in store. The value of holding them in store is the sum of the accessibility they provide over a period plus their value, measured in terms of either future consumption or future storage, at the end of that period. As stocks are withdrawn for consumption, the supply of accessibility will fall and the use charge will rise. This is why spreads tend to be more negative later in the crop-year, as was seen previously for wheat and soybean oil in Tables 1.2 and 1.3. With a new crop, or with the opening of a major mine, the supply will increase, and the forward use charge fall. Consequently, the most distant spreads are less likely to be extremely negative, as was seen in the pattern of spreads for copper in Table 1.4.

Clearly, all the prices in the array react to new information. For example, the prospect of a crop larger than previously expected necessitates many adjustments in the equilibrium array to increase consumption over the period before the harvest. One result of the increased consumption is for spreads covering periods before the harvest to move farther from full carrying charges as the amount in store falls. In contrast, those spreads covering periods after the harvest move more toward full carrying charges as the forward use fee falls with the prospect of larger quantities becoming available. That the various use charges, representing different periods in the future, do not react in parallel is the reason for several futures contracts.

4.7. The demand for accessibility and the supply of storage

This interpretation of the mysterious negative component to spreads as the price paid to borrow commodities is related to that of Holbrook Working, who proposed the concept of the supply of storage to explain the paradoxes of spreads (1948, 1949, and 1953b). Working approached the problem from the perspective of carrying charges rather than from the perspective of a use charge for the commodity. The perspective of a use charge for the commodity has several substantial advantages over the perspective of carrying charges, as will now be shown. The empirical evidence of the relationship between spreads and aggregate inventories is better explained by the formal theory behind the demand for accessibility. Even so, Working's concept of the supply of storage affirms what is fundamental to futures prices, namely the behavior of spreads.

Working's first insight (1949: 1258) was that

> A known return for storage is, in essentials, a price of storage. The fact that the price of storage is not quoted directly, but must be derived by taking the difference between quoted prices of wheat for two different dates of delivery is immaterial to the economic reasoning. The price difference is . . . in all essential respects itself a price of storage, determined in a free market through the competition of those who seek to supply storage service.

Before Working, no one had adequately explained "inverse carrying charges," that is, negative spreads.[28] Working, following Kaldor (1939), argued that inventories provide a "convenience yield" whenever a firm needs to fill orders promptly or smooth out production.[29] For this convenience yield, firms will incur inverse carrying charges. A firm balances the advantages of convenience yield against the costs of maintaining an inventory: warehouses fees, insurance, and interest. To determine how much to store, the firm constantly compares its net marginal cost of storage at each level of inventory to the implicit price of storage. That is to say, the behavior of an elevator or flour mill is just like that of any firm producing more conventional products than storage. As a consequence, the aggregate

---

[28] Vaile (1948), however, objected to Working's definition of the price of storage as a residual, claiming that no firm paid attention to a residual. But as demonstrated in Chapter 2, an implicit price has all the economic significance of an explicit price.

[29] Weymar (1966) corrected a technical flaw in Working's theory. Goss (1970) and Plisker (1973) have also contributed to the theory of the supply of storage.

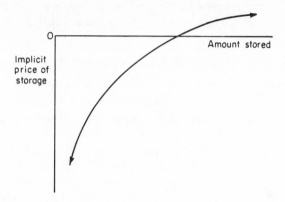

Figure 4.2. The supply of storage

behavior of all firms holding wheat is simply an industry supply curve for storage.

As mentioned in Chapter 1, Working and many others have observed a strong relationship between aggregate inventory behavior and spreads. Figure 4.2 portrays a generalization of the supply-of-storage function Working found for wheat, previously portrayed as Figure 1.2. Here, in Figure 4.2, the quantity stored is plotted against the implicit price of storage. At small quantities the marginal convenience yield dominates, so that the implicit price of storage is negative.

Despite such strong empirical support, the theory of the supply of storage fails to deal with a number of important points. First, the costs of physical storage are nearly constant regardless of the amount of wheat in store, as noted in section 4.1, and as such do not account for the patterns in spreads. Rather, convenience yield must alone be responsible for movements in spreads. Second, there are often separate and distinct markets for the two components, although the theory analyzes them as one. Third, and most important, when convenience yield is examined separately, it does not behave at all as a conventional supply curve behaves. Rather it behaves as the mirror image of a conventional demand curve.

The alternative concept of the demand for accessibility can explain everything covered by the theory of the supply of storage, but without its weaknesses. Where the theory of the supply of storage combines the costs of physical storage services with convenience yield and analyzes them as one, the theory of the demand for accessibility distinguishes clearly between these two components. It should not be surprising that the combination of a price the firm receives

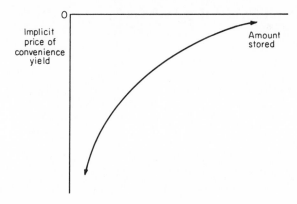

Figure 4.3. The supply of convenience yield

for its service of physical storage with one the firm pays for accessibility is sometimes negative.

The theory of the demand for accessibility also emphasizes the more important of the two components associated with holding commodities over time. Physical storage, itself, constitutes a small part of the so-called supply of storage, and because its price is virtually constant, it is not important to an understanding of price movements. It is a much better use of terms to reserve the "supply of storage" for the supply of warehouses, insurance, and so forth, and to dismiss pure storage costs from consideration.

If the physical costs of storage were paid for in a separate market, the spread between the spot and futures prices would simply reflect the marginal convenience yield. In that case, one would have to deal expressly with the market for convenience yield. This separation of pure storage from convenience yield can occcur in practice, not just in abstraction. Mills and county elevators may own the grain in their care, but the public warehouses in Chicago, for example, carefully distinguish the storage service from the convenience derived from owning the grain, which is retained by the person holding the warehouse receipt. Although the prices of futures contracts reflect these warehousing fees, the transaction for the service of physical storage takes place in a separate market.

In any case, the stable fees for warehousing in cities with futures markets allow one easily to derive the implicit price of convenience yield from the implicit price of storage. A similar adjustment can be performed on the general curve graphing the supply of storage in Figure 4.2. Here, in Figure 4.3, a constant marginal physical cost of

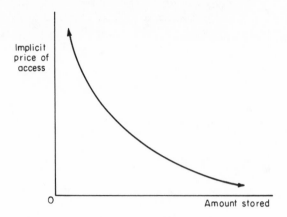

Figure 4.4. The demand for accessibility

storage including interest expenses has been subtracted out, leaving only the supply of the marginal convenience yield.

This supply curve for convenience yield hardly looks like a normal supply curve. In the first place, goods and services are usually supplied at a positive price, not at a negative price as in Figure 4.2. Second, a price ordinarily must increase more and more (or as here become less and less negative) to draw forth each additional unit. Yet in Figure 4.3 this is not the case. In fact, this curve looks just like the mirror image of a conventional demand curve, as in Figure 4.4.

The supply of convenience yield, and with it the so-called supply of storage, is being looked at upside down. It is nothing but the mirror image of the demand for accessibility, seen previously in Figure 4.1. Although the benefits of inventory are balanced against the cost of holding them, regardless of whether the problem is called the supply for storage or the demand for accessibility, it is more natural to view the relationship between spreads and storage as the demand for accessibility.

The advantages of the perspective of the demand for accessibility can be appreciated by considering which perspective applies in the market for money. A firm holding cash either forgoes interest income if it owns the money or must pay a bank interest for a loan. Yet in either case, the firm is portrayed as paying a price, namely interest, for the cash it has demanded. It is true that cash provides the convenience of avoiding expensive conversions of illiquid assets, but it would hardly be sensible to refer to the supply of convenience yield of money. It is no more sensible in the case of other goods held in inventory.

The money market also demonstrates why it is advisable to separate out pure storage costs from the other costs of holding commodities over time. Early deposit banks were simply warehouses for specie, and goldsmiths naturally charged for this storage service (Richards 1929: 35-37, and Horsefield 1977). Goldsmiths soon discovered, however, that it was profitable to pay interest to attract deposits because they could in turn lend the currency to someone who would pay an even higher premium for having it immediately. Consequently, goldsmiths as primitive deposit bankers were doing two things at once: supplying storage for specie and demanding currency for immediate use. (Remember, bankers borrow from depositors.) Likewise, modern banks often charge separately for each check and for a monthly statement, services that correspond to the physical storage of a commodity like wheat. Yet banks pay out interest to depositors, which corresponds to the use charge on the commodity. The rate of interest, rather than the service fees, is of primary importance in markets for money, just as its counterpart is in commodity markets.

Compared to Working's theory of the supply of storage, the theory presented here of a market for accessibility is a much simpler and more informative way to obtain similar results. A market for accessibilty, with a positive rather than a negative price, is easier to comprehend. Moreover, it more obviously resembles many other markets, especially markets for money, allowing the insights from those markets to be applied to the spreads between futures prices.

This approach can also expand on the insights of the supply-of-storage concept, for the impression remains that the implicit price of storage, although important for the allocation of stocks, is incidental to the main purpose of futures markets. Somehow the full implications of the price-of-storage concept have not been appreciated. Even Working was led to state that firms who do not hedge all their inventories (1962: 442) "increase the efficiency of their participation in the price forming process, instead of largely withdrawing from such participation, as they do when they practice routine carrying-charge or operational hedging." This statement, which implies that a spot purchase and a sale of a futures contract cancel each other out in their influence on prices, flatly contradicts Working's major insight about the supply of storage. Routine hedging is instrumental in determining spreads. Hedging operations are simply the purchase of accessibility. If dealers did not conduct so many hedging operations, for instance because their demand for accessibility fell, the use charge would be lower. Dealers who routinely hedge participate in the price-forming process by changing the use fee for the commodity, and as a result, by changing spreads. If Working can make this mistake, it is not surprising that some researchers still misunderstand the relationship of futures prices to both spot prices and the implicit price of storage, and have developed models at odds with the theory of the supply of storage.

4.8.   The reasons for borrowing commodities

The real advantage of the perspective of the demand for accessibility comes from its implications about the reasons firms use futures markets. The perspective of the supply of storage tells little of why firms use futures markets, at least not directly. Working argues eloquently that spreads are implicit prices of storage. But he fails to emphasize how firms would construct an implicit position in the good he calls storage, comprising physical storage services and convenience yield. They do so, of course, through short hedging operations, buying spot and selling for future delivery, that is, they use futures markets as part of a set of trades to take a position in spreads.

The theory of the supply of storage leaves unanswered whether or not firms need to use futures markets. The spread between the spot price and the nearest-term futures price does guide a firm in selecting how much inventory to buy in the spot market. But what determines whether it sells a futures contract against its spot purchase? Why does it need to sell a futures contract? The firm would, on average, earn the implicit price of storage whether or not it sold a futures contract. Actually, because of the transactions costs in the futures market, the firm would earn less on average if it practiced hedging operations rather than outright purchasing. Seemingly then, futures contracts would be useful only to those firms that were risk averse. A risk-neutral firm would be content to earn the average without resorting to futures markets. As a result, the theory of the supply of storage inadvertently encourages the belief that firms use futures markets because they are averse to risk. Even granting the concept of the supply of storage, the story about futures markets follows its familiar course: Perhaps in order to sell a futures contract, risk-averse storers must pay a risk premium. That is, spreads might be biased downward as a return to storage; realized returns to storage on average would be higher. Thus, there is nothing in Working's view of his theory of the supply of storage to supplant the view of futures markets as markets involving risk aversion.

Working has, however, argued elsewhere that firms use futures contracts as temporary substitutes for merchandising contracts to be arranged later (1953b and 1962). Taken on its own, this argument also seems to imply that the motive for using futures markets is risk aversion. Why else would risk-neutral firms care whether they had a temporary substitute for a merchandising contract? Yet they should care even if risk neutral. Working was attempting to articulate the ideas later developed in search theory and the theory of financial intermediation, although the reasons could have been seen in the phenomenon called convenience yield. Had Working formally synthesized his two arguments, he would have been able to establish that risk-neutral firms have reason to use futures markets.

The theory of the demand for accessibility, however, establishes that dealers will use futures markets even if they are risk neutral. The perspective of the demand for accessibility leads naturally to the synthesis able to explain both why firms hold inventories and why they use futures contracts. All depends on a hierarchy of transformation costs. These transformation costs include both the costs of speeding up processing or transportation and the transactions cost in particular markets. Obtaining material for immediate delivery involves the highest transformation costs. Second must be the cost of selling quickly. Third must be the cost of arranging a purchase or sale in advance. Fourth and lowest must be the cost of consummating agreements made previously. Because of this hierarchy of transformation costs, risk-neutral firms hold inventory, some of it borrowed, just as they hold cash, some of it borrowed.

Delving into the reasons why firms hold inventories, the theory of accessibility establishes that firms are well advised to hold inventories because of shortage costs and transformation costs. A consideration of convenience yield would likewise uncover the reasons for holding inventories, but no one has studied convenience yield carefully. Consequently, no one has appreciated that firms hold inventories to have a secure supply of commodities. They do not want the commodities themselves; access to the commodities suffices. They can acquire access by borrowing the commodity instead of buying it outright. Given the choice between a loan of a commodity and an offer for sale, they will choose the loan. If done implicitly through a hedging operation, borrowing a commodity involves a futures contract. This position in futures does not result from risk aversion.

Calculated as a difference between the spot price and the price of a futures contract, the price of accessibility is implicit. But of course this price could be explicit; there could be a formal, organized exchange for trading accessibility. If such a market existed, a contract denominated in units of accessibility would be traded. Yet, as Chapter 2 emphasized, nothing of substance changes if a firm buys accessibility implicitly rather than explicitly, that is, through a hedging operation rather than through an outright loan.

This assertion of a firm's contentment with implicit borrowing ignores one problem: the extra transactions costs involved in constructing a loan implicitly. Because an implicit loan requires two transactions costs, and an outright purchase only one, perhaps an outright purchase is preferable. That is to say, borrowing commodities implicitly through a hedging operation requires the brokerage fees of initiating and later offsetting a position in futures. In a system of trading with an explicit loan market, an explicit futures market, and an implicit spot market, clearly a risk-neutral firm would borrow rather than own outright since two transactions, one in the loan market and one in the futures market, would be necessary to create the effect of a transaction in the spot market. But why should a risk-neutral firm pay the higher expenses of borrowing implicitly rather than owning outright? (Note, however, that these costs to hedging are brokerage fees, not the backwardation in prices, as is presumed in theories emphasizing risk aversion.) Do transactions costs, however small in active futures markets, preclude their use by risk-neutral firms?

This issue of borrowing versus owning outright is also ignored in the literature on the demand for money. For example, the standard model of the transactions demand for cash does not investigate whether a firm should hold cash outright or borrow. But just as important as an understanding of the reasons for holding money is an understanding of the empirically observed practice of both long-term control of money and short-term loans. Granted that it needs cash, should a toy manufacturer, whose needs are highly seasonal, issue stock or long-term bonds sufficient to have enough cash for its highest possible needs, or should it depend on temporary trade credit granted by its bank? The answer depends on what the toy manufacturer is able to do with its extra cash during its seasonal lulls. If the bank is a more effective intermediary than the toy manufacturer, which the bank should be since intermediation is the bank's main line of business, then the toy manufacturer should borrow. In fact, the toy manufacturer will find it advantageous to borrow at least some money through temporary trade credit even if temporary loans are more expensive than long-term financing.[30] That is to say,

---

[30] For examples of models treating both the demand for cash and the proportion borrowed, see Gupta (1973) or Aigner and Sprenkle (1973).

a risk-neutral firm will find it perfectly rational to borrow from a bank at 10% per annum for a few months even though it could issue long-term bonds at 8% per annum (the difference being the bank's fee for its service of intermediation). The reason is that if the firm issues long-term bonds, it must find a use for the money when its short-term needs have passed. When it tries to lend, being ill-equipped for the business, it obtains only 7% per annum. It will pay the premium for short-term borrowing in order to avoid becoming a lender itself. A short-term loan allows the firm to give the money back to the bank, leaving the bank with the problem of finding someone to whom to lend it again. In effect, a short-term loan arranges for the firm in advance what it can do with its cash after its seasonal need passes.

Analogously with short-term trade credit, an implicit loan of a commodity offers a dealer or processor the advantage over outright ownership of greater ease in disposing of excess inventory. In the extreme, a firm can simply deliver on its futures contract, avoiding any costs of using the spot market quickly. Consequently, even a risk-neutral dealer or processor will find it advisable to borrow implicitly at least some of its inventory even if the extra brokerage fees on futures contracts make it more costly to borrow than to own outright. That is to say, risk-neutral firms have reason to use futures markets.

Several of these themes can be brought together in one last formal model. The starkness of this last model highlights its two important features: (1) The firm is risk neutral, concerned only with average costs and not their variance, and (2) use of the futures market incurs a brokerage fee. As in previous models in this chapter, the firm has an uncertain need of raw material in the next period. Thus, the model asks, alongside the question of the derivation of the precautionary demand for inventory, the further question of the proportion of that inventory against which a futures contract is sold.

For simplicity let the need for raw material x range equally for 0.0 to a normalized 1.0 unit; $f(x)$ follows a uniform density function. Whatever the firm does not have on hand, it must buy hurriedly in the spot market and ship hurriedly to its plant. Picture a miller in Chicago, who must rush around, locating a seller, perhaps needing to offer the seller a premium in price because of his hurry, and who must then pay a premium for fast freight. Let t_b comprise all these costs of hurried buying. To avoid this high per-unit cost of buying hurriedly, the firm can acquire inventory I ahead of time. Holding inventory costs P_A per unit, as before.

In this instance, the firm also selects the optimal number of futures contracts, H, to sell short. A transaction in the futures market, whether initiating the hedge or lifting the hedge, costs t_f. Because of this transactions cost, seemingly there is no reason for the firm to sell any of its inventory. But the firm must also consider what happens if its needs for raw material are such that it has too much inventory. Suppose it must liquidate all its positions, whether futures or inventory, in the second period. If it has too much inventory, it must sell in the spot market at a per-unit transaction cost of t_s. Although the firm must accomplish the reverse of its actions as when it had to buy hurriedly, perhaps it is not quite as pressed as when its mill threatens to stand idle. Hence t_s is probably less than t_b. What is more important is that the costs of delivering on a futures contract, t_d, are considerably less than t_s. It has the advantage of having already arranged a sale. Therefore, it is reasonable to suppose a hierarchy of costs with $t_b > t_s > P_A > t_d > t_f$. A more realistic formulation of the problem would make all transactions, whether in the futures market or the spot market, an increasing rather than a constant function of the amount transacted. This complication would preclude an explicit solution for the amount of inventory and the amount of hedging. As it is, the firm must balance the costs of using the spot market to aquire raw material quickly with the costs of holding inventory and balance the cost of brokerage fees on futures contracts against the relative ease of delivering on them.

The firm, being risk neutral, seeks to minimize its expected costs,

$$EC = \int_I^{1.0} [t_f H + t_b(x - I)]dx + \int_{(I-H)}^I \{t_f[H - (I - x)] + t_d(I - x)\}dx$$

$$+ \int_{0.0}^{(I-H)} \{t_d H + t_s[(I - x) - H]\}dx + P_A I + t_f H$$

The first of these five terms applies whenever the need for raw material is greater than the level of inventory. New supplies are acquired through purchases on the spot market and indirectly through the lifting of hedges. The second term applies whenever the amount of raw material is less than the amount of inventory but more than the amount not committed for delivery on futures contracts. Those futures contracts must be bought back. The third term applies whenever inventories are too large. The last two terms do not involve the random variable x, being set in the first period.

Solving the first-order conditions yields formulas for the optimal amount of inventory and the optimal amount of short hedging,

$$I^* = (t_b - P_A - 2t_f)/(t_b + t_d - t_f)$$

$$H^* = I^* - 2t_f/(t_f - t_d + t_s)$$

As is apparent in these formulas, a risk-neutral firm will sell futures contracts despite brokerage fees. It will short hedge (although that expression, indicative of risk aversion, is no longer appropriate). For example, if t_b is 2.0%, t_s 1.5%, and P_A 0.75% for the length of time involved, and if t_d is 0.5% and t_f 0.1%, then the firm will hold .44 units of its raw material (its average need being .50 units), and it will sell futures contracts against 58% of its inventory. To put the matter slightly differently, with those costs, it would like to keep .44 units on the spot of its mill, owning outright 42% of that amount while borrowing the other 58%. What influences its extent of hedging, that is, the proportion it borrows, is not its degree of risk aversion but the brokerage fee (or more generally the bid-asked spread) in the futures market and the relative advantage of disposing of excess inventory with the help of futures contracts. Specifically, it is worth paying t_f because t_d is smaller than t_s. As the difference between disposal through spot markets and disposal through futures contracts increases, the proportion of inventory hedged increases. As brokerage fees fall or the liquidity of the futures market increases, the proportion of inventory hedged increases.

This model also applies to those dealers not located at the delivery point for the central futures market. In fact, this model can help explain why futures markets become centralized. As already developed, the model can explain why dealers would use a futures market if it were local. If t_f, the cost of a trade in a futures contract, were lower on a centralized exchange, they would have an incentive to transfer their trading to there. Working in the other direction, however, are the relatively higher costs of disposing of excess inventory through the central futures market. At first glance in fact, it would seem that t_d is above t_s. For a dealer away from the central market, to dispose of excess inventory, he must both lift his hedge and sell locally. Thus, t_d would seem to equal $t_f + t_s$. But a strong case can be made for t_d to remain below t_s. In the first place, the dealer has always the option of sending his excess inventory to the central market (presuming the natural flow of the commodity is in that direction). With a previously arranged delivery for there, his only expense is the cost of arranging transportation. That should be less than t_s. Second, the dealer's search costs would be reduced by the expansion of the number of people he could trade with. Consider some trader who owns the commodity in one of the warehouses in the central market but who is indifferent between holding it there and at the desperate seller's local market. That trader could offer the desperate seller an exchange. The exchange would do the seller little good if he then had to worry about a hurried sale in the central market. If, however, he had a commitment to deliver already arranged, as with a futures contract, he would be home free. Thus, with t_d below t_s, a risk-neutral dealer, wherever his facility is, has reason to use, to some extent at least, futures contracts on a central exchange.

Firms use futures markets for much the same reasons they use banks when the commodity is money rather than wheat or soybean oil. Banks reduce search costs, monitoring costs, and placement costs for firms that would otherwise need to invest their idle funds themselves. Futures markets provide a service comparable to financial intermediation. As a result, an issue uniting money markets and futures markets concerns the scope of the firm. One must believe that there are some advantages to specialization, since most firms are specialized. Belief in the advantages of specialization is equivalent to maintaining that there are nonlinearities in the capacity and skills of management. In the case of dealers in commodities, limits on the breadth of management makes it advisable for the firm to limit itself to inventory control rather than speculation, that is, to borrow commodities rather than to own them outright. One could also make the point slightly differently by saying that these are limits on a firm's capacity to digest information. Working (1953a, 1953b, and 1962) has repeatedly stressed that futures markets allow firms to concentrate on price relationships rather than price levels. However described, a nonlinearity in the capabilities of firms is once again crucial in determining why firms use futures markets. But also once again, that nonlinearity is not in their utility functions; it has nothing to do with risk aversion. It is in the technological and organizational features of the firm itself.

The perspective of the demand for accessibility is only subtly different from the perspective of the supply of storage. Yet that subtle change in perspective leads to a powerful conclusion about the function of futures markets. All the interesting features about futures markets, especially the existence and persistence of negative spreads, can be explained without recourse to risk aversion. Negative spreads are the amount firms are willing to pay in order to borrow commodities to minimize their expected transactions, transformation, and shortage costs. Firms buy and sell futures contracts as part of more complex transactions that leave them implicitly borrowing commodities. Firms are content to borrow commodities rather than buy them outright because what they need is quick and secure access to the commodities for a period of time rather than the commodity itself. Such a demand for accessibility and the resulting desire to use futures contracts as part of an implicit method of buying accessibility is true even of risk-neutral firms.

On close inspection, besides commodity dealers' use of futures markets, many activities thought to be responses to risk aversion are not. For example, inflexible production processes can lead, in the case of uncertainty about the output's price, to changes in the demand for inputs, as has been studied by Hartman (1976). In his model he assumed (p. 676) that

the firm is risk neutral in the sense that it chooses the capital input (the quasi-fixed input) to maximize the expected value of long-run profits. An obvious implication of this assumption is that all uncertainty results . . . arise from the non-linear nature of the technology rather than risk aversion.

Cukierman (1980) has studied the response in terms of investment of a risk-neutral firm using a Baysian framework. Mayers and Thaler (1979) have reexamined the much-noted phenomenon of sticky wages, which is the practice of paying a set hourly wage or a weekly salary. They argue that instead of being a response to the risk aversion of employees, as commonly presumed, sticky wages are well explained by the transactions costs associated with resetting a wage continuously. Even insurance itself, it seems, can be explained without risk aversion. According to Mayers and Smith (1982), risk-neutral firms have sufficient reason to pay premiums for property and liability insurance, rather than to self-insure, in order to, among other reasons, reduce expected transactions costs involved in bankruptcy, achieve efficiencies in administering claims, and lower expected tax liabilities. Similarly, the ability to explain satisfactorily the paradoxical features of futures markets without recourse to risk aversion is the principal point of this chapter and of this book.

CHAPTER 5

The contribution of futures markets

The previous chapter emphasized that firms hold inventory as a response to the costs of producing, moving, and processing commodities quickly. Not surprisingly, there are other possible responses to inflexible and uncertain production and processing, such as vertical integration, horizontal integration, or versatile equipment. But even if other responses are used to some degree, in many instances it will be cheapest for firms to buy access to materials. To borrow a commodity implicitly through a hedging operation involving a futures contract is one method of obtaining accessibility for a stretch of time. Thus, it is a demand for access that leads to the contribution of futures markets as organized implicit loan markets for commodities. This chapter will put the contribution of futures markets into a more general setting, and will seek to explain why futures markets are the dominant institution for borrowing and lending commodities.

Others, of course, have argued that the contribution of futures markets is something besides that of organized implicit loan markets for commodities. The idea of futures markets as markets for price insurance has been discussed in Chapter 3, and the idea of them as markets for information will be discussed in the next chapter. Yet another strand in the literature has emphasized the features of futures markets as institutions, namely the standardization of contracts, the margin system, and the operation of clearinghouses, as what makes them special. The discusssion of the institutional responses to inflexibilities in producing and processing commodities extends naturally to a consideration of this theory that futures markets are superior to informal forward markets because futures contracts allow impersonal, highly organized trading. Although true, these advantages of futures markets should not be overemphasized. On close inspection futures markets are found to borrow heavily from forward markets, and more important, many forward markets are found to be highly advanced institutions themselves. Furthermore, many explicit loan markets have standardized contracts, enforcement of contracts through margin, and clearinghouses.

Thus, a search for the reasons futures markets exist is not espe-

150

cially fruitful if the position is taken that what is special about them is their degree of organization. Rather, the reasons that futures markets exist instead of essentially equivalent ways to trade, such as explicit loan markets, hinge on the small advantages the legal system gives to particular systems of trading and the small conveniences gained in arranging transactions in particular patterns. These transactional and legal reasons for implicit loan markets are explored in depth in the second half of this chapter.

5.1. The demand for access in general equilibrium

Although one can deduce the reasons for holding inventory given the uncertainties and costs of producing, moving, and processing bulk commodities quickly, one does not so readily see why those inconveniences and uncertainties persist. The fact of the matter is that they persist because doing away with them is often even more costly.

Once again, an analogy with money is helpful. Given the inconvenience of frequent visits to the bank and the uncertainty of receipts and expenditures, it is natural to hold currency. On the other hand, it would seem so easy to reduce the uncertainty and mismatching of receipts and expenditures. People might be expected to avoid the opportunity cost of holding cash by rearranging their method and pattern of payments and receipts. If, after a regular paycheck, a tenant must hold funds idle for several days before his rent falls due, he might recontract with his landlord to pay less rent earlier or with his employer to receive more pay later. Similarly, instead of paying with currency, which has no chance of being returned for insufficient funds, a customer might offer a small premium to a merchant to take a personal check from an interest-bearing account. The potential for this conservation of currency has motivated many predictions of the arrival of a cashless society.

Prophets of a cashless society have not seen their new world arrive precisely because rearranging methods and patterns of payments and receipts is costly. Forgone interest on currency is cheaper that other methods, such as certified checks, of ensuring a merchant that the payment he is taking from a stranger is good. For each employee to receive his pay on the day most suitable for him, necessitating a whole schedule of premiums and discounts for later or earlier payment, would raise the employer's administrative costs far above the forgone interest on the employee's idle balances. Moreover, its employees' wishes might well exacerbate the firm's own problem of coordinating its receipts and payments so as to keep its idle cash to a minimum.

Currency holdings result from an economywide balancing of the costs of converting interest-earning assets back and forth into cash, the costs of monitoring credit ratings, the costs of administering checking accounts, and the cost of planning receipts and expenditures far in advance. Of course, innovations lowering these costs might induce people to hold less cash. The invention of ready-teller machines, for example, reduces the costs, especially that of time, of visiting a bank, and changes the demand for currency at all interest rates. Similarly, if some invention like payroll processing with computers made it easier for employers to adjust their schedule of paychecks more to their employees' personal patterns, less money would be held. Meanwhile, currency persists because it is often the most convenient and least costly method of conducting many commercial transactions.

The demand for access to raw materials likewise results from a delicate balance among possible ways of minimizing shortage and transformation costs. Besides holding inventories, firms might integrate vertically, integrate horizontally, or employ flexible workers and machines. For primary commodities these other techniques are relatively ineffective. Consequently, stockpiles of primary commodities will have a prominent place in this balance among ways to minimize shortage and transformation costs.

Firms, by integrating vertically, might improve the coordination of their orders with their needs as well as avoid possible opportunistic behavior on the part of suppliers who know their delivery of inputs is vital.[1] Much the same improvement in reliability might be accomplished less formally through repeated use of the same suppliers, so that both firms come to depend on each other. A firm could also respond to uncertainties in the arrival of supplies by horizontal integration or similar expansion, since the reserves of materials, spare parts, and labor could be increased less than in proportion to the size of the facilities if the interruptions were independent of each other.

Yet horizontal and vertical integration, which require more managerial effort, are not costless. Moreover, because the inherent and unalterable uncertainties in commodities ebb and flow in magnitude

---

[1] A large literature, including Goldberg (1980), Klein, Crawford, and Alchian (1978), and Williamson (1979), has explored the responses to opportunistic behavior, including the response of vertical integration.

while the scope and scale of a firm are much less elastic, neither vertical nor horizontal integration can eliminate the need for access to raw material.

An entirely different reaction on the part of a firm to uncertainties might be for it to specialize less in one line of business. A firm repeatedly confronted with interruptions in its supplies of raw material and buffeted by large swings in the demand for its product might install more flexible machinery and hire fewer workers skilled in only one task. A flour mill might have the range of equipment to mill wheat of different hardness and perhaps even the flexibility to switch to the production of corn meal.

Yet such flexibility sacrifices the advantages of specialization. Further, for many processors of commodities, flexibility is prohibitively expensive compared to specializing in one line of business. Although hog raisers can substitute feed grains fairly readily, they can hardly switch from fattening hogs to raising chickens, just as soybean crushing facilities would have to be radically different in design to do anything but crush soybeans. Copper firms find it difficult to build smelters even flexible enough to handle copper ores of different sulfur content, let alone capable of smelting lead.

All these responses, horizontal integration, vertical integration, flexible facilities, and stockpiles of raw materials, arise from a fear that contracts promising timely delivery of a specified quantity of raw material cannot be fulfilled. The simplest reaction to this anxiety would seem to be stricter enforcement of contracts. (This approach, of course, is not costless either, whether resulting in more surety bonds or more courts and lawyers.) Yet promises of raw material may be negated not because of dishonesty on the part of suppliers but because acts of God make it impossible for anyone to make the scheduled deliveries. Vagaries in weather, either in growing or moving crops, affect large areas. Under such circumstances, stockpiles of raw material are far more effective than horizontal integration, vertical integration, and flexible facilities. Vertical integration can little remedy disruptions in supply when a miller's own farms suffer the same shortfall of wheat as other farms. Consolidation of several mills in one region into one large enterprise offers little advantage if all the mills would have been short of wheat at the same time. There would also be much less advantage to a flour miller from the flexibility of grinding cornmeal if all other mills in the region convert at the same time. Consequently, in industries handling or processing primary commodities such as those traded on futures markets, the tendency to desire access to raw materials will be pronounced.

In this context it is clear that access to raw material also is not costless. At any moment in time the quantity of a commodity, and hence the supply of accessibility, is limited. Consequently, spreads often are below full carrying charges. The supply of agricultural commodities, in particular, is bounded by harvests. Even with a new harvest, the stock of raw material may not increase enough to satiate the demand for accessibility. After all, it is costly to increase plantings in order to add to stocks. In general, production of a commodity will be increased only up to the point where its marginal cost equals the value of the material delivered or, in other words, the sum of the value of the material at the end of the following production cycle plus the value of accessibility over the interim. This is just like the equilibrium in the money market under a gold standard between the demand for specie and the cost of mining gold. Although more gold reduces the opportunity cost of holding currency, an extra supply of gold is forthcoming only to the extent that the currency price of gold, the present value of all of the interest it earns, is greater than or equal to the current cost of mining that gold.

5.2.   Warehouse receipts and grain banks

Whatever the balance at any given time among the many possible responses to the inflexibility and uncertainties in producing, transporting, and processing commodities, a new balance is constantly sought since the relative advantages of the various responses are constantly changing with the incessant pressure to invent new responses or improve the old ones. All responses are costly, and any improvement in managerial techniques, storage facilities, or machine design changes these costs. As the advantage of vertical integration, for example, increases compared to flexibility in machinery, access to raw material, and so forth, the extent of each in the equilibrium among the responses shifts.

This pressure to reduce costs applies equally forcefully to the costs of holding inventories. Many institutions in the commodities trade, including futures markets, can be understood as ingenious efforts to reduce the costs of holding inventories by making more efficient use of the existing inventories. Many have been spontaneous creations, often poorly recognized as advances.

One such reaction to the cost of holding reserves of commodities was the mid-nineteenth-century development of negotiable warehouse receipts issued by public grain elevators in shipping centers like Chicago. By transferring evidence of title to grain through an easily circulated piece of paper, negotiable warehouse receipts reduced the expense of and damage from moving the grain itself. This invention is comparable to the rise of *giro* banks for specie in Venice and Amsterdam in the seventeenth century. A customer could direct the transfer of funds to the account of another by written or oral order and so reduce considerably the time and expense of extinguishing a debt. The new holder of the funds could then use them as the basis for further transfers in bank.[2]

A *giro* bank was a warehouse only and always kept a sufficient amount of specie on hand to back all deposits. A natural evolution of *giro* banks was fractional reserve banking. Banks can create credit in the form of checking accounts (money in bank) or in the form of printed bank notes. The acceptance of bank credit, whether in the form of checks or bank notes, as a means of payment allowed the community to make do with much less of the actual legal medium of payment, namely gold or silver coins. A bank, by pooling the actions of many individuals, reduces the total reserve necessary for emergencies. In effect, a fractional reserve banking system lowers the price of holding money without the addition of more resources. Consequently, it makes holding money, in the form of bank notes, more attractive than, for example, adjusting the timing of receipts.

A similar effort to reduce the costs of holding inventories by expanding effective supply was developed by Chicago grain elevators in the 1860s. Chicago's warehousemen practiced an incipient form of fractional reserve banking in grain. Their activity was covert, however. It was deducible only from scandals of elevators caught with false bottoms to their bins, or scandals after fires when insurance companies would collect more receipts than the capacity of the elevator.[3]

From the available evidence, Chicago's warehousemen showed considerable sophistication in their use of fractional reserves. Like conventional bankers, a grain warehouseman had two principal means of overissuing receipts. First, he could speed up the printing presses for receipts. Second, a warehouseman, with every appearance of virtue, could issue only receipts for grain put into store, all the while surreptitiously shipping out grain on his own account, and so leaving more receipts outstanding than grain. From the few avail-

---

[2] *Giro* comes from the Latin word meaning to rotate.
[3] A detailed account of grain banking along with references to the statutes making it illegal can be found in Williams (1984).

able instances, it would seem that warehousemen could hold only 50% reserves and still meet their obligations to deliver grain on demand.

Far from seeing the overissuing of grain receipts as a great invention comparable to fractional reserve banking, many farmers, grain shippers, and commission merchants viewed the warehousemen's actions as simple fraud, a breach of their fiduciary duties to depositors. As early as 1851 the legislature of Illinois had prohibited warehousemen from issuing receipts for grain unless the property was actually in store. Despite the law, which had no sanctions, there was frequently a discrepancy between the amount Chicago warehousemen kept in store and the face amount of receipts outstanding. In 1859 the directors of the Chicago Board of Trade voiced their disapproval of this practice; nonetheless, complaints abounded in 1862 and 1867. By 1870 resentment against warehousemen's abuses, from the issuing of false receipts to acting in concert with the railroads in order to monopolize the storage business, helped establish a state agency, which undertook a system of registering the receipts for all new arrivals into store and canceling receipts for all shipments.

Warehousemen in Chicago persisted in overissuing warehouse receipts for as long as they did despite these legal prohibitions for the same reason modern banking relies on a system of fractional reserves. Just as banks can be relatively certain only a small proportion of their depositors will ever withdraw their money at one time, large public elevators were sure everyone would not ship his grain out at the same time. While some people were receiving shipments, others were making arrangements for shipments out. Consequently, a fraction of the total amount deposited, whether money or grain, sufficed to cover withdrawals. Had the warehousemen been able to use a fractional reserve system legally, shippers, concerned with loading their vessels quickly, would have held for the same opportunity cost more warehouse receipts payable on demand (or the same number at a lower price). Fractional reserve banking in grain would have reduced the costs of holding inventories.

5.3.   The economic function of futures markets

Although the citizens of Illinois outlawed fractional reserve banking in grain, they permitted the development of futures markets, another invention that reduces the costs of holding inventory. Simply put, the contribution of futures markets is to be an organized part of an inplicit loan market for commodities. A functioning loan market for commodities improves the allocation of reserves over time and among those holding stocks at any one moment in time. A loan market directs stocks to the firm whose need for them is most immediate. Such improvements in the allocation of reserves effectively lowers the price of holding them.

Perhaps the issue can be understood by considering what a firm obtains if it cannot borrow a raw material but can only buy it outright. A commodity on the spot is a bundle of two characteristics: access to the good over some period of time and the right to future use beginning at the end of that period. The contribution of futures markets is precisely to accommodate these two separate markets, a market for accessibility and one for the good's future use. It slices the commodity into different periods, effectively making many goods out of it. Without a futures market, a firm wanting to secure access must buy the full amount outright. With a futures market, a firm buying a good on the spot can sell its right to that commodity in the future by contracting to deliver in the future. The firm is left with only what it really desires, namely accessibility over the first period. Just as separate markets for telephones and telephone service allow people more flexibility and choice, separate markets for accessibility and forward wheat or forward cotton allow firms to better adjust to the uncertainty and delay in their production processes.

The nature of the argument is even more obvious in the case of money. Firms are frequently in need of cash for short periods above their long-term needs. Imagine, however difficult, the state of affairs if there were no functioning loan market for money. Typically, a firm raises money for long-term needs by issuing stock, since stock never obliges the firm to return the money. If the firm could raise cash only through the sale of stock, it would need to sell enough to raise the largest amount of invested capital and cash it would ever require at one time. It is hard to imagine a firm with a hoard of cash periodically far above its needs precisely because it will do everything possible to reduce its idle funds. Perhaps it will resort to the cumbersome and expensive procedure of repurchasing its own stock, only to reissue it when its seasonal needs are high. Clearly, an active loan market in money with a range of maturities allows a firm much more flexibility in managing its cash. The result of an effective loan market is that it holds less cash on average, an outcome for the economy as a whole equivalent to the discovery or creation of more money. Through a loan market, cash is passed to the firm that most needs it at that moment, to be passed on again when some other firm needs the cash more.

A loan market in commodities in a similar manner improves the distribution of physical inventories and reduces the average amount that firm must hold. For example, suppose that an anticipated bulge in the demand for a miller's flour has induced it to hold extra wheat. The miller's neighbor, however, may enjoy the next bulge and need access to inventory when that time comes. The total inventory would be better used if it were always in the hands of the merchant who most needs secure access at any particular moment. In this case it makes more sense for each mill to borrow wheat for a short period of time, rather than buy it outright. If each mill needs accessibility over only a particular period, why should it own forward wheat that allows access over all other periods? Futures markets enable those two flour mills to improve the use of their inventory, just as banks improve the use of money by lending it to firms who need it immediately but only temporarily.

Because a single futures market allows for trading in a number of different months, it comprises several implicit loan markets for a particular commodity. One loan market covers the period from the present to the futures contract with the nearest delivery, and requires both the futures market and the spot market. This requirement is the reason why the contribution of futures markets must be qualified as being only part of a loan market for commodities, although if a contract for immediate delivery is included conceptually in the array of contracts for different dates of delivery, then the futures market encompasses the present loan market. Another implicit loan market, fully within the futures market, covers the period between the nearest delivery month and the next futures contract, another market, the next pair, and so on. The spreads between the different pairs of months represent the interest rates on forward commodity loans over these periods. The more months in which there is trading of contracts for delivery, or, in other words, the greater the range of the forward loans, the more flexibility a firm has when selecting the term and amount of accessibility.

Of course, if there were an explicit loan market in commodities, the contribution of futures markets would be redundant. Even so, what is most important economically is to have a loan market in some form. It matters much less whether the loan market is explicit or implicit. Likewise, it is of much less importance whether the loan market, implicit or explicit, is an informal collection of dealers trading by telephone or a formal, central exchange like the Chicago Board of Trade. The allocation of commodities through an informal explicit loan market would differ only slightly from an organized

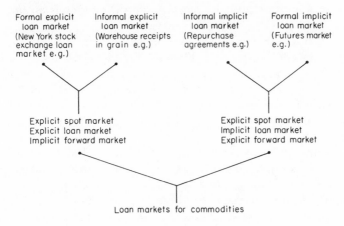

Figure 5.1. The contribution of futures markets

implicit market. They are essentially equivalent ways to trade. Without any kind of loan market, however, the allocation of commodities is very different.

Much confusion over the contribution of futures markets arises from the trouble in defining the circumstances taken as given. Given that a loan market for commodities exists, whether it is implicit or explicit becomes a major distinction. Likewise, given that a loan market exists and is implicit, the distinction between an informal forward and an organized futures market becomes relevant. Yet the conditions accepted as given must not be forgotten. For example, inspection of explicit loan markets, formal or informal, provides an immediate test of attributes thought special to futures markets.

The contribution of organized futures markets can best be understood with the help of a tree-like structure such as that shown in Figure 5.1. At the base of the tree is the need for a loan market in commodities. Extending from that base are two branches, one representing an explicit loan market and the other an implicit loan market achieved through the combination of explicit spot and forward or futures markets. At the end of each of these two branches are two twigs, one representing an informal market, the other an organized, centralized exchange. More specifically, given an implicit forward market, one twig represents an informal explicit loan market like that for lending warehouse receipts, while the other twig on that branch represents a formal loan market such as that operated by NUEXCO for uranium. On the other hand, given an explicit forward market, one twig is an informal implicit loan market, a combination of spot and forward markets, and the other is an organized implicit loan market, or futures market.

Just such a tree is accepted as a matter of course when approaching the market for money. Throughout the ages, many different items, from cowrie shells to electronic signals, have served as the medium of exchange. Even more varied have been the institutional arrangements for borrowing and lending these various forms of money. Nevertheless, men of affairs, regulators, and theorists of money have penetrated the facades of these many institutions and have, generally speaking, recognized that their function fundamentally concerns borrowing and lending money. Unfortunately, people have been slower to recognize systems of trading equivalent to those involving futures markets, for instance, loan markets for grain receipts, and hence have missed the common feature of borrowing and lending commodities common to all.

Among the many methods of organizing the market for loans of money, the most obvious arrangement is an explicit loan market with an explicit interest rate. An easily comprehensible variant of an explicit loan market for money is discounting, in which the interest rate is implicit in the difference between what a borrower can raise in current funds and what he promises to pay at some date in the future. The borrower must also pay the same interest on the loan whether it is called a loan outright or an overdraft. For their part, many large borrowers such as banks and securities dealers raise money through repurchase arrangements involving government securities. Although Chapter 2 stressed the aspect of these repurchase agreements for borrowing securities, these agreements also provide a loan of money to the party lending the securities. Less obvious as a loan of money, but a loan nonetheless, are the many deals providing one party with money in one location in return for his promise to deliver money at some later date at another location, most often a money center like New York, London, or, as in earlier times, Florence. Such a contract is called a bill of exchange, of course. When the money to be returned is the same currency as obtained, the transaction is categorized as domestic exchange; when another currency is returned, say guilders for florins, the transaction involves foreign exchange. So-called dry exchange was an even more complex repurchase agreement arranging a loan of money.

More often than not these various institutions for lending money are on a twig representing informal rather than organized markets, that is, dealer networks rather than central exchanges. Yet such centralized institutions have existed, such as the "money desk" on the New York Stock Exchange. Perhaps the U.S. Treasury bill auction, with its weekly ritual of bids from all dealers, should also be considered as a formal market, an organized implicit loan market to be exact, since bills are sold at a discount rather than at an explicit interest rate.

It makes little difference whether a loan of money is arranged as dry exchange, as an overdraft, or as a discounted note; all serve the same purpose. None is significantly more cumbersome and more expensive than the others; all would result in much the same interest rate. Likewise, what matters most in commodities is a functioning loan market, which many systems of trading could provide reasonably well. The particular system of trade among essentially equivalent systems of trading is much less relevant.

Admittedly, the institutional form of a market has some effect on the prices that emerge. The phrase "equivalent systems of trading" exaggerates the similarities of institutions. Even if extreme, it serves as a useful antidote to the more common exaggeration of accepting different institutions as being only distant substitutes. Without a clear understanding of the economic function of an institution and its similarities with other systems, one is too easily led to ascribe importance and uniqueness to its method of trading. It is too easy to confuse the facility with which an institution performs a function with the function itself. One should suspect that the coexistence of several different institutional forms, as for example in the collection of loan markets for money, demonstrates first and foremost how little different they really are. If one were clearly superior, it would dominate for long stretches of time and over wide areas.

Even if many systems of trading are close substitutes, the institutional form of a loan market is not devoid of interest. The reasons why, in the case of money, checking accounts are used as opposed to domestic exchange are still worth study, as is the question of whether the money market is highly organized with elaborate rules or an informal collection of traders with few standardized procedures. One can also investigate which institutional form for lending money is least susceptible to shocks or which permits the participation of more traders. Likewise, it is interesting to explore why futures markets, namely an organized implicit loan market, have become the dominant institution providing commodity loans.

The remainder of this chapter puts forth several hypotheses for the reasons futures markets have become the dominant institution for loans of commodities. Consistent with the observation that the institutional possibilities are not profoundly different, the reasons deduced for the dominance of futures markets seem almost trifling. It appears that futures markets have a transactional convenience compared with explicit loan markets. Whenever the lender does not want his good back, as would apply in the case of farmers wanting to market their crops, it is easier for all concerned if borrowers construct loans implicitly rather than explicitly. One can be on firmer ground when putting forth legal reasons for one institution over another. If one institution is at a legal disadvantage, whether it itself has been outlawed or whether particular contracts move more easily through the courts, then it is not likely to be the dominant market form. Explicit loans of securities and commodities are at a disadvantage compared to implicit loans because they have become more ensnarled in bankruptcy courts. Actually futures contracts were nearly outlawed in the nineteenth century by courts confusing them with proscribed gambling contracts.

On closer inspection, it does not appear that futures markets differ very much from informal forward markets, even though a large literature makes much of this distinction. In other words, the issue of why contracts for future delivery are traded on organized exchanges appears to be the least significant issue of all. Nor do the techniques of protecting contracts through margin and offsetting contracts through the payment of differences explain why futures markets rather than explicit loan markets exist.

In the following sections, it might seem that short shrift is given to the advantages of margin and clearing. Far from denigrating these techniques, the point is precisely to show that because of their considerable advantages they emerge in many other places than futures markets. Consequently, they cannot explain the particular contribution of futures markets. People have failed to perceive futures markets in the setting of the tree in Figure 5.1 and, hence, have ascribed to futures markets attributes they share with other markets.

5.4.   Futures markets and forward markets

Telser (1981) posits that organized futures markets exist because they are superior to informal forward markets. An organized futures market has elaborate written rules, standing committees for adjusting disputes, and a limited membership. According to Telser, futures contracts are also exceptionally secure due to their system of margin and the role the clearinghouse takes, as party to all trades, in backing the contracts. In contrast to futures contracts, forward contracts rely on the good faith of the individual parties. Also in contrast to standardized futures contracts, a typical forward contract, according to Telser, is tailored, through substantial negotiations, to the individual parties and the particular lot of the commodity. Therefore, they cannot be offset by identical contracts, and there is no scope for the advantages of clearinghouses and settlement by the payment of differences. At the sacrifice of many different contracts tailored to specific situations, futures markets concentrate trading in just a few contracts, greatly increasing the number of people willing to trade any one of the remaining contracts. The resulting liquidity understandably makes the futures contracts even more attractive to traders.

Telser suggests that the superiority of futures contracts over forward contracts can be understood by drawing an analogy between currency and personal checks. Although checks can be written for any amount, an advantage that eliminates the inconvenience of making change, they depend on the credit of one person. The government, on the other hand, backs Federal Reserve notes, which, because they are impersonal, can pass freely between strangers. The consciously limited number of denominations of bills, by greatly increasing the circulation of a particular denomination, increases the ease of handling currency. Although bills can be used over and over again, checks must be laboriously returned to their drawers. In short, according to Telser, currency and futures contracts, because they are impersonal and standardized, and as a result are far more liquid, are superior to checks and forward contracts respectively.

By viewing a futures contract as a temporary and liquid store of purchasing power in the manner of currency, Telser is expanding on a view of futures contracts long held by Working. Working (1953b: 560) maintained, "Hedging in futures consists in making a *contract to buy or sell on standard terms, established and supervised by a commodity exchange, as a temporary substitute for an intended later contract to buy or sell on other terms*" (emphasis in original). Thus, according to Working, standardized futures contracts temporarily take the place of merchandizing contracts; once these specific contracts have been negotiated, the futures contract is canceled by offset. Many others besides Telser and Working have emphasized the differences between forward and futures contracts; Kaldor (1939) and Dow (1940) are early examples. A gulf between futures contracts and forward contracts is so widely accepted that a disclaimer about forward contracts appears in almost every article on futures markets. This view of the contribution of futures markets might be succinctly called the "liquidity theory of futures markets."

Despite the common appeal to analogies with money, the liquidity theory of futures markets emphasizes very different features of futures markets than does the view propounded in this book. The two views are not necessarily contradictory. In fact, as the common analogy with money suggests, both are complementary. Yet the liquidity theory is concerned with the tertiary issue of why some markets are organized.

The common analogy with money can illuminate the place and relative importance of the two explanations of the contribution of futures markets. Telser's analogy concerns whether Federal Reserve notes or personal checks serve as the medium of exchange. True, checking accounts may pay some interest net of processing charges and minimum balances while currency pays none, but holding either one incurs a severe opportunity cost compared to holding bonds. When studying the money market almost everyone lumps checking account balances and currency together. The difference between them is a minor issue. What is important about money, whether Federal Reserve notes or balances in checking accounts, is the insight it gives into why firms hold inventories of commodities, and why they might want to borrow them. In terms of Figure 5.1, the tree representing the contribution of futures markets, the full interest rate lost when holding money broadly defined corresponds to whether or not there is a functioning loan market of some type for commodities. The further issue of whether there is any difference in the interest rate lost holding checking accounts compared to currency corresponds to whether the loan market for commodities is a formal futures market or an informal forward market.

Perhaps this analogy with money is unfair to the liquidity theory. Although the distinction between currency and checks may be a secondary issue in understanding loan markets for money, it is possible that the corresponding difference between futures and forward markets is much more important to an understanding of loan markets in commodities. As it happens, the actual differences between forward and futures markets are small. The contrast that the liquidity theory presumes exists between sophisticated futures markets and clumsy forward markets is too sharp.[4] What differences exist are

---

[4] Trouble for the liquidity theory can be anticipated from the fact that Federal Reserve notes and checks are much more alike than Telser admits. For many transactions, it is a matter of indifference to both parties whether currency or checks settle debts. The problem with Telser's analogy can also be seen in the history of money. Developed after coins, checks are conventionally portrayed not as inferior, as Telser claims, but as a superior invention that reduces the need to transfer actual cash.

more of degree than kind. Many so-called forward markets are highly sophisticated, often with means of clearing and enforcing contracts much like those of futures markets. Conversely, futures contracts are not actually impersonal. These statements, and their elaborations in section 5.5, are not meant to imply the liquidity theory is wrong. Rather these criticisms are meant to correct the overemphasis on futures markets as organized exchanges.

Futures contracts do not actually have the highly impersonal nature of currency because the backing of the clearinghouse protects only a small proportion of outstanding futures contracts. A clearing member's account, recall, is kept on a net basis with the clearinghouse.[5] If he sells twenty contracts as a commission merchant for various customers, and buys thirty for others, he deposits original margin with the clearinghouse only for the ten net he buys. Likewise, the clearinghouse only guarantees and passes through variation margin for the ten net. The futures commission merchant himself must transfer funds among his customers' accounts on behalf of the twenty other contracts. Thus, the performance of all fifty contracts relies on the futures commission merchant and his ability to police the creditworthiness of his many customers to keep their margin accounts current.[6] With the exception of a member of the clearinghouse who deals only on his own account, futures contracts are actually agreements between a clearing member and his customers. For customers of a futures commission merchant who is not a clearing member himself but instead has a special account for the net of his contracts with a clearing member, the collective backing of the clearinghouse is yet another step away.

In addition, clearinghouses like that of the Chicago Board of Trade did not interpose themselves as guarantors of futures contracts nor as collectors of margin for many years, including the 1880s and 1890s when trading in grain futures markets was more active than at any time before the 1970s. Surely the markets in the 1980s are not appreciably different from those of the 1880s. Likewise, even though the London Metal Exchange has no system of margin, no one would maintain that it does not offer the advantages of a futures market. Members of the LME, who are very few in number, dispense with margin among themselves (even though they require margin from their customers), because they are confident of

[5] A few exchanges require more margin than on a net basis, but on none are all contracts covered (Edwards 1983).
[6] For this reason, some have proposed that original margin be deposited on a gross basis.

the fulfillment of contracts between one another. From these instances, one can conclude that the backing of the clearinghouse and its role in the system of margin are not what make organized futures exchanges stand apart.[7]

Thus, futures contracts are less secure than the liquidity theory portrays them. The liquidity theory also ignores how forward contracts often rely on more than the good faith of the contracting parties. For example, a party to a forward contract in foreign exchange or government securities can expect the equivalent of a margin call if prices move too far against him, although the security deposit is not adjusted as frequently and meticulously as in futures markets. (Of course, forward contracts always rely on the courts.)

Forward contracts also are often highly standardized contracts. This can be seen most clearly in dealings in foreign exchange and government securities. After all, the majority of such dealings are in round lots of millions of dollars. For their part, banks issue certificates of deposit in denominations of $100,000 and $1,000,000.

The real advance in the practice of canceling contracts by offset and payment of differences comes not in the move from informal ringing up (as practiced in the early days of the Chicago Board of Trade) to an official clearinghouse but rather from the original standardization of the contract. Forward markets, not futures markets, are generally the first to standardize the size of lots, the grades allowed for delivery, and the circumstances of delivery such as whether in railcars or in elevators. Indeed, there is considerable evidence that the first futures markets, the Chicago Board of Trade, the New York Cotton Exchange, and the Liverpool Cotton Ex-

---

[7] The properties of variation margin itself are the center of the literature begun by Black (1976), with articles by Breeden (1979 and 1980), Cox, Ingersoll, and Ross (1981), and others. Forward contracts are not paid for until delivery, while futures contracts involve variation margin, with the effect that the futures contract can be paid for in part before delivery. Consequently, much is made of the distinction between forward and futures contracts. Although theoretically valid, "the mean differences between forward and futures prices are insignificantly different from zero, both in a statistical and economic sense," in the words of Cornell and Reinganum (1981: 1045), who studied futures and forward markets for foreign exchange. The history of futures markets also supports this conclusion. As it happens, early futures contracts allowed for monetary differences to be discounted because they represented early settlement of the contracts (e.g., see the rules of the New York Cotton Exchange [1891]). That these rules are no longer on the books suggests that this difference between forward and futures contracts is of little practical significance. A proposal in 1882 by the Settlements, Clearing House, and Bank Committee of the Liverpool Cotton Association would have set an average discount rate for all differences "to facilitate office work and calculations on Contracts" (attached to minutes of 18 December 1882, 380 Cot 5/1, Liverpool Records Office).

change, which officially recognized futures trading in the mid-1860s or early 1870s, simply adopted contracts already standardized in informal forward markets (Williams 1982). Forward contracts in breadstuffs reported in the 1840s and 1850s already showed the round lots, 500 or 1,000 barrels of flour or 1,000 or 5,000 bushels of grain, used later in futures contracts on the Chicago Board of Trade. Recently, in much the same way, new futures contracts have been patterned after existing standardized forward contracts, whether the terms of forward delivery in the fuel oil market or the terms of forward delivery of mortgage certificates. Whenever the specifications of the futures contracts were written differently from prevailing forward contracts, futures trading in the commodity has failed. The contract on the Chicago Mercantile Exchange for pork bellies languished until its provisions in regard to shrinkage, storage time, transportation allowances, and grades were brought into closer correspondence with trade practices (Powers 1967). In designing its plywood contract (which began trading in 1969) the Chicago Board of Trade matched forward contracts as closely as possible, and it had much greater success than the New York Mercantile Exchange had with its plywood contract, which had a different method of delivery than forward contracts (Sandor 1973). With all futures contracts, the exchanges are forever attempting to bring them more into line with the predominant forward contract in the trade.

One must also be careful not to conclude that markets without well-developed clearinghouses are unsophisticated and enjoy none of the benefits of offsetting contracts. After all, the Chicago Board of Trade was called a futures market long before it established an official clearinghouse. Clerks arranged alphabetically by their firms' names in one large room passing warehouse receipts among themselves, as begun in the early 1880s on the Chicago Board of Trade, accomplish nearly all that a formal clearinghouse does.

In essence, standardized contracts and the offsetting of contracts are common not only in organized futures markets but in many other markets as well. Further, forward markets often protect contracts through margin, while futures contracts are not particularly impersonal. Therefore, Telser and others subscribing to the liquidity theory of futures markets base their theory on too sharp a contrast between forward and futures contracts, and they consequently overstate the contribution of centralized exchanges.

The existence of standardized forward contracts traded by offset should put to rest another controversy over the difference between futures and forward contracts. Kaldor (1939) and then Dow (1940) argued that inventories committed for deliveries on forward contracts do not provide the benefit of accessibility, or in their terminology, convenience yield. If a dealer has signed a forward contract committing him to deliver a specific lot to a specific person, he seemingly has no recourse but to hold and deliver that lot. If he sells it to someone else, he can never get the precise lot back. On the other hand, if a dealer has committed his inventory to delivery through a futures contract, he can rescind his agreement in the event he needs the inventory for another purpose by the expedient of buying an offsetting futures contract. This flexibility is what induces him to pay the opportunity cost of spreads below full carrying charges for a hedging operation.

The exception to this state of affairs is when the forward contracts are themselves standardized agreements traded by offset. Since this exception applies to most commodities with futures trading, prices in the forward market are no different from those in the futures market. From a broader perspective, the argument made by Kaldor and Dow could have been dismissed without mention of active forward markets. Even a highly specific forward contract for commodities usually designates a particular grade for delivery rather than a particular lot. Another lot of the same grade could be substituted for the original lot, and the buyer would be none the wiser. As long as the commodity itself is fungible, the seller can use his original holdings, if the need should arise, buying an equivalent amount later at his convenience. From his perspective, it should matter little whether he buys an additional amount and proceeds with his scheduled delivery or cancels that delivery ahead of time by purchasing an offsetting contract. Since commodities with futures trading must be fungible, it follows that the commodities themselves are fully as fungible for forward contracts.

5.5.   Futures markets and organized markets

Actually, this emphasis on the centralized and organized nature of futures markets is misplaced for an even more important reason. The issue would arise even if loan markets were explicit rather than implicit. In other words, the dispute about the advantages of a central organized market over an informal market would arise even if there were neither futures markets nor forward markets, but explicit loan markets instead. Consequently, the resolution of that dispute has only a limited amount to say about the reasons futures markets exist.

The loan market for shares on the New York Stock Exchange in its halcyon days before the regulations of the 1930s illustrates most forcefully that a loan market can be highly organized. Loans of shares were protected by margin and passed through an advanced clearing system exactly in the manner Telser believes distinctive to futures markets. Recall that the explicit loan market on the New York Stock Exchange is a double loan market in which money is lent in return for a loan of shares. The amount of money involved was adjusted every day according to the direction in which the stock's price moved, exactly as futures contracts are marked to market with variation margin. Beginning in 1892, a highly sophisticated clearinghouse accommodated both outright purchases and loans of shares, working a considerable advance in the ease of using the loan market (Emery 1896).

A similar system of ensuring and offsetting contracts could evolve if the good lent were wheat or copper instead of stock certificates. Indeed, those speculators who borrowed warehouse receipts in grain in the 1850s and 1860s in Chicago deposited a large part of the worth of the receipts as collateral, deposits akin to original margin, for repaying loans. Whether they were also required to pay variation margin if prices moved against them (or whether the commission merchants were required to give back some of the deposit if the price moved lower) is impossible to tell from the scanty descriptions left. In any case, it is obviously possible to construct a working system of margin for an explicit loan market in commodities.

Although no advanced system of clearing has operated for loans of commodities, a so-called Cotton Bank in Liverpool cleared spot transactions in cotton (Elison 1905). Spot transactions in Liverpool were not for delivery seconds after the deal was struck but rather the next day, as indeed most spot transactions in any commodity are in practice.[8] Consequently, there is time during the day for a trader to enter into several transactions, in which case a clearing bank would help in reducing actual deliveries to the net amount of both cotton and money. Once this system was in place in Liverpool it would have been an easy matter for it to accommodate loans of cotton in the manner of the clearinghouse of the New York Stock Exchange. As it happened, the clearinghouse for futures transactions absorbed the Cotton Bank.

Much the same argument used to dismiss the notion that margin

[8] Consequently, such nominally spot transactions are a futures contract with one day to maturity.

and clearing are special to futures markets applies to the role of speculators. The extensive speculation on futures markets, in the popular eye the dominant feature of futures markets, does not come from futures markets' special connection with the future but rather from the great ease and assurance of trading made possible by central, supervised exchanges. There is little speculation in many markets because trading is cumbersome. If there were a formal, highly liquid loan market and an implicit market for future delivery, speculators would have all the same incentives to seek out information about the future.

To be more specific, although extensive short selling is necessary for a market to absorb all available information, it is not unique to futures markets. Because futures markets facilitate short selling, Gray (1979) has argued that this is one of their major contributions. However, the practice of lending warehouse receipts also makes extensive short selling possible. Indeed, it was speculators wanting to sell short who were seemingly the principal borrowers of the warehouse receipts in Chicago. By selling their borrowed receipts on the spot market, they were commited to deliver in the future something they no longer possessed. Likewise, it is obvious how a futures market encourages long speculation, but the system of lending warehouse receipts can also induce more long speculation. A long speculator can buy on the spot market and lend his receipt, his net position being equivalent to owning a futures contract with delivery at the time the loan matures.

The role of speculators in futures markets can best be assessed by comparing the London Stock Exchange with that of New York. In London, recall, stocks are traded for future delivery while in New York they are lent or sold for immediate delivery. It could hardly be argued that London is the more speculatively inclined market, even though the market is a futures market. It is much more likely that the behavior of prices is the same in both cities. After all, several issues are traded in common, and if prices diverge, arbitrage quickly brings them back together. This assertion that prices would behave the same regardless of whether there is an explicit futures market is not to say that either exchange would operate the same if there were no speculators. On both exchanges, speculators were crucial to the depth of the market. The important message is that futures markets are not uniquely connected with speculation; any advanced market attracts speculators. Consequently, speculators are the key to understanding futures markets only to the extent that their trading adds to the depth of the market.

Once again an attribute thought to be special to futures markets, in this instance the extensive short selling, turns out to be much more common than imagined in the liquidity theory of futures markets. That is not to say the advantages of extensive speculation and the advantages of enforcing, standardizing, and clearing contracts are inconsiderable. Rather, they do not distinguish futures markets. What advantages the liquidity theory credits to organized futures markets are, in fact, properly attributed to organized markets in general rather than futures markets in particular. It would be better to study these features of futures markets in the broader field of formal versus informal markets.

5.6.   Transactional reasons for implicit loan markets

Much less explored than the reason for a formal versus an informal market are the reasons some markets are explicit and some implicit. In weighing the merit of certain systems of trading, there are advantages simply from the ease of transacting. In the case of an implicit versus an explicit loan market, whether or not the lender wants his good back seems to go far in determining the system of trading. A person who makes a time deposit in a bank, that is, who lends money to a bank, has use for that money when the loan matures and so wants it back. Transactions like these where potential lenders want the good back are accomplished most easily with both the loan and its price explicit. A farmer who has brought wheat to market, however, is not likely to want it back. The form of market that can best accommodate borrowers when potential lenders really do not want their good back, or at least not back in the same condition and location, is implicit.

Consider a farmer in Peoria who lends his wheat to a local miller, although he would have preferred to sell it instead. He agrees to lend to the miller because he can still sell his wheat indirectly. He has in hand an agreement with the miller in which the miller promises to return the wheat by a particular date to the bearer of the agreement along with a fee for having borrowed the wheat. Suppose someone in Chicago would like to receive wheat at about that time. He could buy the loan agreement from the farmer and contract to have the wheat shipped to Chicago upon its return in Peoria. If many farmers in Peoria and merchants in Chicago transferred such loan agreements, a secondary market would spring up. Such a secondary market would enable all parties to be satisfied, the farmer who wants to sell his wheat, the local miller who wants to borrow wheat, and the merchant who wants wheat in the central market.

But this combination of an explicit loan market and secondary market for such securities requires extra transactions and instructions. The result of (1) the loan agreement, (2) the sale of the loan to the merchant in Chicago, (3) the instructions to the miller to deliver to the Chicago merchant's local representative instead of the farmer, and (4) the merchant's contracting for freight to Chicago, is that the farmer hands over the wheat to the miller in Peoria and the wheat reappears in Chicago. How much more expeditious it would be for all parties taken together if the miller were to conduct a hedging operation and borrow the wheat implicitly, (1) buying from the local farmer and (2) selling a contract for future delivery on the futures market in Chicago. In effect, the miller would borrow from the market as a whole rather than from a single party. Although the miller now has the extra expense of a second transaction, and possibly a third if he must arrange for freight, from the farmer's and merchant's perspective, transactions costs are reduced considerably. The farmer and merchant can share their savings with the miller, directly or indirectly. How much more convenient is this arrangement even for the miller if he, in the course of events, decides to use the wheat in his milling operations. Rather than locate the farmer and renegotiate the loan into a sale, the miller can more easily purchase the wheat by lifting his hedge and canceling its obligation to deliver in Chicago. He could do the same if he wanted to pass the wheat to another miller. In any event, the farmer is not likely to want the wheat back. Consequently, an implicit loan saves all parties expenses collectively and gives them more flexibility than an explicit loan whenever there is a natural flow of a commodity from one location to another, one form to another, or one owner to another.

These transactional advantages appear to explain a shift in the institutional form from an explicit loan market to an implicit loan market for grain in Chicago in the 1860s. Recall the practice among commission men in Chicago in the 1850s and early 1860s of lending grain receipts. While the commission merchants were awaiting instructions from the parties whose produce they had on consignment or waiting for navigation to open so that they could ship those goods, they controlled warehouse receipts needed only later. Naturally, they were tempted to lend them over the interim, as long as they got them back. Once railroads began to transport produce from Chicago during the winter and a better network of telegraphs improved communications with customers, commission merchants began to hold warehouse receipts for shorter periods of time. Moreover it became much more common for ownership to change as the grain flowed from one place to another; when grain stopped in Chicago it usually changed hands. Under these circumstances, the explicit loan markets ceased to function, and futures markets took their place. Because these circumstances have not changed yet, implicit loan markets retain their transactional advantage.

A telling example of how the natural flow of a commodity encourages a loan market to function implicitly is the money market whenever its principal purpose is to finance trade, either domestic or international. If a dealer in Chicago needs to borrow money to purchase a commodity he plans to ship to New York City, rather than arrange an explicit loan with someone in Chicago, he could raise the funds by drawing a bill of exchange on a correspondent in New York City. The bill would direct the correspondent to pay the bearer of the bill in New York a specified amount at a particular time after presentation of the bill. After the dealer's shipment will have been sold in New York, it will be much easier for him to pay back a loan in New York than repatriate his funds to Chicago. He obtains the funds he needs in Chicago by selling (i.e., discounting) his bill of exchange to someone locally. The person who buys the bill will send the bill to New York, where it will either be presented on his behalf by one of his correspondents or sold to a New York investor who will then present it.

A bill of exchange allows a person to obtain a good, namely money, in one location, with the promise to return that commodity in another location. A short hedging operation works in a similar manner. Through a short hedging operation a miller obtains wheat locally with a promise to return wheat in Chicago, just as a soybean crusher in Peoria obtains beans with a promise to return meal and oil in Chicago. These borrowers, whether of money, wheat, or soybeans, do not borrow directly from a single party. Rather they conduct business in their own local market with one person and in the central market with another.

Indubitably, the purpose of a domestic bill of exchange is to borrow money implicitly. Such bills are of great advantage to al' shippers, even if their goods are not intended for New York City. They can either ship their money to New York to pay their debt or, more commonly, sell their funds locally for a bill promissory in New York, which they can use to offset their own obligation. Incidental to any domestic bill of exchange is an implicit short position in the freight charge for shipping money from the place where the goods are actually sold to New York. This rate can fluctuate if, for example, money becomes especially tight in that local market, say Buffalo, although its movements are limited by the relative ease and speed of shipping currency back and forth between Buffalo and New York. This risk to issuing domestic bills of exchange corresponds to basis risk in commodity markets, specifically the basis risk for a commodity that is of the contract grade but is outside the immediate area of the futures market. The basis for wheat other than the contract grade held in Peoria combined with a short futures position in the Chicago market corresponds to the risk of a bill for foreign exchange, since in both cases something other than the precise commodity obtained locally must be returned in the central market. This correspondence between basis risk and the risks incidental to bills of exchange is well worth contemplation. What is important to comprehend is that these risks little impede the drawing of bills of exchange, and for that reason, basis risk is not of great significance to standard hedging operations. In neither case should the risks obscure the main purpose of the transactions, which is to borrow, either money or commodities as the case may be. The borrowers are simply employing an implicit method because of collective transactional advantages to all the parties involved.

5.7.   Legal reasons for implicit loan markets

Regardless of the advantages of implicit markets to potential lenders who do not want their good back, the existence of implicit markets depends upon other factors, primarily legal. If one system of trading is illegal or involves considerable delay when entangled in court, it suffers a substantial handicap. It might seem that if one system of trading is superior for transactional reasons, the legal system will eventually adjust to that way of conducting business. And in fact, in the legal history of commodity markets, there are many instances where the courts have ultimately recognized a new practice. Yet there are also many instances of sustained legal opposition, often because a particular practice in commodity markets conflicted with a higher legal principle.

Although legal complications can deter a particular system of trading, the handicap of illegality need not be absolute. Options, for example, were illegal during the 1870s and 1880s in Illinois, and yet trading flourished after hours at the Chicago Board of Trade. No one would prosecute the traders. Similarly, in the 1840s, most transactions in New York for shares of stock were contracts for future delivery, which the courts had failed to uphold as valid. Such trading persisted because the traders agreed among themselves to have no recourse to the courts, and anyone who breached his pledge was blackballed.

That legal prohibition can be a considerable deterrent is clearly seen in the case of grain banks. The laws against overissuing warehouse receipts for grain were made even stricter in Illinois in the 1860s and 1870s, and eventually all warehouses kept 100% reserves. Whether or not this was wise public policy, it surely had a significant effect on the institutional form of grain markets. Judging from the behavior of banks for money, most likely a network of branches would have developed among grain banks due to the advantages of concentrating reserves. Grain branch banking would probably have reduced the number of futures contracts used to transfer commodities implicitly from one location to another (i.e., buy in City A and sell for future delivery in City B). At least that has been the case for money. According to Scammel (1968: 164, 171) and Mishimura (1971), branch banking in England reduced the number of domestic bills of exchange. More important, with flourishing grain banks there would probably have been no organized central futures exchanges for grain. Banks, it is true, lend money implicitly through the practice of discounting. But each bank deals with its customers on its own premises, approaching other banks through informal channels. Therefore, an informal implicit loan market would have been more consistent with grain banks.

In the 1870s and 1880s the developing system of settling futures contracts by the payment of differences came under considerable legal attack. First, payments of monetary differences appeared to the courts to be bets, which were not valid contracts. Second, settlement by the payment of differences altered the agent-principal relationship between futures commission merchants and their customers. Had the legal battles come out differently, which they came close to doing, many of the advantages of settling futures contracts by offset would have been lost, and organized futures markets might well have atrophied.

Futures contracts became entangled with the statutes against wagers because a wager is difficult to define legally. A wager has all the requisites of a legal contract: parties, consideration, subject matter, and the meeting of minds (Dewey 1886: 9). Yet in the law's eyes such a contract is invalid because it is not to the mutual advantage of both parties, one party gaining at the expense of the other. The payment of money to settle differences, the method of fulfilling the great majority of futures contracts, appeared to the courts to be a case where one party gained at the expense of the other. Truthfully, in a most literal sense, a futures contract really is a wager on uncertain events, but then so is nearly every commercial transaction.

Faced with the commercial prevalence of futures contracts, the courts laboriously constructed two additional tests to determine whether futures were wagers (Bisbee and Simonds 1884). First of all, the written contract had to require delivery unconditionally, which left options outside the protection of the law because their delivery was conditional. Second, at least one of the parties to the contract had to intend to take or make delivery; for if there was a mutual understanding that the provisions for delivery would not be enforced, the contract was nothing more than a wager. Of course, this test placed courts and juries on the dangerous ground of interpreting parties' intentions, a task made even more difficult by having written evidence only in the form of a cryptic telegram, "Buy 5,000 bushels July corn at 54¢."

Inevitably, some new judge, observing that only a few percent of futures contracts were settled by delivery regardless of the provisions calling for delivery, would cut through the tortuous logic of his peers and once again declare futures contracts void, and the controversy would continue.[9] For example, in *Beveridge* v. *Hewitt* (1881), which dealt with the ringing up done on the Chicago Board of Trade, the court maintained that "the business of the board being so organized as to facilitate fictitious transactions in the settlement of differences, an inference arises, whenever the course of dealing is shown where one of the parties intends to settle in that manner," that the very futures contracts, and not just the settling procedure, are void.[10] The scars of this judicial hostility can still be seen in the greater attention American exchanges give to terms of delivery than do English exchanges, which found their courts more willing to accept futures contracts on their face.

On the other hand, some American judges grasped "that these customs are founded on commercial convenience; that they are not in contravention of law."[11] In the case of *Clarke* v. *Foss* (1878), involv-

---

[9] See *Gregory* v. *Wendell*, 39 Mich. 337 (1878), *Sawyer, Wallace & Co.* v. *Taggart*, 77 Ken. 727 (1879), or *Union National Bank of Chicago* v. *Carr*, 15 Fed. Rep. 438 (1883).

[10] 8 Ill. App. 467 (1881); also see *Melchert* v. *American Union Telegraph Co.*, 11 Fed. Rep. 193 (1882).

[11] *Williar* v. *Irwin*, 30 Fed. Cas. 38 (1879). The U.S. Supreme Court (110 U.S. 499 (1884)) held this instruction to the jury was in error. It did so not on the ground that the custom of ringing up showed the transactions were wagers, but because ringing up worked a material change in the principal's rights and in other parties' obligations to him, to which he could not give his consent because he was not aware of them.

ing contracts for corn on the Chicago Board of Trade, the court emphasized testimony that said "this adjustment of differences is a mere matter of convenience to the members of the board and to their customers . . . [and] frequently saves to their customers the costs of insurance and storage." The court concluded, "If the transactions disclosed by this case were illegal, then the greater part of the banking and clearinghouse transactions in our great commercial centers are illegal also. I am persuaded that to hold them so would be treading too severely upon the business of the commercial world without any corresponding benefit to be expected from it."[12]

This contradictory legal standing of the system of settling contracts through the payment of differences was only clarified through the U.S. Supreme Court's decision in *Higgins & Gilbert* v. *McCrea* (1885) in favor of ringing up.[13] The legal logic in this important case, incredible as it is, also involved the effect of ringing up on the relationship between a principal and his agent.[14] Higgins & Gilbert, Chicago futures commission merchants, placed a speculative order in June of 1883 for August pork on behalf of McCrea. Prices in late June turned against McCrea, who refused to forward additional variation margin. The commission house had routinely rung out the party who had originally sold to McCrea, but the party replacing the original seller delivered the pork in August. Higgins & Gilbert paid the contract price and immediately sold the pork at the lower price then prevailing, suing McCrea for the discrepancy. McCrea countersued for the margin money he had lost. First, he argued that he intended (and Higgins & Gilbert knew this) for his trades to be gambling transactions. Second, he claimed that the substitution achieved by the ring violated his rights as principal, because it substituted another seller without his permission. The judge instructed the jury that if they found the transactions to be gambling, neither party could recover from the other, and if they found the original transactions to be legitimate, then the defendent was entitled to recover his margin money because the plaintiffs had not followed his interests in the ringing up. Naturally the commission firm objected to the judge's charge to the jury. On appeal, the U.S. Supreme Court overturned the award in favor of McCrea.[15] But the Court did not rule in favor of the plaintiffs. It seems that they were in the habit of ringing out trades while only keeping track of the balance in each

---

[12] 5 Fed. Cas. 955 (1878).   [13] 23 Fed. Rep. 782 (1885); also see Bonney (1885).
[14] Also see *Oldershaw* v. *Knowles*, 4 Ill. App. 63 (1879) and 6 Ill. App. 325 (1880).
[15] 116 U.S. 671 (1886).

account. When produce was delivered they would apply it to the oldest contract on their books. The Court ruled this practice did not coincide with the regulations of the Board of Trade, which required a new principal officially to be substituted after a ringing out, so that every trade had an explicit opposite party. In accepting the regulations of the Chicago Board of Trade, the Court pronounced payment of differences a legitimate business practice.[16]

Had futures markets been declared illegal in the course of these disputes over settlement procedures, it is probable that explicit loan markets would have replaced them. Indeed, during the early 1890s when Congress, responding to farmers who held futures markets responsible for declining prices, nearly outlawed the short selling of futures contracts, the organized produce exchanges gave active consideration to setting up a system of trading modeled after the New York Stock Exchange with its loan market in shares.[17]

The legal standing of particular transactions also goes far to explain why at present some loan contracts are written implicitly through the technique of repurchase agreements. Blau and Barber (1982) observe this effect in the management of loans of money by futures commission merchants from the funds their customers deposit as original margin. Although the funds belong to the customers, the interest accrues to the futures commission merchant (who lowers his brokerage fees accordingly). The laws regulating brokers limit their investments from these fiduciary accounts to the safest possible securities, such as U.S. Treasury bills. The futures commission merchants, however, prefer to invest in banks' certificates of deposit, which pay a higher rate of interest because of their greater risk. Unable to lend explicitly to a bank, futures commission merchants arrange a repurchase agreement in which they buy a T-bill from a bank and agree in advance to resell it to the bank at a stipulated price. This repurchase agreement, even with its high-grade collateral in the form of T-bills, still amounts to a loan of money to the bank. Through repurchase agreements, futures commission merchants can circumvent the law. The point is not that

---

[16] Despite this decision, the controversy over ringing up and settlement by the payment of differences did not die. The issue reappeared before the courts on and off until the 1930s. Other prominent cases include: *Ward* v. *Vosburgh*, 31 Fed. Rep. 12 (1887); *Clews* v. *Jamieson*, 182 U.S. 461 (1901); *Board of Trade of the City of Chicago* v. *Christie Grain and Stock Co.*, 198 U.S. 236 (1905); *Gettys* v. *Newburger*, 272 Fed. Rep. 209 (1921); *Lyons Milling Co.* v. *Goffe & Carkener, Inc.*, 46 Fed. Rep. (2nd) 241 (1931); and *Palmer* v. *Love*, 80 S.W. Rep. (2nd) 100 (1934).

[17] For a history of the campaign against futures markets, see Dewey (1905) and Cowing (1965).

repos are reprehensible, but that the law's major effect is on the method of making loans.

Bankruptcy laws as well influence the form of transactions. If Party A lends something, money or commodities, to Party B, and B declares bankruptcy, A may never recover his property. Even if A holds sufficient collateral, it may be months or years before the court allows him possession. That delay may harm him considerably if he has other commitments, as for example if he himself had borrowed what he lent to B. With a repurchase agreement, on the other hand, Party A has clear title to the collateral, since he had ostensibly bought it. This speed in liquidation has been the advantage of lending implicitly through a repurchase agreement. Following the failure of Lombard-Wall, Inc., in 1982, however, the bankruptcy judge ruled that the securities the firm had sold to others as part of repurchase agreements through which it was borrowing money were collateral and that all were enjoined from disposing of them.[18] Although one cannot fault the judge for perceiving that the repos were the same as explicit loans to Lombard-Wall, his ruling reduced considerably the attractiveness of implicit loans over explicit loans. The Federal Reserve, which conducts much of its monetary policy through repurchase agreements, prevailed upon Congress to reverse the judge's ruling through an amendment to the bankruptcy law.[19]

Much the same legal issue arises when a bankrupt has a position in a futures contract. Traditionally, parties have acted as though variation margin money paid by a defaulter belonged unequivocally to his futures commission merchant, or if the bankrupt was a clearing member, to the clearinghouse. (Variation margin, recall, is paid over immediately to someone else.) But in the 1970s, a case was brought in which it was argued that margin money was a deposit still belonging among the bankrupt's assets.[20] If a dollar deposited as margin money might actually represent only the 5¢ paid to a general unsecured creditor, the whole system of margin as a method of ensuring the performance of futures contracts collapses. A new law passed in 1982 has ended this threat. Had it not, one large advantage of conducting commodity loans implicitly through futures markets would have disappeared.

[18] *Wall Street Journal*, 20 September 1982.
[19] *Wall Street Journal*, 3 May and 29 June 1984.
[20] *Seligson* v. *New York Produce Exchange*, 394 Fed. Supp. 125 (1975).

CHAPTER 6

The optimal number of futures markets

Considering the significant advantages of functioning loan markets in commodities and the dominance of futures markets as the institution for providing such loan markets, one might wonder why organized futures markets are so few in number. There are probably no more than forty or fifty worldwide with sufficient volume to be deemed active markets. The number of exchanges, like the Chicago Board of Trade, is even smaller. Further, the same commodity is rarely actively traded on more than one exchange. The London Metal Exchange and Comex in New York do survive side by side, but because the LME closes just as Comex opens they do not compete directly. Likewise, the cocoa and coffee markets in London and New York, even though they trade different varieties, are more naturally considered as part of one worldwide market chasing daylight hours. In any case, for metals, cocoa, and coffee, either New York or London dominates, attracting the large majority of volume and open interest. Similarly, the markets for wheat in Kansas City and Minneapolis, which offer contracts for different varieties, are also small in comparison to the primary market on the Chicago Board of Trade. Otherwise, futures trading is overwhelmingly concentrated in one location for a particular commodity. In that one market trading is rarely in more than five or six delivery months, spanning a year or two.

The small number of active futures markets is perfectly reasonable. Few commodities have a pronounced term structure. That is to say, few have spreads sufficiently volatile to justify delivery months stretching far into the future. The same is true for one commodity in several locations and for the full multitude of delivery months within a calendar year. The number of organized futures markets is small because, in effect, the prices for many related commodities and many related delivery dates can easily be deduced from the few explicit futures prices.

What determines which spreads are volatile concerns the inflexibilities in demand or supply. In most instances either demand or supply is sufficiently supple. Only when something is known about

180

the future but both demand and supply cannot adjust will there be a reason to express the appropriate spread and to have a futures contract. Inflexibilities are another way of saying high transformation costs. Once again, therefore, transformation costs emerge as central to the reasons futures markets exist.

The failure to understand the function of futures markets leads to much confusion about the appropriate number of such markets. For example, the large swings in commodity prices during the 1970s prompted many people to remark that prices would be more stable if futures trading extended into delivery months much farther ahead.[1] Supposedly, without distant futures contracts, the price system cannot absorb information about the prospects of an event far in the future.

What is more important, many people see the absence of distant futures markets as an indication that the market system itself is flawed. According to Arrow (1978), "The very concept of the market and certainly many of the arguments in favor of the market system are based on the idea that it greatly simplifies the informational problems of economic agents, that they have limited powers of acquisition, and that prices are economic summaries of the information from the rest of the world" (p. 161). "The crucial empirical point is that markets for most future commodities do not exist" (p. 160). If economic agents cannot observe distant futures prices but must themselves calculate the prices, the "economic agents are required to be superior statisticians, capable of analyzing the future general equilibria of the economy," which of course they cannot be.

These views seriously misinterpret the economic contribution of futures markets. Confusion arises because of a failure to distinguish a hypothetically inclusive set of markets from those economically justifiable. These views also argue for the benefit of an additional distant delivery month or a futures market in an additional city as being substantial. The truth is that beyond a small number of contracts, the marginal benefit is close to zero. A sufficient number of futures markets is little larger than the observed number.

After it is developed further in the next section, this perspective of the sufficient number of futures contracts rather than the conceivable number will be applied to, first, the number of exchanges trading futures contracts in the same commodity, second, the number of different grades, third, the number of delivery months within a calendar year, and fourth, the number of years ahead futures con-

---

[1] For example, see G. W. Smith (1978).

tracts cover. A final section will contrast this perspective with other theories that have been put forward to explain the small number of active futures markets.

Attempting to deduce what futures prices would be if many more markets were active, the arguments in these sections must be mainly theoretical rather than empirical. Evidence from futures markets themselves is missing, by the very nature of the problem. Deducing what the missing prices would be can be accomplished indirectly by considering the nature and inflexibilities of shipping, cleaning, processing, and storing commodities. Fortunately, the nature and inflexibilities of these services are clear enough, so this chapter will not become mired in such technical details as the mechanics of drying corn.

6.1.   The number of economically justifiable markets

Because of the many characteristics of goods and because prices allocate resources, one would expect a fine division of markets and prices to improve the allocation of resources. The allocation of agricultural commodities, for example, has been improved by distinguishing on the basis of weight and cleanliness, among other characteristics. Similarly, in the storage and use market for such commodities a finer division of time or geographical distribution could improve the allocation of the goods. It is possible, for instance, to imagine as of 1 January discrete markets for future delivery of cotton on 1 June, 8 June, 15 June, and so forth, or carried to the extreme, a separate contract for delivery on each day of the year. It is also possible to imagine functioning markets for future delivery in many different cities. A complete set of markets would include a market for every imaginable location, grade, and delivery date.[2]

Figure 6.1 illustrates an inclusive set of markets for corn. These corn markets cover a full range of delivery dates in the two western lake ports of Chicago and Milwaukee and the recipient eastern lake port of Buffalo.[3] An inclusive set of markets also has explicit markets for corn freight from Milwaukee to Buffalo and from Chicago to

---

[2] One could also include options by indexing each commodity by the random state of the world. The arguments concerning such contingent contracts would run much the same as those for delivery not contingent on a state of the world. As the issue here is to show that the economically justifiable number of markets is below the number in a complete set, restricting the definition of a complete set does no harm.

[3] These three ports are used not because they remain important in the grain trade but because they are clearly terminal points.

	s	*s*	*s*	*s*	*s*	*s* ...	
Storage and use (*s*)	Immediate		Near forward			Distant forward	

	d	*d*	*d*	*d*	*d*	*d*	*d* ...
Delivery in Milwaukee of No. 2 corn (*d*)	Immediate		Near future			Distant future	

	f	*f*	*f*	*f*	*f*	*f*	*f* ...
Freight from Milwaukee (*f*)	Immediate		Near forward			Distant forward	

	d	*d*	*d*	*d*	*d*	*d*	*d* ...
Delivery in Buffalo of No. 2 corn (*d*)	Immediate		Near future			Distant future	

	s	*s*	*s*	*s*	*s*	*s*	*s* ...
Storage and use (*s*)	Immediate		Near forward			Distant forward	

	f	*f*	*f*	*f*	*f*	*f*	*f* ...
Freight from Chicago (*f*)	Immediate		Near forward			Distant forward	

	d	*d*	*d*	*d*	*d*	*d*	*d* ...
Delivery in Chicago of No. 2 corn (*d*)	Immediate		Near future			Distant future	

	s	*s*	*s*	*s*	*s*	*s* ...	
Storage and use (*s*)	Immediate		Near forward			Distant forward	

	c	*c*	*c*	*c*	*c*	*c* ...	
Cleaning (*c*)	Immediate		Near forward			Distant forward	

	d	*d*	*d*	*d*	*d* ...		
Delivery in Chicago of No. 3 corn (*d*)	Immediate		Near future			Distant future	

	s	*s*	*s*	*s*	*s* ...		
Storage and use (*s*)	Immediate		Near forward			Distant forward	

Figure 6.1. An inclusive set of markets for corn

Buffalo, and for forward freight as well as transportation begun immediately. Because of the time required to transport corn, the market in Buffalo connected to Chicago by freight is for delivery that interval ahead. Cleaning of corn likewise has a lag, although possibly a shorter one than for lake freight. As illustrated in Figure 6.1, cleaning and freight both require a set amount of time. More generally, such services can be accomplished slightly faster with the inducement of a higher price. Another dimension to Figure 6.1 would be necessary to express the time for execution as well as the time of execution of a service. The activity of storage and use, by its very nature, takes a set amount of time. For storage and use, each location and each period of time is distinct.

Figure 6.1 comprises 74 distinct markets: 14 freight markets, 6 cleaning markets, 25 storage and use markets, and 29 distinct delivery dates. (One could also describe this as 74 distinct contracts, whether for freight, cleaning, storage, or delivery, all encompassed in one corn market.) Actually the number could be even larger. The various delivery dates, and with them the times for the various services, could be finer or could stretch farther into the future. For each period they are begun, cleaning and freight could have an array of markets ranked according to the time taken to completion.

Of course, an inclusive set of explicit markets, such as that in Figure 6.1 for corn, is not feasible. In the first place, the sizable costs of building, operating, and supervising an exchange limit the geographical distribution of futures markets. Second, the more dispersed are locations, grades, and dates of delivery, the fewer the number of people likely to trade each contract. With fewer individuals interested in any single contract, buyers and sellers must wait longer for one another to express interest in a trade. Such illiquidity itself further discourages trading, with the result that the posted price of a particular contract is not a reliable guide for allocating resources, being either out of date or no more than a guess at what price the contract might trade.

Although operating costs and illiquidity may eliminate many of the markets in an inclusive set, markets are not eliminated at random. Those eliminated are superfluous because they can be well provided for implicitly through other markets. The important consideration in judging the proper number of explicit markets is not which markets constitute a complete set but which are economically justifiable. The distinction between inclusive and economically justifiable is particularly relevant when the absence of an explicit market is thought to intimate a failure of the market system. That explicit

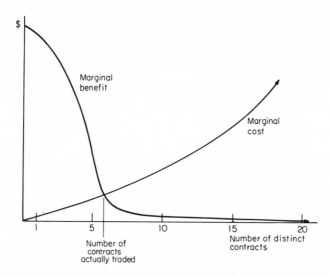

Figure 6.2. The costs and benefits of additional contracts

market may not be vital because its price can be approximated well from other explicit markets.

The economically justifiable number of markets represents the equilibrium of the marginal benefit just equaling the cost of an additional market. Such an equilibrium is illustrated in Figure 6.2. An additional market (or delivery month) surely imposes some costs, whether measured as the actual building housing the exchange or as the loss of liquidity in related markets. The marginal benefit of a market can be thought of as the savings it provides by an improved allocation of resources. (Carlton [1983a] develops a rigorous measure of the benefit of an additional market.) A ranking of markets by a stepwise inclusion, so that the first market provides the greatest benefit given no other markets exist, the second market provides the greatest benefit among the contenders given the first market exists, and so forth, produces a declining marginal benefit curve. The intersection of the marginal benefit curve with the rising marginal cost curve determines the economically justifiable number of markets, as in Figure 6.2.

The argument here is more subtle than that a market must justify its cost. The argument here concerns the slope and shape of the marginal benefit curve. Because of the suppleness of demand and supply when given adequate notice, prices for distant delivery dates or for different locations need adjust only little for large swings in knowledge. Consequently, the prevailing prices cannot seriously misallocate resources. In short, beyond a small number of markets, the benefit of an additional market is close to zero. Before that number, however, the benefit of an additional market is substantial. Consequently, the marginal benefit curve is steeply sloped over a small range and then is essentially flat at a value of zero, as it has been drawn in Figure 6.2. Regardless of the shape and position of the marginal cost curve, the economically justifiable number of markets is much the same. In that sense, some markets can be described as indispensable, and those with small marginal benefits as superfluous. A sufficient number of markets, specifically futures markets, is little larger than the observed number.

The power of the argument is clear in the case of explicit markets for services. A contract for delivery of corn in Chicago in conjunction with a contract for delivery of corn in Buffalo an appropriate time ahead implicitly defines a contract for corn freight. Those who want to engage or offer corn freight can do so without a formal market. Likewise, the cleaning markets and storage and use markets function well implicitly. Of the full 74 contracts in Figure 6.1, all 45 for services can be deduced from the prices of corn for delivery in various places, conditions, and times. The point, as stressed in Chapter 2, is that one market among related markets is likely to be implicit. That these markets for services do not exist is neither surprising nor alarming, everyone should agree.

Not as obvious but true nonetheless, many of the remaining 29 contracts for delivery provide little opportunity not provided elsewhere. As the remainder of this chapter will demonstrate, many of the contracts for delivery, because of the consistency in the forward prices for cleaning and freight, are likely to be in a stable relationship. Consequently, the prices of some contracts can be deduced effortlessly from other prices. Positions in some other contracts are nearly perfect substitutes for those contracts, at least for a period of time.

A market can be implicit not only when its price can be deduced as the difference between other prices but also when prices move in a stable relationship. For example, if wheat and oats are both shipped by weight, then either freight rate can be deduced from the general rate per ton. For that matter, it should also be possible to deduce the price for shipping oats even if the quoted freight charge is for wheat, since the weights for wheat and oats per bushel of dry measure are known.

The same logic applies to the price of a contract for future delivery in Chicago and the price of a contract for future delivery in Buffalo. If those two prices move in lockstep, regardless of the size of the premium for Buffalo over Chicago, there is a need for only one market, once that premium is established, say by observation of the difference between another pair of contracts in the two cities. The spread between the two contracts is, itself, implicitly the forward price of transportation. Whether one or two contracts are needed revolves around whether the forward price of transportation is stable in relation to the price for immediate transportation. Thus, the question of the necessary number of explicit futures markets becomes a question of which spreads are predictably and persistently variable. If the relationship between the prices for two different delivery dates in the same location, say one and two years ahead, is stable, the price of a contract calling for delivery in two years will be implicit in the price of a one-year contract. This relationship can also be thought of as the forward price of storage and use over that one-year interval. If such spreads representing the forward prices for storage and use are stable or predictable, far fewer futures contracts than the theoretical maximum are necessary.

The issue at hand can also be approached from the perspective of how the prices of various contracts are correlated over time, rather than how they are related at one moment in time. Consider a speculator who believes he has some inside information about the size of the corn crop two years hence. He would like to take an appropriate position in corn for delivery in two years, with the intention of holding it for one week, until his news breaks publicly. If the price of corn for delivery in one year moves over that holding period of one week in close correlation with the price for delivery in two years, regardless of what news comes on the market and regardless of which way prices move as a group, the speculator would be just as content with the contract for delivery in one year. Over that one week the contract for delivery in one year would be a reasonable substitute for the contract requiring delivery in two years. Trading in both contracts is redundant.

For as long as two prices are closely correlated, one price can be readily inferred from the other. What matters then is the length of time over which the two prices are correlated. To represent this symbolically, let P_{T-t} represent the price of corn for delivery at time T, say November '92, as of time t, say 1 June 1984, $T - t$ being the time until delivery. Compare this price with $P_{(T+1)-t}$, say the price for delivery in December '92 as of 1 June 1984. Suppose that P_{T-t} as it moves over time, with new crop reports coming in, new farm programs being announced, exports being controlled or subsidized, is closely correlated with $P_{(T + 1)-t}$ as long as $T + t$ is greater than a length of time L. Up until L months ahead, therefore, the contract for delivery at T is a close substitute for the contract for delivery at $T + 1$. At time $T - L$ trading in the $T + 1$ delivery contract should begin, because at that point two distinct contracts are needed. Those who previously used the T delivery contract as a substitute for the $T + 1$ delivery contract should switch their positions to the new contract, offsetting their positions in the old while establishing the same long or short position in the new. The question is, how protracted a stretch of time is L? Do contracts for delivery of corn in December '92 remain closely correlated with contracts for delivery in November '92 until only 1 May 1985 or until much later, say 1 April 1991? The answer determines when trading begins in two distinct futures contracts. Those who puzzle over the absence of an inclusive set of futures contracts are, without realizing it, maintaining that L is very large, on the order of decades. Here it will be argued instead that L is on the order of a few months, or at most a year or two.

An investigation of the length ahead, L, leads to the same conclusion whether conducted from the perspective of correlation over time or from the perspective of spreads. Two prices are closely correlated when the spread between them is stable. They are not closely correlated when the spread between them is volatile. This point is valid whether the two contracts in question are for two different delivery dates in the same city, in which case the spread represents the price for storage and use, or whether the two contracts are for delivery in two different locations, in which case the spread is the implicit price of freight. The degree of correlation between two contracts depends on the movement over time in the spread between them. Much about the movement in one particular spread can be deduced, however, from looking at several spreads as of one moment in time. A particular spread must first refer to a time far in the future, then, as time passes, a nearby spread, and ultimately the immediate spread. Presumably, a snapshot as of the same moment in time of the relationship among immediate, nearby, and distant spreads, each a distinct spread, tells much about how a particular spread moves over time. If in many snapshots the nearby and distant spreads are observed to be always the same, the immediate spread alone showing different values, then one can conclude, without a detailed statistical analysis, that the length L at which the close correlation ceases is very short. This line of reasoning will be used repeatedly in the next sections.

6.2.   The number of trading locations

The distinction between inclusive and economically justifiable markets can be applied first to the number of cities with futures trading in the same commodity. An inclusive set of markets would include explicit futures markets in every important center in a particular commodity's path of shipment. In each location the array of prices for various times of delivery, from the immediate to the distant future, might differ from those in other locations in two ways. First, the quotations differ if the premium for early delivery of a commodity over a particular period is higher or lower in one location than in others, because the array of prices at one location implicitly defines the array of storage and use charges. Second, the pattern of the arrays differs if the prices of transportation contracted for now and executed at different moments in the future varies, since the spread between two cities' arrays implicitly defines prices for immediate and future delivery of freight.

The need for futures prices in many locations hinges on either the currently listed prices of storage and use of the commodity over various periods differing among the locations or the currently listed prices of transportation differing for various periods in the future. At least some differences must be expected. For any number of reasons, the supply of a commodity in a particular city at a particular moment might be excessive or deficient. Bad weather may have retarded shipments. By happenstance, many farmers may have come to market on the same day, or many exporters may all have arranged by chance to make large shipments on the same day.

In the short term, nothing can be done to change the local supply or demand. Consequently, the local price of storage and use for a short term or the price for immediate use of railcars or freighters will be highly dependent on local circumstances. On the other hand, given time, arrangements to compensate for any particular local conditions are possible. The contrast, then, is between periods distant from the present, in which local differences cannot persist, and periods a short time ahead, during which local conditions matter. At the time ahead beyond the latter, there is no longer a need for contracts for local delivery. Consequently, the issue of whether a locality can sustain futures trading depends upon the length of the short term. If the short term is less than a span of two or three months, futures trading is unlikely because the number of contracts traded simultaneously would fall below the minimum of different delivery months necessary for an active futures market. In most actual cases the short term will be even less than a few months, more likely a matter of days or weeks.

Because what must be defined as the short run is closely connected to how quickly one good or service can be transformed into another, once again the crucial issue about futures markets becomes transformation costs. As it happens, it is a relatively easy matter to transform freighters for corn into those for wheat, or reroute boxcars from Iowa to Kansas. Thus, for the service of transporting bulk commodities the short run is a matter of days. For a commodity like gold, which can be shipped air freight economically, redistributing stocks requires only a few hours. Consequently, little need exists for formal futures markets in many different cities for the same commodity.

The forces working to dispel the impact of local conditions are beneath the surface, and their effect on the arrays of futures prices is even more so. Basically the forces are arbitrage and the law of one price. As long as there is enough time to ship from one location to another, and at the same price, the storage and use charges over comparable periods will be equal. If stocks carry a higher value in City B than in City A, the natural response is to ship from A to B right away, assuming transportation costs no more now than later. The result, of course, is to increase the stock in B at the expense of stocks in A. If the price in B were lower than in A, the same forces would work to withhold shipments until comparable storage and use charges were equal. If it takes one month to ship from City A to City B, then a period from the present to one month ahead in City A corresponds to a period in City B from one month ahead to two months ahead, and those storage and use charges in both cities will be the same. Beyond the time of transportation, futures markets in many locations to distinguish separate local storage and use charges are unnecessary.

The remaining possible reason for differences in the arrays of futures prices in different locations is that the price of transportation as of the current period may not be the same for various periods in the future. Yet differences in the prices of transportation for bulk commodities like corn are extremely short-run phenomena.

Imagine the situation where a commodity is shipped from a number of locations to a central market. The traffic in corn from the western lake ports that funneled into Buffalo is a good example and one previously depicted in Figure 6.1. The top part of Figure 6.3 shows a reworking of Figure 6.1 so that freight rates from Chicago to Buffalo are explicit. Moreover, Figure 6.3 attempts to show the

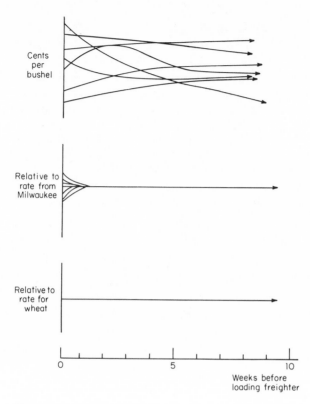

Figure 6.3. Possible arrays of freight rates for corn, Chicago to Buffalo

variation possible in the array of freight rates from Chicago to Buffalo. Corn freight for immediate loading might be low relative to later loading, or for that matter, higher. Prices for both loading times together might be high one shipping season and low another. The arrays of freight rates from Milwaukee to Buffalo would have similar patterns and similar variation. Clearly, the array of freight rates from either western port is highly variable. But what determines the need for distinct corn futures markets in Buffalo, Chicago, and Milwaukee is not the behavior of these arrays of freight rates. Rather it is the behavior of the array for Milwaukee-Buffalo relative to the array for Chicago-Buffalo, and even more important, the array for corn freight relative to the arrays for wheat freight, oat freight, and soybean freight. These comparisons, also shown in Figure 6.3, tell a very different story than the array for Chicago-Buffalo corn freight itself. In these comparisons there is little variability. Spreads are constant. Distinct futures markets are not necessary.

Would the rates for corn from Milwaukee to Buffalo (adjusted for distance) ever vary from the rates from Chicago to Buffalo? This question concerns not just the prices of immediate freight, from either Milwaukee or Buffalo, but also forward freight. At any moment, there might be many ships in Milwaukee and few in Chicago, making the price of immediate transportation lower in Milwaukee. The higher price for shipping corn out of Chicago, however, would be only temporary. With a few weeks' leeway, vessel owners could be certain of being in Chicago in time to fulfill any agreement. Consequently, they could safely contract in advance for freight out of Chicago. For the same reason, with adequate time to adjust their schedules, vessel owners could be certain of avoiding Milwaukee. Therefore, beyond the time necessary to direct freighters to a particular port, the expected return to vessels laden with corn leaving Milwaukee must be comparable to that of those leaving Chicago. Carrying corn is the same service, whether from Milwaukee or Chicago. Since the same good must sell for the same price, forward freight rates must be the same from Milwaukee to Buffalo and Chicago to Buffalo, when adjusted for distance.

The speed with which vessels can be transferred among Chicago and other western lake ports assures that the forward price for freight is the same in all cities. Differences between Chicago and Milwaukee can exist only in the price for immediate transportation of corn, and these arise only with unpredictable events. If the possible arrays of corn freight rates for Chicago to Buffalo, immediate through distant forward, were expressed as a ratio with the comparable arrays for Milwaukee to Buffalo, virtually all the possible variation in the patterns would disappear. The possible arrays in the top third of Figure 6.3 collapse to the essentially flat line in the middle third of the figure. Because the forward prices for corn freight are the same from Milwaukee and Chicago, two separate forward freight markets are hardly necessary. Consequently, one of the full corn futures markets, in either Milwaukee or Chicago, is superfluous. These corn markets, recall, implicitly define the array of freight rates in conjunction with the corn futures market in Buffalo. If both give the same price for freight at one moment in time and both record the same changes in freight rates as time passes, then one is redundant.

Similar circumstances eliminate the need for both a futures market representing the western lake ports, say in Chicago, and another in Buffalo. A single market in either Chicago or Buffalo suffices, because of the behavior of the spreads in the array of forward freight rates for corn implicit between the futures prices in the two cities.

The demonstration of this proposition employs complex and unfamiliar combinations of positions, the idea of spreads between freight rates for different times being far from common currency. Freight rates themselves are the differences between corn prices in Chicago and Buffalo. Spreads between freight rates are thus a difference in differences. It helps, therefore, to view the freight rates as a formal, explicit contract.

At first glance it might seem that the price of, say, a contract calling for the performance of the service of shipping corn in July as of April would bear little relationship to the same for September as of April, because haulage to be performed in July cannot be stored until September. For the same reason it would seem that the two prices would change independently with news, which is to say the spreads between them would be highly volatile, and in consequence separate quotations for each freight rate would be necessary. Such is not the case, however. Although it is impossible to store a service like freight, it is possible to store the corn to be transported. The storability of the commodity to be transported affects spreads in the array of freight rates by placing bounds on the relationships between freight contracts. Obviously, if it is twice as expensive to ship corn in September as in July, it pays to take corn out of storage in Chicago, ship it to Buffalo, and store it there. Such substitutability will drive closer together the prices of freight to be performed in July and in September whenever the freight rate is higher for September than for July. Such substitutability can also drive the prices for corn freight closer together even if the price of freight is higher for performance in July than for September. A shipper intending only to store his corn in Buffalo can store in Chicago and ship later, reducing the price of the July freight relative to that performed in September. All this is not to say that the forward prices of transportation do not change. Rather the spreads between the forward freight rates are likely to be stable.

Because of the ease in adjusting shipments of corn to be kept in storage, there could be persistent differences in the spreads in the implicit array of freight rates only if there is a sustained and foreseeable demand for early delivery and immediate transshipment of corn in Buffalo. Whenever someone wants corn in Buffalo immediately, he puts pressure on the demand for near-term freight. Some shippers might be induced, by the bargain of lower rates for more distant periods, to postpone shipments, but if enough people in Buffalo want corn quickly, the array of freight rates is likely to show declining prices with increasing time to performance. That is to say, they might be in backwardation.

Yet, even if there is sustained demand for immediate delivery of corn in Buffalo, the freight rates for corn for different times of performance will not differ very much. Other users of bulk freight put bounds on the shape of the array of corn freight rates. Although the pattern of freight rates might not induce shippers of corn to postpone delivery, it does induce other shippers to do so. When owners of wheat, oats, and soybeans postpone their scheduled shipments even slightly, they release a considerable quantity of freight services to corn shippers, the same vessels being used to ship any of the grains. After all, bulk carriers are designed precisely to be flexible. In such circumstances, the price for immediate or near-term shipment of corn will not rise much above that for corn freight contracted far in advance. Spreads in corn freight will remain essentially stable. Because the services of shipping wheat, oats, and soybeans are easily transformed into the service of shipping corn, there is hardly ever a need for a premium for immediate corn freight over more distant corn freight.

Here, too, transformation costs are crucial, in this instance the cost of transforming one type of freight service into another. Only if there are persistent and substantial costs in adapting one type of freight service to another are futures markets for the same commodity necessary in several locations. Because it is a relatively quick and easy matter to transform Milwaukee-Buffalo freight into Chicago-Buffalo freight, there is no need for distinct markets in Milwaukee and Chicago spanning delivery dates many months ahead. Since it is also a relatively easy matter to transform general-purpose bulk freight into corn freight, only one futures market for corn, in either Chicago or Buffalo, is necessary. In the extreme there is no need for any means of constructing freight rates specifically in corn. If bulk freighters can ship wheat just as easily as corn, then freight rates for corn must be the same as for wheat (adjusted for weight or volume as appropriate) regardless of whether the grain is shipped immediately or months later. Relative to wheat, the array of freight rates for corn must look like the plot in the bottom third of Figure 6.3, namely a horizontal line. In these circumstances, no delivery date in Buffalo for corn specifically is necessary beyond the time it takes to ship corn from Chicago to Buffalo.

In the extreme situation of general bulk carriers, which can instantaneously transform wheat freight into corn freight, the whole argument concerning the number of distinct locations with futures trading in a particular commodity ultimately rests on the law of one price. No owner of a general bulk freighter would ever rationally carry corn for less than he could earn carrying wheat. In other settings to be considered in the rest of this chapter, such rationality is also an unstated assumption, being such a reasonable one. Farmers, for example, will rationally grow the most advantageous variety or crop, constrained only by the ease with which they can adapt their resources.

Perhaps the nature of the argument can be summarized as well as illustrated with an example. Imagine someone who, based on information he has as of now in April, wants to buy corn for delivery in Buffalo during the first week of September. Suppose there is no corn futures market in Buffalo. Is he thwarted? Does the market system fail to absorb his information? The answer to both questions is no, as long as a few conditions hold: (1) Freighters are equally prepared to carry corn or wheat. (2) Wheat and corn will be shipped from Chicago to Buffalo, which always takes one week, continuously from April through September. (3) Although no explicit freight market exists, futures markets in wheat exist in both Buffalo and Chicago, as does a corn futures market in Chicago. (4) Someone will exploit any opportunity to make money at no risk. Under these conditions, anyone wanting to buy corn for future delivery in Buffalo can accomplish exactly that implicitly with three other transactions. He must simultaneously go long in Buffalo wheat, short in Chicago wheat, and long in Chicago corn. The whole argument hinges on seeing the economic content of these combined positions. By definition corn in Buffalo is corn in Chicago plus the value added of transportation from Chicago to Buffalo. Thus, the trader could buy corn for delivery in Buffalo the first week in September by going long in corn for delivery in Chicago the last week of August while simultaneously going long in corn freight to be performed the last week of August. Although there is no freight market for corn, wheat freight is a perfect substitute. A position in wheat freight must be constructed implicitly from a short position in Chicago wheat for delivery in the last week of August simultaneously with a long position in Buffalo wheat for delivery the first week of September. Although not immediately recognizable as such, a long position in Chicago corn plus a short Chicago wheat and a long Buffalo wheat amount to being long in Buffalo corn, and collectively must have the same return as prices change. Strictly speaking, these three simultaneous positions amount to Buffalo corn only as long as enough time remains to ship grain from Chicago to Buffalo. Once late August arrives, the trader will find himself needing to make delivery of wheat in Chicago while taking delivery of corn in Chicago. He should then unwind his three positions while buying corn for delivery in Buffalo the first week of September. This would be a "to arrive" market in modern terminology, because of its relatively short span. The corn market for delivery in Buffalo during the first week of September is finally active as of the last week in August precisely because only with one week or less to go to delivery will Buffalo corn prices begin to move independently of Chicago corn prices and freight rates. No longer can additional supplies reach Buffalo. In the more general terms introduced in section 6.1, L, the time within which corn in Buffalo is no longer perfectly correlated with some linear combination of other prices, is a matter of only one week. Corn futures in Buffalo for more distant delivery dates are superfluous.

What is necessary in addition to one fully formed futures market per commodity is a market in immediate bulk freight, and a local market for the commodity with delivery dates covering the period transportation takes, a few weeks at most. These markets will often be highly advanced "to arrive" markets. While extra local markets add nothing to the information within a central futures market for periods far into the future, they are essential for short periods if the web of existing markets is to convey all available information.

Without a need for a full array of implicit freight rates for each and every commodity, the frequent efforts to establish more than one exchange in a particular commodity regularly fail. For example, only one exchange has survived the competition opened in March 1983 between the Chicago Board of Trade and the New York Mercantile Exchange over a crude oil futures market. The Chicago Board of Trade, eager for a successful new contract, encouraged its floor traders to spend time trading, thereby increasing the liquidity of its contract, which calls for delivery in the Gulf of Mexico. Yet the New York Mercantile Exchange, whose contract calls for delivery at the large storage depot in Cushing, Oklahoma, prevailed. By early 1984 daily volume on the New York Mercantile Exchange was regularly 2,000 contracts compared to 30 on the Chicago Board of Trade.[4]

---

[4] Even the 2,000 contracts on the New York Mercantile Exchange, each for 1,000 barrels of crude, was only on the order of a few large tankers, tankers being the unit of trading in the interfirm crude market. Volume by early 1985, however, was five times as large as in early 1984, and prices on the New York Mercantile Exchange were beginning to influence oil markets worldwide.

Whether the Chicago Board of Trade failed because of the experience of the New York Mercantile Exchange with its markets in fuel oil and gasoline, or because of a poor specification of the delivery procedures in the contract (which it rewrote in early 1984), the fact remains that both markets had little chance of coexisting. More than one futures market in crude oil is unnecessary because the array of prices for oil in the Gulf of Mexico would bear too close a relationship to that for delivery in Oklahoma.

When futures trading in gold first began in the U.S. in 1975, five exchanges competed for the new business. Only two markets survived the first year. Of the two survivors, the market on the Chicago Mercantile Exchange, once with volume of more than 10,000 contracts per day, not far from the 40,000 traded daily on Comex, collapsed in 1983. Once trading began to fall on the Chicago Mercantile Exchange's gold market, more and more of the business went to Comex. That the Chicago Mercantile Exchange held out as long as it did is surprising enough. Transportation costs for gold are insignificant relative to its value. One charter flight with a cargo of bullion can restore a normal relationship between New York and Chicago. A full array of gold freight is not needed. Consequently, one market, in New York as it happens, suffices.

The same result is a foregone conclusion in financial futures. On the same day in 1981 three exchanges introduced essentially identical contracts for the future delivery of domestic certificates of deposit (CDs) issued by large banks. All three heavily promoted their market, and while at first volume was equally distributed, today trading persists on only one exchange, the Chicago Mercantile Exchange.[5] That only one market survived is precisely because one clerk with a briefcase full of domestic CDs can end a relative shortage in one city within the time of an air flight.[6]

The origin of the particular contracts traded on the London Metal Exchange also illustrates why distant futures contracts are necessary in a particular location only up to a point.[7] Members of the LME can initiate only contracts for immediate delivery or for delivery thirty or

---

[5] By 1984, the market for domestic CDs was languishing even on the Chicago Mercantile Exchange, to the benefit of the exchange's own Euro CD market. Domestic and Euro CDs being closely related, only one market should be expected to persist. This is an application of the principle of the economically justifiable number of markets to the number of grades, the subject of section 6.3.

[6] For other examples of markets that failed to persist in more than one city, see Silber (1981) and Carlton (1984).

[7] Contracts in copper on Comex in New York now stretch farther ahead than in London.

ninety days later. Founded in 1876, the LME dealt at first primarily in copper imported from Chile.[8] Ships took three months to travel from South America to England. Whenever the use charge for copper over a period more than three months ahead was higher than for other periods, enterprising traders could arrange for slightly more production in Chile, passage to England, storage on the spot, and profitable delivery on a futures contract. In other words, the high price did not persist beyond three months ahead, because there was sufficient time to transport supplies to England. Therefore, the spreads over periods far in the future were in a stable relationship, and only one futures price was necessary to convey the price for all delivery dates far in the future. It was hardly a coincidence that trading on the London Metal Exchange goes no further ahead than for delivery ninety days ahead, for it is only within that period that the price of storage and use in London fluctuates relative to other locations.

6.3.   The number of grades

Related to the issue of the number of separate locations with futures markets is the matter of how many grades and varieties have separate markets. These issues are related not only because the same theory serves to answer them but also because trading in different varieties occurs most often in different locations. The growing region for soft wheat is near Chicago, and the region for hard wheat is tributary to Kansas City, so naturally the prices in these two futures markets reflect their regional varieties.

Moisture content, foreign matter, and color are the common criteria for distinguishing grades. As a result, the different grades serve as a means of implicitly pricing drying, cleaning, bleaching, and so forth.[9] Not surprisingly, the question of whether markets for future delivery of different grades are indispensable becomes again a matter of whether differences in prices for such services, contracted for now and executed at various times now and in the future, can be foreseen and yet not compensated for. Perhaps rainy weather during the harvest prevented corn from drying naturally. Although No.

---

[8] The year 1876 was the first time the metals traders in London had their own organization, although the first move toward a specialized exchange was in 1869 (Economist Intelligence Unit 1958).

[9] Sometimes a lower grade would need to be both cleaned and dried to turn it into a higher grade. This possibility clouds the interpretation of the spread between prices for those grades as the price of a particular service, but it does not alter the conclusion that separate futures markets will emerge only when the array of that spread displays sufficient variability among different periods.

2 corn may be in greater demand and tighter supply than No. 3 at this moment, it may not have been possible to predict and to incorporate that weather into prices beforehand. Furthermore, even if the weather were predictable, it is unlikely that a difference in prices would have emerged. If, months ahead of the delivery date, the price of No. 2 stood unusually higher than No. 3, there would have been plenty of time for drying, cleaning, and sorting No. 3 in order to convert it into No. 2.

The forward price of a single grade is probably closely correlated with all the forward prices of the many grades for delivery beyond more than a few weeks ahead. Within less than a few weeks, however, there is not enough time to adjust to changes in demands and supplies for various grades. Consequently, spot markets that distinguish grades are indispensable.

The New York Cotton Exchange applies such logic to the problem of which grades to certify for delivery on its futures contracts. All contracts are made in terms of the price of the grade "middling," yet almost any grade can be delivered. Deliveries of "prime" and "fair" are adjusted according to the premiums and discounts from middling in the spot market on the day the seller gives notice of his delivery, a practice that greatly expands deliverable supplies. In effect the New York Cotton Exchange's rule recognizes that for a delivery date more than a few weeks ahead the grades are in a stable relationship and one explicit price suffices, while at any particular moment discrepancies in the prices for immediate delivery are common and must be accounted for.

In one case, wheat, active futures trading exists simultaneously in three distinct varieties. Futures trading in wheat on the Kansas City Board of Trade and the Minneapolis Grain Exchange persists because their varieties of wheat do not exactly parallel movements for comparable delivery months in the price of the variety traded on the Chicago Board of Trade. These varieties move separately because hard wheat, which has a protein content suitable for breads, can neither be converted into nor substituted for soft wheat, primarily used for cakes and cookies. Additional supplies of a particular protein content being unobtainable until the next harvest, prices for delivery far in advance can be predictably and persistently different. Depending on the time of year, L can range from six to twelve months, a sufficient time ahead to induce futures trading in several contracts in all three grades. (Even so, volume and open interest on the Chicago Board of Trade are on the order of four times that in Kansas City and ten times that in Minneapolis.)

Precisely because there is much less substitutability or convertibility among the varieties of wheat, the pattern of prices in the three wheat futures markets can demonstrate why other commodities do not have futures trading in more than one grade. Wheat is the extreme. Yet even the prices of the various varieties of wheat are nearly perfectly correlated further ahead than one year before delivery. This evidence for nearly perfect correlation can be deduced from a comparison of snapshots at frequent intervals rather than a complete statistical study of the time series. Table 6.1 shows the relative prices among all three American wheat futures markets for the four delivery months, March, May, July, and September, as of early February for ten years. Of more interest, Table 6.1 also shows the standard deviation over the ten years of the relative prices for these four months. If the relative prices for the more distant delivery months have relatively low standard deviations, which is to say indirectly that they are much the same from year to year, compared to the nearer delivery months, one can infer that the futures prices in the three cities are relatively closely correlated until only a few months before expiration of the contracts. Unmistakably, in Table 6.1 the standard deviation declines with increasing time until delivery. For example, the standard deviation over these ten years of the Minneapolis price relative to the Chicago price for March delivery is .085, while for September delivery it is .040. Extrapolated out another year to the following September, the variance of that relative price would be effectively zero. For that reason, there is no trading in those distant September contracts. The patterns among the delivery months within individual years only reinforce these observations about the wheat markets. Whenever the relative price for March delivery is above average, the other delivery months trend downward to the long-run relative price. Whenever the relative price for March is below average, the other delivery months trend upward.

As of early February, exceptional weather may already indicate a surging Mississippi will delay barge traffic in the spring. As of early February, exceptional weather may already indicate the Great Lakes being closed to shipping much later than usual, landlocking wheat in Chicago, and depressing the price for delivery there in March relative to Kansas City and Minneapolis.[10] Similarly, the weather may

---

[10] For example, foreseeable but unavoidable bottlenecks in transportation and storage explained the extreme patterns in 1979 (Gray and Peck 1981).

Table 6.1. *Relative prices of wheat varieties, 1974-1983 (closing prices as of the first business day in February)*

	March delivery	May delivery	July delivery	September delivery
	Kansas City relative to Chicago			
1974	0.967	0.969	1.017	1.018
1975	0.999	1.000	1.012	1.042
1976	1.017	1.009	1.012	1.012
1977	0.987	0.984	0.984	0.987
1978	1.012	0.993	0.986	0.985
1979	0.903	0.946	0.982	0.985
1980	0.953	0.966	0.982	0.983
1981	0.959	0.968	0.993	0.995
1982	1.100	1.040	1.022	1.007
1983	1.114	1.067	1.036	1.030
Mean	1.001	0.994	1.003	1.004
Stand. dev.	0.062	0.035	0.019	0.020
	Minneapolis relative to Chicago			
1974	0.947	0.969	1.058	1.009
1975	1.091	1.102	1.097	1.061
1976	1.141	1.137	1.104	1.072
1977	1.064	1.050	1.047	1.037
1978	1.045	1.022	1.007	1.004
1979	0.879	0.942	0.988	0.987
1980	0.913	0.920	0.933	0.933
1981	0.965	0.970	1.008	0.999
1982	1.083	1.049	1.043	1.024
1983	1.096	1.091	1.086	1.062
Mean	1.022	1.025	1.037	1.019
Stand. dev.	0.085	0.069	0.051	0.040
	Minneapolis relative to Kansas City			
1974	0.978	1.000	1.041	0.992
1975	1.092	1.102	1.084	1.018
1976	1.122	1.127	1.091	1.060
1977	1.078	1.067	1.064	1.050
1978	1.033	1.029	1.022	1.019
1979	0.974	0.995	1.006	1.003
1980	0.957	0.952	0.950	0.949
1981	1.006	1.002	1.015	1.003
1982	0.984	1.008	1.021	1.017
1983	0.984	1.023	1.049	1.031
Mean	1.021	1.030	1.034	1.014
Stand. dev.	0.054	0.050	0.039	0.029

already foretell unusually early or late harvests of particular varieties, which appear as different relative prices for July delivery as of February. From the vantage point of February, no one can foresee any bottlenecks in transportation or harvesting without sufficient time to be worked out before September, by which time all wheat is harvested. Of course, by September one variety may be in short supply. What matters to the patterns among futures prices is whether such circumstances are apparent as of February. Most likely only a few are apparent as of February; of these, seven months' flexibility in transportation and consumption may eliminate the majority. Earlier than February there would be even more flexibility and even less foresight. Hence relative prices as of October for delivery the following September would be much closer to their long-run average values. By February farmers can adjust the acreage of spring wheat only and not winter wheat too. Moreover, by February prices can reflect the effects of the winter weather on the winter wheat crop, information that could not have been incorporated into futures prices the previous fall since it was not yet known.

If futures prices for the different varieties of wheat show little relative variation when for delivery more than six months ahead, then a commodity with much greater convertibility and substitutability among varieties needs distinct contracts stretching even less than six months ahead. Consider the case of corn. Grades of corn are mainly a function of moisture content and extraneous matter, both of which can be changed through drying and cleaning in a much shorter time than the protein content of wheat. Moreover, different varieties of corn can be much more readily substituted for one another in animal feed than can millers use different varieties of wheat. If futures markets were to exist for several varieties of corn, and if a table like Table 6.1 were to be constructed, the variance of the relative corn prices, say No. 3 versus No. 2, would fall off even faster than for wheat. The variances would be effectively zero within a month or two. Precisely for this reason full-fledged futures markets for more than one grade of corn are superfluous. For much the same reason a sorghum futures market has failed to take hold. Sorghum and corn are interchangeable as animal feed. Their relative price for immediate delivery varies only little, let alone how little it would vary between contracts for delivery six months into the future.

The conditions under which futures trading in separate grades persists are an application of a more general principle encompassing all processing services. In effect, drying, cleaning, and transporting are all services employed to alter a commodity. Crushing soybeans, milling flour, and fabricating copper are other examples of the same activity. A full array of processing margins for several periods of execution into the future are necessary only if both the demand for and supply of that service are inflexible. The supply of crushing facilities for soybeans is relatively inflexible because such facilities cannot be installed or dismantled quickly and cannot be used for processing other commodities. On the other hand, elevators, which perform much of the drying and cleaning of grains, are equally able to treat corn, oats, rye, barley, soybeans, and wheat. Whenever the demand for cleaning corn is especially high, cleaning of all the others need be postponed only briefly to release collectively considerable facilities for cleaning corn. Thus, although there is reason for an active futures market in soybean crushing, achieved implicitly through a combination of futures markets in soybeans, soybean oil, and soybean meal, there is much less need for a separate market in cleaning, drying, and warehousing each grain.

The flexibilities in cleaning, transporting, and using various grades of corn dictate a considerable revision of the number of distinct contracts in the corn market as depicted previously in Figure 6.1. In Figure 6.1 there were 74 distinct markets (or contracts), although it was clear that the 45 markets for services could be easily inferred from the 29 contracts for future delivery. That list of necessary contracts can now be condensed further, to 12. Figure 6.4 shows this revision, assuming that there is a market for general bulk freight and that Chicago has the surviving futures market in corn. The dates for delivery in Buffalo beyond the time it takes to transport corn from Chicago to Buffalo are unnecessary because the prices for Chicago delivery plus the appropriate prices for general bulk freight give exactly the same prices. For the same reason all but the spot market in Milwaukee disappears. Figure 6.4 presumes that the immediate price of cleaning corn may differ from the price of nearby performance. Consequently, two delivery dates are shown for No. 3 corn. Farther ahead, however, the price of cleaning is the same for all times of performance, and as a result the price of No. 3 can be inferred from the price for No. 2. Full-fledged futures markets in Milwaukee and Buffalo add little to the prices conveyed by a short-term cleaning market, a market for general bulk freight, and the No. 2 corn futures market in Chicago.

Delivery in
Milwaukee of   *d*
No. 2 corn (*d*)   Immediate

Storage
and use

Freight
from Milwaukee

Delivery in
Buffalo of   *d*   *d*
No. 2 corn (*d*)   Immediate

Storage
and use

Freight
from Chicago

Delivery in
Chicago of   *d*   *d*   *d*   *d*   *d*   *d*   *d*   . . .
No. 2 corn (*d*)   Immediate   Near Future   Distant future

Storage
and use

Cleaning

Delivery in
Chicago of   *d*   *d*
No. 3 corn (*d*)   Immediate

Storage
and use

Figure 6.4. A sufficient set of markets for corn

6.4.   The number of months within a year actively traded

Just as the inflexibilities in transformations determine the number of
futures markets in a particular commodity, they influence the number of delivery months traded. In terms of Figure 6.4, the question
has now become whether the number of contracts in the one remaining futures market, No. 2 corn in Chicago, can itself be reduced. Attention now turns from the services of transportation and
cleaning to the service of storage and use. The price of storage and

use is implicit between two contracts for delivery in the same location but at different times.

Different delivery months are necessary whenever the storage and use charge for one stretch of time is different from the charge for another period, with both prices being measured as of the same moment. A difference in storage and use charges occurs if there is a break in the demand for or supply of commodity loans. Several breaks in the supply of commodity loans are both substantial and foreseeable. The most important is the harvest. The change in supply with a new harvest disrupts the continuity in the array of prices of loans over particular times of the year. What matters for the number of distinct futures contracts actively traded is not simply the uncertainty in the size and timing of the harvest, however. Rather, it is the combination of seeing some facts about the harvest in advance of the harvest and yet being unable to do much about them. Although the exact time of the harvest is not constant from year to year, reasonable predictions can be made several months ahead based on knowledge of planting time and weather patterns. Many months before a harvest, there exist three distinct intervals where the supply of loanable commodities is predictably and persistently different: The first is the interval up to the beginning of the harvest, during which time the available supply is fairly steadily consumed. The second is the interval from the first part of the harvest to the middle of the harvest. The supply of loanable commodities over this period differs from year to year with the crop's maturity and capacity constraints. The third interval in which the supply of loans differs is after the harvest is complete. The size of the harvest, of course, determines the precise supply of loanable commodities over this third interval, but the deviation from an average supply can be discerned and predicted some months ahead based on the size of plantings and weather to date. Differences in the supply of loans during these three intervals—just before, during, and just after harvest—persist because it is impossible to transfer the commodity from the period after the harvest when it is abundant to the period before when it is scarce.

Breaks in the demand for storage and use, although far from insignificant, are less important than breaks in supply. Because the demand for loans of commodities derives from the demand for final products, the demand for such loans is likely to differ only when final demand differs. In many cases, the derived demand for loans at any given price is nearly constant, because firms such as flour millers and spinners try to run at full capacity all of the time and because the consumption of baked goods and textiles is steady. In contrast, the demand for lumber is tied to the winter lull in the construction industry. The exporting, shipping, and marketing businesses, likewise, have more variable demand, depending on the seasons and the prospects for transportation. Furthermore, such seasonal variation in the demand for commodity loans is predictable.

With many modes of transportation today, this seasonal variation in the demand for commodity loans is less pronounced than when most bulk commodities moved by water. Therefore, the typical contractual terms of a less flexible age of transportation are instructive for demonstrating that breaks in the array of futures prices, and hence a need for distinct contracts, are at those points in time when transportation becomes either more or less flexible. In the years before 1860 if the Great Lakes were frozen, southern rivers at flood, and the North Atlantic stormy, nothing would move. As a result, contracts for goods to arrive or for future delivery, in order to distinguish them, often designated the time "as soon as the vessels can arrive," "fifteen days after opening of lake navigation," "at the opening of the canal," or "at the opening of the river."[11] Other contracts were for goods "to arrive before the close of navigation."[12] Even as many contracts were directly tied to specific natural events, more called for delivery during some stretch of time on the calendar. When designated by months, trading was most often in those months coinciding with the commencement or close of transportation. Long before traders knew the severity of the winter and the thickness of the ice, the price of storage and use for the months after that in which transportation normally resumed would differ considerably from the price of storage and use before that month.

In summary, different prices of loans over periods in the future are likely to emerge at these breaks during the crop-year: at the start of the harvest, the completion of the harvest, the opening of transportation, and the close of transportation. Because these natural divisions mark the major differences in the prices of loans, a finer division of the year into many delivery periods would add little additional information. Prices between these breaks could be inferred closely with a simple interpolation.

These considerations about the foreseeable and yet unavoidable

[11] *Buffalo Morning Express*, 2 April 1847; *Buffalo Daily Courier*, 8 February 1848; *Chicago Daily Journal*, 24 April 1851; *Buffalo Morning Express*, 5 March 1847, report for New York City market.
[12] *Chicago Tribune*, 2 January 1860.

breaks in the array of periods in the storage and use market go far in explaining the particular delivery months in various futures markets. In the various wheat futures markets today, the delivery months are precisely the months coinciding with the persistent and predictable breaks in the supply of or demand for wheat loans. Trading is confined to five different months of delivery: March, May, July, September, and December. These five months for delivery are the minimum number for separating the important periods for wheat loans. May corresponds to the period right near the end of the crop-year; July is the month that reflects whether the harvest is early or late; September represents the period after the harvest. These three months, then, display the breaks in the supply of loanable wheat. December and March, for their part, correspond to the breaks in the demand for such loans, namely when the Great Lakes freeze and thaw.

In the first decades of organized trading in cotton futures, the 1870s and 1880s, trading for delivery in all twelve months was possible.[13] Even so, there was a marked predilection for trading in certain months, exactly those that marked abrupt changes in the prices of loans of cotton. Table 6.2 lists estimates for the average daily volume for each month of delivery on the New York and New Orleans cotton exchanges compiled from daily market reports in the 1880s. These figures relate not the average volume for all contracts during each day but rather the average for a particular contract, say January delivery, over the entire year.[14] In New York two contracts were particularly popular, January and August, being traded approximately twice as heavily as the delivery months before and after them. August is the end of the crop-year, and January marks the beginning of the winter shipping season. Three other months were

---

[13] Although in American markets delivery was for a period covering a single month, on the Liverpool Cotton Exchange delivery was in coupled months. For example, delivery could be at the seller's option on any day in September and October or in November-December. Although particular pairs were more popular because they represented important breaks in the crop-year, there was no way to predict a persistent difference in the price for individual months because the uncertainty in the time of arrival of shipments destined for England from the American South was two months. As shipments became more reliable, contracts in Liverpool called for delivery in one month only.

[14] These estimates are based on a sample of a week's trading (5-1/2 business days) at the start of each month. Because the increased volume of trading that occurs in all contracts as they approach maturity may have distorted the average volume, a second column is presented in which the average volume refers to the amount of trading in a contract excluding the three months before it expired. The same contracts emerge as more popular whether this adjustment is made or not.

Table 6.2. *Average daily volume in cotton contracts, 1883-1886*

Month of delivery	New York		New Orleans	
	Over entire year	Over period more than three months ahead	Over entire year	Over period more than three months ahead
January	106	60	32	17
February	65	33	21	11
March	83	47	33	20
April	63	37	29	15
May	87	47	29	14
June	72	33	22	7
July	48	29	25	13
August	103	66	15	10
September	40	13	13	9
October	47	25	12	7
November	38	21	12	7
December	56	38	25	15

Sources: New York Herald, 1883-1886; New Orleans Picayune, 1883-1885.

important demarcations in the course of the crop-year and, thus, were relatively popular: March, May, and to a lesser extent, October. A similar though weaker pattern according to differences in the supply and demand of loanable cotton was also present in the average volume on the New Orleans Cotton Exchange. Today, the New York Cotton Exchange has acknowledged in effect that markets in only a few delivery months are indispensable. Accordingly, it allows trading only in March, May, July, October, and December contracts.

6.5.   The number of years ahead actively traded

A discussion of the months in which there is active futures trading leads naturally to a final question: How far ahead should futures trading cover? Granted that for commodities like wheat and cotton a subset of the calendar months is needed, how many years ahead should that subset be traded? One, two, five, or ten years? A related issue is that of which commodities have futures markets at all. These two issues are connected because the establishment of futures markets in many more commodities would represent a major extension of the length of time ahead that explicit forward prices are available for these additional commodities.

An inclusive set of markets would require trading for delivery in particular months many years ahead. Few of these markets, however, would be indispensable. Recall that the price of a near-term futures contract differs from the price of a distant-term futures contract by the price of the spread over the interim. If that spread is constant as time passes, the two futures prices move parallel to one another, and the nearer-term contract adequately conveys all information available about the more distant contract. Therefore, the answer to the question of how far ahead futures trading should stretch is yet again dependent on whether spreads are persistently and predictably different, in this case spreads between periods far in the future.

This argument is similar to that concerning the number of short-term versus long-term instruments for borrowing and lending money. Money can be borrowed overnight, or for the next week, month, or quarter. Yet no comparable agreements exist for borrowing money now for overnight ten years or eleven years from the present. The reason, of course, is that the forward interest rate on an overnight loan arranged now for ten years from the present would be the same as that arranged now for an overnight loan eleven years from the present. Therefore, there is no reason to quote them separately. Put another way, because the term structure of interest rates is flat between ten and eleven years ahead, there is no reason for separate bonds maturing in each and every day, week, and month during the tenth year. Separate maturities are necessary only when they help to define a term structure of interest rates that is not flat, and the term structure is likely to be pronounced only a few years ahead and exceptionally pronounced only a few months ahead.[15] Likewise, maturities of futures contracts are necessary only where they mark changes in the yield curve on loans of commodities like wheat and cotton.

Perhaps in the setting of commodity markets the issue can best be understood from the perspective of a speculator.[16] Imagine a speculator has learned that a major manufacturer of farm equipment has just patented a greatly improved corn shucker. Once this machine comes on the market, in two years as a result of the need to retool a plant and allow for testing, it will significantly expand the supply of corn. The speculator, of course, wants to profit from his private knowledge, to be public in a matter of days, that in two years the price of corn will be lower than it otherwise would be. If a two-year futures contract exists, the speculator can sell contracts and buy them back at a profit when the whole market drops as his news becomes general knowledge. Suppose, however, that the longest maturity is only one year ahead, so that he cannot go short in the two-year contract. Does this hinder the speculator? Suppose he proceeds to sell the one-year futures contract. By selling an earlier term than he wanted to, the speculator has been forced to assume, in addition to the short position in the two-year contract he desires, a bear position in the spread from year one to year two. This is because the sale of a one-year contract equals the sale of a two-year

[15] This statement is true even though many maturities are traded because the issuing of ten-year bonds is staggered. At any one time there might be 9-year, 37-week bonds traded alongside of 9-year, 38-week bonds. At any one time, however, a borrower will typically issue maturities of 30 days, 90 days, 180 days, 1 year, 5 years, 10 years, and 30 years. Obviously, the short-term instruments are present in greater numbers because the interest rate on 30-day bills is likely to differ from that on 90-day bills, while that on 10-year bonds is unlikely to differ from the interest rate on 10-year, 30-day bonds.

[16] The issue could also be approached from the perspective of a processor who wants to sell ahead all of his output for the next two years. Is he thwarted by having no contracts calling for delivery farther ahead than one year? The crucial evidence and the conclusion are the same as from the perspective of a speculator. As long as distant spreads are stable, the processor can achieve his purpose by "stacking" contracts in the most distant delivery month currently traded and rolling them over as new delivery months become active.

contract plus {the sale of a one-year contract plus the purchase of a two-year contract}, the positions in braces being a bear straddle. When the news becomes public, the speculator short the one-year contract will make the same amount of money on his implicit position in the two-year futures contract as if he would have had sold it to begin with, but he could lose money on his bear spread if it were to move farther away from full carrying charges with the news. This could happen because a larger supply of corn beginning in the second year reduces the need to carry stock over from the first year to the second year. With less inventory held over, the supply of loanable corn would be lower, raising the price of a loan, contrary to the interests of a bear spreader whose spread commits him to lend. In practice, for him to make less money than possible with a full choice of contracts, the one-year futures contract would have to drop less than the two-year futures contract would if it could be measured.[17] If this were to happen to many speculators, their incentive to obtain information would be reduced and prices would be less accurate signals than they are otherwise.

Crucial to the speculator is the movement in the spread because that is where he could lose out on some of his profit. If the price of the spread were not to change with the news, the speculator would be just as content to trade in the nearer-term futures contract as in the one to which his information properly applies.[18] Further, he would have the same incentive to seek out information about the distant future. Clearly, then, whether or not the distant spread changes critically determines whether the price system is missing some important markets. By this standard it does not appear that distant futures contracts are especially important. Because of the suppleness in storage and production over the span of several years,

---

[17] Suppose before the news that the price of corn for delivery in one year was 360¢ a bushel and for two years 329¢ a bushel. These prices drop to 347¢ and 315¢ respectively. Clearly a short makes less money on the one-year contract. His profit of 13¢ on the one-year contract can be decomposed into a 14¢ gain on a two-year contract and a 1¢ loss on the bear straddle (short one-year and long two-year).

[18] Even if the news breaks not in a matter of days but in a matter of years, this argument holds. Suppose an engineer working for the manufacturer of the corn shucker knows that his firm will achieve a breakthrough in technology sometime in the next few years, but he does not know exactly when. He would like to sell corn short, perhaps a five-year contract if that were available. Instead he could sell a one-year contract and roll it forward while it is still fairly distant. His final return will differ only if the spreads implicit between the one-year contract and the five-year contract have moved by when he rolls the contract forward. Movements in such distant spreads are small. Hence, he is as content with a one-year contract as with a five-year contract.

distant spreads would change only slightly with substantial new information.

In the other questions in this chapter about the need for particular contracts, the time necessary to adjust has determined whether different spreads can emerge. As long as there is insufficient time to move supplies in or out, the price of storage and use varies among locations. Given adequate time, however, shippers can be sure of having supplies where they are most wanted. The same logic applies to how far ahead differences in spreads can emerge at a central location. Within a particular crop-year, the total supply of a loanable commodity is fixed, being equal to the stocks on hand and what has been planted. There is little opportunity to increase the amount that crop-year gives to the next without a large change in the current spot price. Likewise, if current stocks are discovered to be too large, it may be difficult to increase current consumption enough to reduce them significantly without a large change in price. Clearly, the farther ahead it is perceived that stocks will be too large or too small, the easier and less disruptive it will be to adjust the stocks to the desired amount. For example, if it is perceived that for a crop-year ten years from now crop rotations will restrict output, there is plenty of time to increase the carryovers from the nine preceding years, by either consuming less or producing more. What is important is that these changes can each be quite small and in total increase substantially the amount carried over into the deficient crop-year. The price of loans over year ten will not remain above that of earlier years because plenty of time exists to increase the stock in year ten.

Although differences in the price of loans among locations cannot emerge for periods farther ahead than it takes to get supplies in or out, which is at most a matter of a few weeks or months if not days, the short run for planting is much longer. Because crops, once planted, cannot be increased or decreased, the scope of adjustments is inevitably restricted.[19] Present consumption must bear nearly all the burden of adjusting the carryover. Given a horizon longer than the growing season, however, farmers can much more easily increase their output. They may still not be completely flexible because of crop rotation or lack of machines or expertise for a new crop, but surely their commitments now to plantings several years ahead are free. The point is not that when a particular growing season arrives farmers can control the level of their output. Rather the issue is

---

[19] Although additional fertilizer can increase yields somewhat, nothing can make the crop mature faster.

whether, given that the price of wheat for delivery three crop-years from the present is low relative to the price for delivery two crop-years ahead or low relative to corn for three crop-years ahead, they cannot make some adjustments to reduce their commitment to wheat three years from now. Surely they can. Therefore, the low relative price for delivery of wheat three years ahead could not be maintained. Even though farmers are restricted in adjusting the amount and blend of production longer than shippers, there is enough flexibility in agricultural supply that differences in forward spreads cannot emerge more than a year or two ahead. Consequently, one will rarely find agricultural futures contracts much farther ahead than one crop-year.

The patterns among futures contracts for cocoa in New York confirm these general arguments. Cocoa is an appropriate crop for such a test, the inflexibilities in cocoa being pronounced. Because cocoa is a tree crop, the scope of adjustments in supply is especially restricted, far more so than for wheat or corn. Four or five years must elapse before trees begin to bear, and they remain productive for decades. For all practical purposes, the supply elasticity is zero, the weather causing most of the year-to-year variation in the size of the harvest.[20] With few substitutes available, the demand for cocoa is also relatively inflexible. In consequence, the spot price of cocoa is one of the most variable among commodities. It would be even more variable without the suppleness in the carryover.

Table 6.3 shows the variablility in the array of cocoa prices.[21] As expected theoretically, the variability falls with increasing time to delivery, as did the relative prices of wheat varieties. The top half of Table 6.3 shows the prices for cocoa for various times of delivery as of early March over a period of ten years. These prices have been adjusted for interest expenses, which varied from 4% per annum to 20% per annum.[22] This adjustment therefore gives the price for, say, September delivery as if it were paid for immediately rather than on delivery. An adjustment of $5 per ton per month was made for warehousing and insurance fees, which have remained relatively

---

[20] Although the crop-year is officially designated as October through September, cocoa does not have as pronounced a crop-year as corn. African and South American cocoa appear on the market at different times; cocoa trees produce two crops a year, one larger than the other. Arrivals in New York are heaviest in the period May through July.

[21] For more on the arrays of cocoa prices, see Weymar (1974).

[22] The percentage spreads between gold futures were used, since they are a good estimate of the private cost of financing. In all years in March the term structure of interest rates on money was relatively flat.

Table 6.3. *Variability in cocoa spreads, 1975-1984 (closing prices in New York as of the first business day in March)*

	March delivery	May delivery	July delivery	September delivery	December delivery	March delivery
	Dollars per metric ton, adjusted for carrying costs					
1975	1,153	1,329	1,241	1,183	1,121	1,063
1976	1,494	1,394	1,314	1,254	1,174	1,115
1977	4,222	4,029	3,876	3,738	3,451	3,270
1978	3,260	2,991	2,854	2,744	2,610	2,497
1979	3,351	3,335	3,302	3,277	3,226	3,160
1980	3,040	2,937	2,855	2,783	2,675	2,594
1981	1,945	1,921	1,915	1,910	1,891	1,875
1982	1,887	1,852	1,832	1,832	1,793	1,747
1983	1,765	1,765	1,761	1,753	1,713	1,686
1984	2,547	2,409	2,343	2,293	2,209	2,132
Mean	2,502	2,396	2,329	2,277	2,186	2,114
Stand. dev.	881	852	827	804	757	727
	Discounts between delivery months in percent per month					
1975	6.94	3.55	2.45	1.85	1.80	
1976	3.57	3.03	2.41	2.29	1.74	
1977	2.39	1.98	1.84	2.77	1.85	
1978	4.48	2.41	2.01	1.71	1.50	
1979	0.24	0.50	0.38	0.53	0.69	
1980	1.76	1.44	1.30	1.35	1.03	
1981	0.63	0.16	0.12	0.34	0.28	
1982	0.94	0.56	0.00	0.73	0.89	
1983	0.00	0.11	0.23	0.77	0.54	
1984	2.86	1.40	1.10	1.26	1.20	
Mean	2.38	1.51	1.18	1.36	1.15	
Stand. dev.	2.06	1.15	0.91	0.76	0.53	

constant beginning with 1974.[23] As can be seen, cocoa prices displayed a strong pattern of spreads below full carrying charges; the average immediate March price, effectively the spot price, at $2,502 was 16% higher than the average price for delivery the following March, $2,114. More important than this pattern of backwardation, ubiquitous in commodities, are the standard deviations of prices for the various delivery months. The standard deviation declines steadily

---

[23] Conversation with Douglas Martoucci, President, Continental Warehouse, New York. Warehouse fees are relatively important for cocoa, which spoils easily and suffers from infestations of insects.

with increasing time until delivery, from $881 for the spot March contract to $727 for the distant March contract. It is as if the more distant contracts converge on a long-run equilibrium price.

The prices of cocoa themselves, in the top half of Table 6.3, actually understate the convergence of prices. The whole array of cocoa prices was moving up and down, mostly up because of inflation. It is not how the whole array moves but rather how the spreads within the array move that determines the distance ahead contracts are traded. The lower half of Table 6.3 reveals the percentage discounts between pairs of months, that is, the spread between the nearer contract and the more distant contract divided by the more distant contract.[24] The variability of the discounts determines the need for trading in the more distant contract; the greater the variability the greater the need. Clearly, the standard deviations of the various discounts fall considerably with increasing time ahead, from 2.06% to 0.53%. Projected yet another year ahead, the variability would disappear. For that very reason, those very distant contracts were not traded. Apparently, the March contract for delivery one year ahead was a satisfactory substitute for all contracts yet more distant.[25]

The same line of reasoning explains the span of contracts in the futures markets for financial instruments. At first glance in might seem improbable that a theory of inflexibilities would explain financial futures well. What inflexibility has the Standard & Poor's 500 Index, a futures contract settled in cash rather than in physical delivery? What increase in inflexibility can explain the explosive growth of the T-bond futures market, contracts for which now stretch into delivery months farther ahead than contracts for any other commodity? Why are there so many successful financial futures markets, even though all seem to express the same term structure of interest rates? Actually, financial futures, far from controverting the theory just successful in explaining cocoa contracts, support that theory. First of all, the growth of the markets has not indicated a need for new markets as much as a shift in the type of market, from informal dealer networks to formal exchanges. Second, increasingly there have been volatile spreads among various financial instruments, which have found expression in new futures contracts. Third, trading in most financial futures is concentrated in a few nearby contracts.

---

[24] Those spreads with a discount of 0.0 were at full carrying charges.
[25] Sometimes the distant May contract was traded, in precisely those years when spreads were especially different among the various periods.

In many cases a financial futures market has grown out of a highly active forward market. One need not explain the growth of financial futures in terms of an increase in inflexibilities. Rather, an informal implicit loan market has become a formal implicit loan market, in the terminology developed in Chapter 5. More accurately still, informal and formal markets now coexist for many financial instruments. The interbank market for foreign currencies existed before and has remained active since the rise of futures markets for foreign currencies. The GNMA futures market, the first successful futures market for long-term debt, grew out of an interbank forward market in certificates of mortgages. The dealer market in repurchase agreements both antedated and grew further after the start of the T-bond futures market, which by 1983 was the largest futures market in terms of volume. This coexistence may eventually be resolved in favor of a formal or of an informal market.

The 1970s and early 1980s were remarkable for the volatility of interest rates. Much less remarked upon were the new extremes and much higher volatility in the term structure of interest rates. These extremes in term structure, either falling steeply as in 1980 or rising steeply as in 1982, imply that forward interest rates are not stably related. For that reason, contracts for the delivery of T-bonds or for the delivery of T-bills have reason to stretch farther into the future. Even less remarked upon but even more important to the number of successful financial futures was the volatility in the term structure expressed in one financial instrument compared to that expressed in another. For example in 1982 the percentage spreads among gold futures were essentially the T-bill rate; both gold and T-bills showed the same rising term structure. In January and February 1980, in contrast, while the T-bill rate was about 15% with a falling term structure, the percentage spread in gold was close to 20% with a much more steeply falling term structure.[26] These differences between gold and T-bills arise from the two being at various times relatively more or less desirable as collateral for loans of money. Because the T-bill market and the gold market do not consistently display the same forward interest rates, two separate futures markets have developed.

The futures market for the Standard & Poor's Index of 500 stocks demonstrates the last point concerning inflexibilities and financial futures. Effectively only one S&P 500 Index contract is traded at a

---

[26] The Federal Reserve in early 1980 actively discouraged banks from lending to speculators in commodities. Hence the high capital costs for those carrying gold.

time. The last column of Table 6.4 gives the proportion of open interest in the various delivery months for this futures market. On the day used for the table, 1 August 1983, 85% of open interest in the S&P 500 Index was in the September contract. Virtually all other open interest was in the next contract, the December contract, even though contracts nominally stretched as far as the following December. This concentration is typical of stock index futures. It is even more pronounced when the first contract has three months to expiration instead of the two as of early August. Open interest peaks in the nearby contract just after the previous contract expires; then, as that contract too approaches expiration, it is "rolled over" into the next contract. In this cycle, one delivery month predominates. In some sense it is surprising that even one active futures contract in the S&P 500 Index is active. After all, a position in the S&P 500 Index can be constructed, to as close an approximation as desired, from spot positions in a portfolio of stocks. Actually, the S&P 500 Index futures contract dominates this spot index, because of its lower brokerage fees (.04% versus 1.0% to 2.0% per round turn),[27] higher liquidity, and lower margin requirements. (Regulators hesitated to approve trading in stock index futures because they would have much lower margin, 5% to 10% of value, than for stocks, normally 50% of value.) In effect, there is only one S&P 500 Index contract traded out of all the possible delivery dates, from immediate delivery to extremely distant delivery, namely the next expiring contract. Consistent with this interpretation is the unusual ratio of trading volume to open interest in stock index futures. In most commodities daily volume is on the order of one-fifth to one-third of open interest. Daily volume in stock index futures approaches twice the level of open interest. So far in their short histories the stock index futures are also unusual for the relative lack of trading by dealers, such as pension funds.[28] This suggests that stock index futures are valuable for their liquidity and ease of establishing positions rather than as a means of displaying a full array of prices for various dates of delivery. One contract at a time suffices for these purposes.[29]

---

[27] The futures contract for the index has another advantage, as noted by Jaffee (1984). As the individual stocks in the index change value, their proportion in the index changes. A spot index constructed from the stocks would incur the brokerage fees of these continuous small adjustments.

[28] *Wall Street Journal*, 10 August 1984.

[29] The great majority of contracts made for the future delivery of shares on the Stock Exchange of London (recall the discussion in Chapter 2 of this method of trading) are for a single delivery date, the next settlement of accounts. A larger array of delivery dates is not necessary.

Table 6.4. *Percentage of open interest as of 1 August 1983 in particular delivery months*

Month of delivery	Corn[a]	Chicago wheat	Sugar	Cocoa	Copper	Mark	T-bonds	S&P 500
September	16.2	26.7	4.2	21.4	43.7	88.5	53.8	84.7
October	nt[b]	nt	47.9	nt	nt	nt	nt	nt
December	56.5	54.4	nt	38.8	32.9	11.2	17.2	14.8
January '84	nt	nt	0.3	nt	0.7	nt	nt	nt
March	17.6	11.2	34.0	24.1	9.6	0.3	7.4	0.3
May	4.4	4.0	9.1	6.2	2.2	nt	nt	nt
June	nt	nt	nt	nt	nt	0.0	9.7	0.1
July	3.6	3.8	2.6	4.0	4.1	nt	nt	nt
September	0.4	0.0	0.5	3.8	3.2	0.0	5.5	0.1
October	nt	nt	1.3	nt	nt	nt	nt	nt
December	1.3	0.0	nt	1.7	1.5	0.0	3.1	0.1
January '85	nt	nt	0.0	nt	0.3	nt	nt	nt
March	0.0	0.0	0.0	0.0	1.2	0.0	1.5	0.0
May	0.0	0.0	0.0	0.0	0.7	nt	nt	nt
June	nt	nt	nt	nt	nt	0.0	0.7	0.0
September	0.0	0.0	0.0	0.0	0.0	0.0	1.0	0.0
December	0.0	0.0	nt	0.0	0.0	0.0	0.2	0.0
Total open interest	165,248	61,199	95,215	29,148	108,651	26,921	165,276	28,843
Percentage beyond January '84	27.3	18.9	47.5	39.8	22.7	0.3	29.0	0.5

[a]Including the Mid-America Exchange.
[b]Contract not traded.

Table 6.4 concerning the distribution of open interest across delivery months brings home the contrast between financial futures and agricultural futures.[30] The eight commodities in Table 6.4 were selected because they have many delivery months in common. What is most interesting in the table is the last row, the percentage of open interest in contracts maturing more than six months after 1 August 1983. As with the S&P 500 Index, virtually all trading in the West German mark is in nearby contracts. Among the financial futures the T-bond market alone trades a proportion close to that of the agricultural markets beyond maturities of six months. This is consistent with one market sufficing to display the distant forward term structure of interest rates on money. Among the agricultural commodities themselves, the pattern of breaks in the crop-year explain much of the variation in the proportion of open interest in more distant contracts. Open interest in corn, for example, is heavily concentrated in the first December contract, the first new-crop delivery month. The more distant December contract also has a reasonable percentage of the open interest, at least in comparison to the mark and S&P 500 Index. The crop-year in sugar is less precise than for corn, but both October and March represent important breaks. Not surprisingly, those two delivery months have much of the open interest in sugar. In Table 6.4 wheat falls off much faster than the other agricultural commodities. This is because early August falls just after the harvest and much before the next planting. As of early August there are few foreseeable and yet unadjustable breaks in the array of wheat futures prices. Accordingly, there is less need for the more distant contracts. Had open interest in wheat been shown for February, by which point planting would have been irrevocable and much of the effect of weather on the size and timing of the harvest would have been known, far more of the open interest would have been in distant contracts.

Similarly, much more open interest would appear in distant contracts if a date had been selected at which time particular commodities were in pronounced backwardation. For example, in early February 1980, a time at which copper prices were far below full carrying charges, 29% of open interest in copper was beyond contracts of six months, compared to the 23% of Table 6.4, August 1983 being a time of close to full carrying charges in copper. In January 1974, when copper prices were in extreme backwardation (recall Table 1.4), the

---

[30] A comparable table for daily volume would show the point even more forcefully than this one of open interest, since trading volume increases more than proportionately with open interest.

comparable figure was 37% of open interest. February 1980 was also a time of large and different premiums in the exchange rate between the dollar and the mark. Accordingly, there was more need for more distant delivery months for the mark. Compared to the 88.5% of the open interest in the nearest contract as of August 1983, only 57.7% was in the comparable contract in February 1980. Likewise in this period of 1980 when the term structure of interest rates was exceptionally steep, 54% of open interest in the T-bond market was in contracts beyond six months.[31]

For agricultural commodities, for which the production cycle is annual or even longer if crop rotation matters, adjustments cannot be completely flexible within less than a year. For copper shipped from Chile to England, adjustments are flexible after three months. For most other goods, however, the time required to alter production schedules or ship supplies from one place to another is much less. For the S&P 500 Index adjustments can be made almost immediately. The forward prices of these goods for delivery dates beyond a few weeks will be stably related because differences in the prices cannot persist. As a result there is no need for separate contracts for delivery dates more than a few weeks ahead. In other words, for most goods fully formed futures markets with many delivery dates stretching many months into the future are unnecessary. Futures markets are indispensable only for the goods whose inflexible production leads to differences in spreads over the intervening periods.

Although this section began by asking how far ahead futures trading should extend, it has ended by considering why particular goods have futures markets at all. The answer to both how far futures trading should extend and what goods should have futures markets is the same: Separate markets for future delivery are likely to emerge only as far forward as the spreads between contracts can be persistently different from a long-term average. For most goods this is a matter of days or weeks. Consequently, there is justification for formal futures markets on organized exchanges for only the few goods whose length ahead, L, is larger than a few months.

6.6.   Comparison with other explanations

This explanation of why so few goods have futures markets differs from the three existing theories of why futures markets exist in such

---

[31] Butterfly spreads involving distant contracts, initiated for postponing taxes, may overstate this figure for T-bonds, however. Changes in the tax laws have removed the advantage of such spreads.

small numbers. These three theories can be described loosely as
"price uncertainty," "costs of liquidity," and "informational content."
Each has a grain of truth for understanding futures markets. But on
comparison with the theory just presented each will appear to have
substantial weaknesses. None contradicts the theory offered here.
Rather all fail to uncover the cause of the number of markets. Their
explanations are incomplete.

The most common reason given for the existence of futures trading is the extent of fluctuations in the price of the commodity. For
those enamored with the theory of risk aversion and futures markets, a highly uncertain price creates more risk, increasing the need
for a futures market. If there is little price risk, there is little need
for a futures market. (Carlton [1984] has most recently summarized
this view of increasing price risk encouraging futures trading.) Carlton (1983b) also argues that the inflation of the 1970s helps explain
the noticeable growth of futures trading over that decade because
inflation brings with it large swings in relative prices even as all
prices rise. These swings in relative prices are an important source
of price risk.

Because those commodities with futures do fluctuate considerably
in value, this perspective of price uncertainty would seem to explain
why they have futures markets. Instead, the fluctuations in price are
a manifestation of the underlying cause. The fluctuations in price
occur because the supply of the good is inflexible for periods of
many months. It is this inflexibility and the speed of adjustments to
it that are the actual reasons for futures trading in the good. With
substantial inflexibility and a long period of adjustment, the price
for immediate delivery differs from near-term delivery and even
more from distant delivery. Consequently, there will be a need for
an institution that will provide these price signals for more accurate
direction of the good to its best temporal use. Even more important,
the spreads among these various delivery dates will change as conditions change, and the more volatile they are, the more there is the
need for a futures market. Because spot prices are variable whenever spreads are variable, it is easy to misperceive the importance of
price risk.

This distinction between price risk and inflexibilities as the reason
for futures markets, even if subtle, is important. To distinguish
them, imagine a situation in which the price of corn for delivery 10
days ahead is always equal to that for delivery 30 days, 90 days, 180
days, and even 360 days ahead. Within 10 days, in contrast, the price
is extremely volatile relative to the other delivery dates. According to

the price uncertainty perspective of futures markets, this volatility, which would imply extreme volatility in the spot price, would encourage an active futures market. But in fact the futures market would be dormant for deliveries beyond 10 days ahead. The futures market would much more likely be active if there were some variation in the relationships among the prices for delivery 30, 90, 180, and 360 days ahead. Volatility in such spreads depends on inflexibilities in supply and demand, foreseeable far in advance and yet unadjustable. The more volatile these distant spreads, the more likely futures trading is to flourish. Inevitably, volatile spreads among delivery dates several months from the present imply at least some volatility in the spot price. But the risk in the spot price is not the reason futures trading develops. Likewise, distinct futures markets in two locations for the same commodity or distinct futures markets in an input and an output emerge not because freight or processing for immediate execution are especially volatile in price but because a whole array of prices for services executed at different times needs expression. Futures markets express price differences, whether between inputs and outputs, two locations, or two delivery dates. When these price differences are volatile and distinct far in advance of the time of execution, futures markets flourish.

The second conventional explanation of the observed number of futures markets stresses the cost of illiquidity when a finite number of traders spread themselves over a large number of distinct contracts. Telser and Higinbotham (1977) use this concept of liquidity and the number of traders in a particular commodity in their empirical study of the existence of futures markets. Telser (1981) for one imagines that exchanges consciously limit trading to five or six delivery months to promote liquidity. If traders could choose among a hundred distinct contracts, say one for every week over the next two years, there would be so few buyers or sellers for any one contract that traders would spend an inordinate amount of time searching for someone with whom to deal. Similarly, whenever a trader would desire to close out his position he, unable to find many people to deal with, would be virtually at the mercy of the other party to his contract.

Although it is unquestionably true that because of manipulation, illiquidity, and high transactions costs a market cannot survive without a minimum number of traders, this factor is subsidiary to whether a futures price conveys any new information. The point is not that the costs of illiquidity do not matter to the number of futures markets. Rather the point is that Telser's argument tells

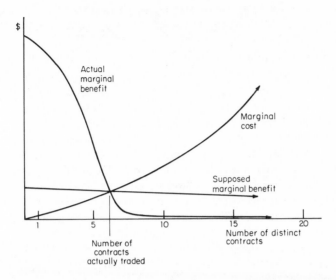

Figure 6.5. The costs and benefits of additional contracts

much less than the whole story. The nature of the dispute can be seen with the help of a diagram, like that shown previously as Figure 6.2, displaying the marginal costs and marginal benefits of distinct contracts, in this case Figure 6.5. (Once again contracts are not ranked along the horizontal axis by the months before delivery but by their marginal benefit.) The difference between the liquidity theory and that presented in this chapter concerns the shape of the curve representing the benefit of an additional contract (the benefit of contracts being measured as before in terms of their usefulness in allocating resources). No one can argue that additional contracts bring additional costs. At the very least an exchange must devote more bookkeeping, surveillance, and space in the pit to an additional delivery month. And as market makers and floor traders disperse themselves over more contracts, the bid-asked spread for a particular contract rises and the speed of execution falls. If such illiquidity increases more than proportionately to the number of contracts, as seems likely, the marginal cost curve will rise steeply, as in Figure 6.5. More problematic is how proponents of the liquidity theory would draw the marginal benefit curve. They do not say. Most likely Telser and others would draw the marginal benefit curve as a horizontal line or one with a slight downward slope. A contract for delivery of corn in December would be only slightly more useful

than a contract for November delivery or one for delivery the following December. The arguments about suppleness and inflexibility
presented in this chapter imply a very different marginal benefit
curve. The marginal benefit of contracts falls steeply, and beyond
some relatively small number of contracts it approaches zero. This
break occurs in the marginal benefit curve precisely where flexibility, keeping spreads in line, allows some contracts to substitute for
others. Only where there are persistent and predictable inflexibilities
are there significant benefits to additional contracts.

Unquestionably the marginal cost of illiquidity helps to determine
the number of contracts traded, as seen in Figure 6.5. If additional
contracts were costless, there would be an inclusive set of them.
Conversely, if the marginal cost of even the most beneficial contract
is extremely high, even that contract will not trade. In that sense, the
word "indispensable," sometimes used in this chapter, is inappropriate. No market is indispensable. Rather its marginal benefit must
justify its marginal cost. The word "indispensable" emphasizes that
some contracts have a substantially higher marginal benefit than
others, that the marginal benefit curve is steeply sloped, as a consideration of the nature of commodity processing, freight, and storage
indicates it must be. Because it is steeply sloped, mainly the marginal
benefit curve determines the economically justifiable number of contracts traded. If it shifted to the left, say because production or
processing became more flexible, the number of contracts might fall
to the point were full-fledged futures trading ceases. This is precisely what happened to the egg futures market. The egg futures
market of the Chicago Mercantile Exchange has not died because
the costs of trading had risen. Rather technical change in egg laying
removed an inflexible seasonal component in production, as noted
by Miracle (1972).

A comparison of the corn and oats markets confirms the relative
importance of the explanations offered. The corn futures market
has on the order of thirty to forty times the open interest and daily
volume of the oats market. With the marginal cost of contracts being
much lower because of the greater volume of trading, the liquidity
theory would anticipate a significantly larger number of contracts
traded in the corn market than in the oats market. In contrast, the
theory argued here would expect little difference in the number of
contracts, because the nature of the inflexibilities in corn and oats
are much the same. As it happens, depending on the time in the
crop-year, the oats markets offers four or five contracts and the corn
market five or six. In both markets the particular delivery months

mark important breaks in the crop-year. Despite the much greater
interest in trading corn contracts, there is need only for those contracts signifying the foreseeable inflexibilities in corn.[32]

The third and last competing explanation of the number of futures markets emphasizes the informational content of futures
prices, their role in price discovery. Much of the recent literature on
futures markets implies that they are primarily concerned with the
future and not with the present. Indeed, many pure theorists working on futures markets imagine them to be solely concerned with
expectations about the future. They begin with an assumption that a
spot market exists but that no storage market and no futures market
do. Then they add in the futures market, in an effort to see what
effect it has on the conveying of information. This approach is particularly pronounced in work on futures markets and their expression of so-called rational expectations. Much recent empirical work
on futures markets also presumes they exist to convey information
about the future. For example, Labys and Granger's study (1970:
89) was "to determine whether futures prices respond to changes in
market expectations, and, as such, anticipate cash prices."

Although it seems plausible to associate futures prices primarily
with the future, this emphasis on futures markets' expression of
expectations about the future is grounded on the mistaken assumption that there can be no explicit market for storage and use. If
there were a storage and use market in conjunction with a spot
market, there would be no need for an explicit futures market. The
spot market and storage and use market together would fully reflect
all information about the future.

Grossman, among others, has been instrumental in perpetuating
the notion that futures markets are concerned predominantly with
expectations about the future. In an influential article (1977) he
proposes that futures markets serve principally as a marketplace for
the exchange of information, arguing that there is an incentive to
trade futures contracts because some traders have information about
the future that others do not, information that uninformed traders
cannot deduce solely from the spot price. The futures price, according to Grossman, reveals to uninformed traders informed traders'
expectations about the next period's spot price. This feature of pub-

---

[32] Carlton (1983a) investigates the related question of whether the entire corn futures
market makes the entire oats futures market redundant. He too approaches the
subject from the perspective of the correlation between prices, concluding that the
oats futures market revived in the 1970s because oat prices began moving less
closely with corn prices than previously.

226 The economic function of futures markets

licly transmitted prices is what Grossman calls the informational role
of futures markets. But once futures prices transmit the informed
traders' expectations, there is no longer an incentive to trade futures
contracts. If, from observing some few traders eagerly selling futures contracts at a low price, other traders know those few know the
price will fall, the uninformed traders will stop trading. And because
the informed traders no longer find trading partners at attractive
prices, they lose their inducement to seek out information. Paradoxi-
cally, the futures market, explains Grossman, with its publicly visible
prices removes the very reason for its creation, different information
about prices. This problem, Grossman believes, is why so few futures
markets are active.

Grossman's view that futures markets both result from and
dampen the incentive to trade information runs counter to the common intuition that the more futures markets, the better. As it happens, Grossman's analysis suffers from a major flaw in his assumptions about the storage and use market. Grossman's whole model
depends on a disequilibrium in the storage and use market.[33]

Grossman, assuming not only that no futures market exists but
also that no storage and use market is operating, ascribes to the
introduction of futures markets the disequilibrium he himself builds
into the storage and use market.[34] There would be no apparent
benefits from a futures market if there were already a functioning
storage and use market. This point should be obvious, since a spot
market coupled with a storage and use market provides an implicit
futures market. An explicit futures market in that situation would be
redundant. A futures market could replace an explicit market for
storage by setting up an implicit market for storage in conjunction
with a spot market. Yet, regardless of whether the storage market is
explicit or implicit, Grossman is studying the benefits of a functioning storage market, which reallocates inventory until it has the same
storage and use charge everywhere, and not as he purports, the
special advantage of obtaining information about the future.

More important, the seemingly harmful effects on the incentives
to gather information, which Grossman associates with futures markets, are in no way unique to those institutions. If there were an
explicit, competitive storage market, all traders, whether informed
or uninformed, would have the same marginal storage costs. Hence

---

[33] I wish to thank Brian Wright for this observation.
[34] Grossman's confusion about the storage market can be seen in his notation for the
amount stored. He fails to make clear whether total storage costs are for an individual, a group such as informed traders, or all traders combined.

it would be an easy matter to compute from the current spot price the future spot price expected by the informed traders. Although Grossman is surely probing a sensitive area in the theory of markets, namely what happens to a trader's incentive to gather information if others refuse to trade with him whenever they suspect he knows something they do not know, the fact remains that this impasse can arise in a system without any futures markets, but with only spot and storage markets. If they know that he intends to buy their stock from them and store it himself in the expectation of profits based on something he alone knows, they are no more willing to sell on the spot than they are to sell a futures contract.

This tendency to associate futures primarily with information about the future comes in part from the observation that the futures price is a reasonable estimate of the spot price that will prevail in the future. At first glance, an equilibrium condition in which the price of a futures contract equals the expected price would seem to confirm rather than refute the relationship between futures prices and expectations about the future. However, an equilibrium condition demonstrates, first and foremost, not what one particular price equals but how all prices are related. If the price of storage and use were always to equal zero, the spot and futures price would be the same. Which price, then, would reflect expectations about the future? Clearly both would. Under more general conditions, all three prices – spot, loan, and futures – reflect expectations about the future. Accordingly, if new information about future conditions becomes known, not only the futures price but the spot and loan prices change. Indeed they must if they are to remain in equilibrium. For that matter, the futures price reflects current conditions just as much as the spot and loan prices. If a huge warehouse filled with cotton burned down, surely the spot price would not be the only price affected. The futures price would change as well because spot prices alone do not record information about current conditions any more than futures markets alone transmit information about the future. All prices reflect all relevant information, and if some other fact becomes known, it affects many prices. Futures contracts are necessary only to the extent information moves the array of prices differentially.

The problems with Grossman's analysis are endemic to numerous papers about futures markets (see, e.g., Cox [1976], Burns [1979], Bray [1981], Kawai [1983a], Turnovsky [1983], and Brannen and Ulveling [1984]). Far too many scholars assess the value of a futures market by supposing that a spot market already exists and examining the effect of introducing futures trading. Although one could well object to this procedure on the grounds that it assumes sophisticated spot markets antedate futures markets, which is not necessarily the case, one should object far more strongly to the unstated assumption of the absence of a functioning storage and use market. If there were already a storage market in addition to a spot market, the introduction of futures trading would have no effect on allocations and prices. Thus, all begin by assuming that prices are not in equilibrium, although that would not be the case if an explicit market existed for holding commodities over time. And all ascribe to futures markets the benefits of removing that disequilibrium. Because the unstated assumption of the impossibility of an explicit storage and use market is untenable, the whole procedure is fallacious and an extremely misleading indicator of the reasons particular futures markets exist. If more commodities had formal loan markets housed in exchanges, few people would be misled to study expectations or markets in information instead of the advantages of an organized market per se.

6.7.   Summary: Economically justifiable futures markets

An inclusive set of markets would include a market for every imaginable delivery date, location, grade, and any other distinguishing characteristic for a particular commodity. In 1876 the Liverpool Cotton Exchange, for example, distinguished contracts by the month of delivery, the time of sailing, the type of ship (sail or steam), the crop (new or old), and the grade.[35] The relevant economic issue, however, is which of these separate markets are economically justifiable.

Because markets exist to communicate prices, an explicit market is useful only when the price cannot be learned somewhere else to an approximation sufficient for most purposes. This logic excludes most of what would make up a complete set of markets. Separate futures markets for different locations are not necessary because futures prices in various locations inevitably settle into a stable relationship. That cleaning and drying to change grades is easily done given sufficient time makes separate futures markets for different grades rarely necessary. Separate contracts for many delivery dates are rarely necessary because differences in the price of storage from a long-term average are rarely persistent and predictable, at least beyond the time producers can increase planned production substantially.

[35] *New York Post,* 19 October 1876.

In fact the list of economically justifiable markets is short. The market system must communicate only these prices explicitly: spot prices for various grades and varieties, although in a few cases such as wheat forward prices of several varieties may be indispensable; local prices for present storage and use; a central market's prices for future delivery, with delivery dates only for those months where there is a significant change in the supply or demand for loans, such as at harvest time or the opening of navigation; and prices in the central market no farther ahead than complete flexibility is possible, which means, in practice, few explicit prices for delivery beyond a year or two.

Although the list of economically justifiable markets is short, particularly when compared to a list of a complete set of markets, the absence of many prices in no way implies a failure on the part of the market system. The great majority of the missing prices are implicit in and easily calculated from the few explicit prices. Indeed, a concentration of trading in truly important markets is optimal, because in that manner liquidity is increased and transactions costs are kept to a minimum.

CHAPTER 7

Conclusion: The economic function of futures markets

Long popular as a stylized representation of the reasons that a handler of commodities uses futures markets is the picture of a miller who sells a futures contract because he is concerned with the fluctuating value of his inventory of wheat. If the spot and futures prices of wheat rise by the same amount, he loses on his short position in futures what he gains in the value of his inventory, and if prices fall, the reverse happens. Because the net is zero regardless of the way the prices move, it is as if the miller has bought insurance against movements in price. Although those dealers actually using futures markets as well as scholars closely studying them know that this stylized representation distorts reality, not least because spot and futures prices do not move in parallel, they insist on employing it, maintaining that it conveys the essential purpose of futures markets.

After observing actual hedging in futures contracts as transactions done simultaneously with those in other markets and examining the reasons dealers hold inventories, it becomes clear that this standardized representation does much worse than ignore a few subtleties of actual hedging practices. The stylized representation of a miller wanting price insurance is fundamentally wrong, and it misrepresents the function of futures markets. Futures markets are not about price insurance.

Others, of course, have proposed explanations of futures markets to replace the simple price insurance view. But for its part, the theory of futures markets as markets for information also misrepresents futures markets, because all markets, not just futures markets, convey information about the future. The liquidity theory is based on too extreme a dichotomy between futures contracts and forward contracts. In contrast to the price insurance theory, the information theory, and the liquidity theory, the primary purpose of futures markets is to serve as markets for implicit loans of commodities.

7.1. The role of risk

The interpretation of the purpose of futures markets hinges on which inflexibilities and nonlinearities are important in the economic

230

system. The conventional analysis based on the view of risk aversion maintains that the principal nonlinearity in the world is in the preferences of commodity dealers toward risk. The view advanced here is that the important convexities are much deeper in the system, and arise from the high proportion of fixed costs in processing operations, the substantial increases in costs to move or process commodities quickly, the extreme inflexibility tied to the cycle of the crop-year in the supply of agricultural commodities, and the limits on the management capacity of firms. These nonlinearities in production and processing are ignored entirely in presentations of futures markets as markets for price insurance. Regardless of whether firms have nonlinearities in their utility functions, the nonlinearities in production are what are important to futures markets. It may well be that the risk aversion of the final consumers induces the pressure to move and process commodities quickly, yet the fact remains that even commodity dealers who are risk neutral have reason to use futures markets, and it is dealers' use of futures markets that is of interest.

All this is not to say that risk has nothing to do with futures markets. On the contrary, the riskiness in agricultural production, transport, and processing has much to do with the reason firms hold inventories and use futures contracts. Because of the large fixed investments in operations like milling, the riskiness in the availability of material is sufficient to trouble the managers of the firm regardless of whether they feel any particular aversion toward risk. These risks in the availability of raw material are unlike the individual risks at the center of the portfolio theory, which presumes that individuals who diversify, pool, or otherwise transfer their own risky position to others can together eliminate most of the risk. The important risks in commodities, however, are much harder to diversify. A small harvest of wheat affects all millers in the region, and pooling that risk among them will not reduce it. An ice jam affects all the region's shippers. Consequently, the perspectives of price insurance and the portfolio theory at their best apply poorly to commodity markets.

Even if a firm is risk neutral in the sense of its preferences, it is called upon to make many decisions in an uncertain world. It is always forced to gamble on whether it should obtain a loan of its raw material far in advance or wait, hoping that prices will move in its favor. A gamble is inevitable in the size of the stock it chooses, and the duration of its loan, whether for three months or for six months. It can never be sure while using its reserve of raw materials that a greater emergency will not arise moments later. These business decisions about inventories are comparable to those about the choice between long-term and short-term financing, the choice of the amount of money to borrow, and the choice of arranging some of the financing in advance. With inventories, as with money, many of the choices will prove wrong, and some firms will be consistently wiser than others. Yet simply because there are business risks involved does not necessarily mean that risk aversion is dominant in explaining the responses firms take.

Nor is all this to say that firms are not risk averse. The point is that the great part of what is interesting, at least about commodity prices, can be explained without the analytical complication of risk aversion, whatever are the actual preferences of firms toward risk. After all, significant advances have been made in understanding the demand for money with the simplifying assumption that firms are risk neutral. When modeling the complex behavior of commodity firms, one can present a simplified view of the technology and scope of the firms in trade for a more complex view of their preferences toward risk, or one can emphasize the complexities of technology and scope of firms while presenting a simplified view of preferences toward risk. This second approach allows more insight into the behavior of commodity markets.

In any case, even if risk aversion were added to the analysis, it is not at all clear that firms would use futures markets more as opposed to less. Given that the firm already owns a flour mill, its first response to risk aversion might be to increase the amount of wheat it borrows, accepting the certain loss of the premium for borrowing as a means of reducing the chance of high shortage costs. If the miller borrows wheat implicitly through the double transaction of buying spot and selling for future delivery, his added borrowings will increase his use of futures markets. In any case, the analysis of risk aversion indicates that a risk-averse miller would want to add long positions in forward wheat to his predetermined position in milling, which he would do by selling fewer futures contracts against his inventory. Whether the net effect on the use of futures markets is positive or negative depends on the particular circumstances of that flour miller. He could well make less use of futures markets if he were averse to risk.

7.2.   Tests of the various theories

However convincing is the argument that a theory of futures markets can be constructed without recourse to the complication of risk aversion, more is required to displace the view of futures contracts as insurance against fluctuating prices. If one theory tightly fits all observed behavior while the others fail to explain some crucial fact, clearly that one is the strongest theory. But because motivations are inherently unsusceptible to measurement, it might seem impossible to gather evidence to test any theory of why dealers in commodities use futures markets. Even so, particular theories imply particular results in the observable behavior in commodity markets.

Previous pages have presented many facts, often unimportant in themselves, about commodity markets, and it is time to draw that evidence together. It concerns the terminology of traders, the number of active futures markets, the delivery months actively traded, industrywide inventory behavior, the extent of bias in futures prices, the patterns in spreads, and such seemingly unrelated institutions as grain banks. Collectively this evidence provides overwhelming support for the view that the function of futures markets is to serve as implicit loan markets for commodities.

To review, the evidence is strongly against theories of futures markets based on risk aversion. In the first place, study after study has failed to find a significant bias in futures prices, let alone a bias of the magnitude required by the theory of normal backwardation. In addition, the theory of normal backwardation cannot explain the observed patterns and volatility of spreads between futures prices. The conclusion of little or no bias in futures prices also casts doubt on the portfolio theory of hedging, which also requires a bias in futures prices. Second, and more important, the observed negative correlation between the return to milling and the return to holding wheat, for instance, implies that a risk-averse miller would want to hold wheat along with his predetermined position in milling, or, in other words, that a risk-averse miller would choose to leave some of his inventory of wheat unhedged. In contradiction to this fact, the portfolio theory of hedging presumes as the starting point of its analysis that risk aversion induces dealers like millers to hedge their inventories with sales of futures contracts. Thus, even on their own terms the theory of normal backwardation and the portfolio theory of hedging are flawed because their basic assumptions are incorrect. In much the same manner, the liquidity theory is suspect in its presumption of a gulf between futures contracts and forward contracts that does not exist.

Because no futures market has long survived without interest from handlers of the particular commodity, the majority of whom use futures contracts in association with their inventories, it follows

that the reasons futures markets exist derive from the reasons
dealers hold inventories. Consequently, it must be counted against
the liquidity theory of futures markets that it offers no explanation
of dealers' inventory practices. The liquidity theory is more properly
viewed as a statement about the difficulty of operating actual markets. It does not stand by itself, explaining only the relative costs of
alternative systems of markets. A broader theory is needed to explain why any system of markets is needed or why firms follow
particular inventory practices, which are perplexing to say the least
because of the persistence of storage in the face of spreads below full
carrying charges. Although the theories of normal backwardation
and the portfolio theory of hedging put forth an explanation of the
use of futures markets given a dealer's level of inventory, they too
offer no reason why the dealer was holding commodities in the first
place. On the other hand, the theory of the supply of storage, as
developed by Working, addresses precisely this issue, answering that
it is as if dealers are supplying the service, which they are willing to
do at times at a negative return because of the convenience yield of
holding inventories. And plots of the so-called price of storage
(which is the spread between the appropriate spot price and the
futures price) against actual holdings of many different commodities
display exactly the regular relationships predicted by this theory.
The theory of implicit loan markets is an expansion of the theory of
the supply of storage, delving into the reasons firms will hold inventories at a seeming loss. Besides suggesting that the supply of storage
is better understood as a demand for accessibility, the theory of
implicit loan markets makes clearer that dealers use futures contracts as part of a more complex set of transactions through which
they borrow commodities. It also explains why they should borrow
rather than own outright.

What the theory of the supply of storage fails to emphasize, and
what the other theories ignore entirely, is that dealers' transactions
in futures markets are conducted simultaneously with other transactions. Contrary to the representation in the theories of normal backwardation and the portfolio theory of hedging, a firm does not first
buy its inventory on the spot market, and then, after contemplating
the riskiness of its position, hedge with a short sale of a futures
contract. Rather, it conceives of and executes the two trades as if
they were one, as seen in the widespread practice of basis trading in
which traders discuss only the difference between the spot price and
the futures price. This pattern of behavior is perfectly consistent
with the theory of implicit loans, in which the principal tenet is that

these various combinations of transactions implicitly amount to the explicit position of borrowing a commodity.

An examination of the particular commodities with active futures markets compared to those with none is less helpful in distinguishing one theory from another. While the theory of implicit loan markets predicts that those commodities with inflexibilities in production, transportation, and processing are most likely to develop active futures trading, the insurance view of futures markets would predict that those with the most volatile prices would have futures markets. Unfortunately, inflexibilities in supply and demand, by their nature, imply large changes in spot prices. There are, however, no active futures markets in commodities without major inflexibilities, as the predominance of agricultural commodities on the roster of futures markets best demonstrates.

Although the evidence of the roster of active futures markets can only weakly distinguish among the various theories, the particular delivery months for each active futures market provide a powerful test. The theory of implicit loans alone accounts for the observed delivery months. While the insurance view of futures markets has little to say about the number of delivery months to be expected, in part because presentations of the theory rarely consider in which contract to place the hedge, the number of delivery months is central to the liquidity theory, which claims that ordinary futures exchanges deliberately restrict the number of contracts traded in order to increase liquidity. The theory of implicit loan markets adds to the liquidity theory the further prediction that the particular calendar months will be those marking breaks in the cycle of production and demand for the commodity, and in any case will not stretch beyond a year or so, a length of time that coincides with a substantial increase in the flexibility of supply. This pattern of delivery months is exactly that found in futures markets, especially the oldest markets like the grains that developed with no conscious control on the part of the Chicago Board of Trade. Moreover, when traders were offered a wide selection of delivery months, as in the cotton markets of the 1880s, they gravitated toward months demarking the important breaks in the crop-year.

Another point of evidence in favor of the theory of implicit loan markets, and against the insurance view of futures markets in particular, is the terminology of commodity markets itself. The term "hedge" with its suggestion of risk aversion became current long after futures markets developed, and it is alien to all other idioms. On the other hand, terms like "contract for future delivery at the seller's option as to time," "to arrive sometime hence," and "on the spot," besides conforming to one another, naturally express the exercises in inventory control underlying the theory of implicit loan markets.

At one time or another explicit markets have existed for the borrowing and lending of a wide range of commodities, from grain, to shares of stock, to uranium, often in place of futures markets. The imagination need not stretch far to conceive of these institutions in place of all futures markets. Although the various theories are intended to explain futures markets, they should be able to allow for such changes in institutional forms. Yet, with the exception of the theory of implicit loans, none of the theories of futures can accommodate explicit loan markets. The possibility of explicit loan markets is especially damaging to the theory of futures markets as markets for information, since explicit loan markets remove any direct informational role for futures markets. Likewise, all theories, besides that of implicit loans, can find no place for institutions like grain banks, which might well have been the dominant institution in the grain trade had the citizens of Illinois not resisted fractional reserve banking in grain.

In short, the evidence supports one and only one theory. The function of futures markets is to serve as implicit loan markets for commodities. Loan markets, whether for money or for commodities, allocate scarce inventories to the firms whose need for them is greatest at the moment. Through the hurly-burly of futures trading, prices emerge, with remarkable order and allocative sophistication, for interest rates on commodity loans.

7.3.   A stylized representation of the function of futures markets

In place of a risk-averse miller wanting price insurance for the value of his inventory, a more accurate stylized representation of the usefulness of futures markets is that of a risk-neutral miller who is worried about interruptions in his supply of wheat. To avoid the costs of his equipment standing idle, he calculates that it would be worthwhile to pay for at least some access to a secure supply of raw material. One way of obtaining temporary access to wheat would be to borrow wheat from someone else for a period of time, paying as it were an interest rate to borrow wheat. The other person is content to lend his wheat because the miller is willing to pay more to have it on hand temporarily. If it happened that the miller did not need the wheat, he could return it. On the other hand, if he needed the wheat suddenly, he could use it immediately. Of course, he would have to find other wheat of the same grade to return to the lender, but he would have the remaining period of the loan to do so. Another way of accomplishing a loan would be for the miller and the lender to write their compact in terms of a repurchase agreement, stipulating that the party with the wheat sell it to the miller forthwith and that the original owner repurchase the wheat some time later at a price fixed in advance. Regardless of the price of wheat, the price for the repurchase part of the agreement will be set lower than the original purchase. Through this difference in price the miller pays the use charge, that is, interest on the wheat. From his perspective it does not matter that he dealt with one party or two. Once he has bought the wheat, he has a contract for the future delivery of wheat. In the jargon of futures markets, he is a short hedger because he has sold a futures contract against his inventory of wheat. Thus, the miller goes short in futures contracts, in combination with his simultaneous spot purchase of wheat, in order to borrow wheat implicitly.

Even if stylized, this representation of the function of futures markets should redirect research on them. The function of futures markets is closely related to the function of money markets. Many of the issues arising in the study of money markets could be profitably pursued in the setting of commodity markets. For example, one could investigate much more carefully the transformation costs involved in processing commodities quickly and hence understand better the demand for inventories. One could also investigate the capabilities of futures markets as the equivalent of financial intermediaries, and their relative advantages compared to explicit loan markets. One could also investigate the behavior of commodity interest rates, both over time and as a term structure at any one time. Few institutions offer the theoretical and empirical challenges of futures markets.

Glossary of trade terms

Actuals: The term actuals encompasses all transactions in a commodity, whether for immediate or deferred delivery, that are not futures contracts (q.v.). Contrary to the implication of the term itself, a seller of actuals need not actually own the commodity, although most often he does.

Arbitrage: Arbitrage is the purchase in one market at a low price while simultaneously selling at a higher price in another market, that price more than covering the relevant transportation expenses, storage fees, interest costs, and so forth. Among commodity traders, arbitrage is sometimes used as a synonym for the risky position of a straddle (q.v.) or spread (q.v.). The term arbitrage is better reserved for those combinations of positions without any risk. Under that definition the phrase risk arbitrage is a contradiction.

Backwardation: A backwardation occurs when the price of a good for later delivery stands below the price of that good for earlier delivery. Of British origin, the term arose from the practice of continuing obligations from one delivery period to another. If a seller wanted to postpone delivery until the next balancing of accounts, he induced the buyer to take later delivery by paying him a fee called a backwardation. Compare with *inverse carrying charges* and contrast with *contango*.

Basis: Basis describes the difference from some other price, one commodity's price being "based" on the price of another commodity. Usually this second commodity is a futures contract (q.v.). Thus, the basis price is like a premium over (or discount under) the price of the futures contract. The basis can refer to location and grade as well as time.

Bear straddle: A bear straddle is a straddle (q.v.) in which the nearer futures contract (q.v.) is the short position (q.v.) while the more distant contract is the long position (q.v.). A bear straddle commits a trader first to deliver a commodity and then to receive it back. Sometimes a bear straddle is called a "bear spread" or a "back spread." Compare with *bull straddle* and *butterfly spread*.

Bucket shop: (1) A bucket shop is a small brokerage house that takes positions opposite those of its clients, rather than acting as a commission merchant (q.v.) to arrange deals with other parties on their behalf. The bucket shop hopes that orders to buy nearly equal those to sell so that it ends up with a negligible position itself. By keeping its margin (q.v.) requirements low and allowing a small minimum order, it seeks the small-time trader.

238

(2) When a regular brokerage house matches orders internally rather than letting everyone on the floor of the exchange bid for them, it too is said to bucket orders.

Bull straddle: A bull straddle is a straddle (q.v.) in which the nearer futures contract (q.v.) (the near leg) is a long position (q.v.), while the more distant contract (the far leg) is a short position (q.v.). Thus, a bull straddle commits a trader first to receive a commodity and then to deliver it. A bull straddle can be constructed from two separate transactions in futures contracts or from one with a trader who specializes in straddles. Compare with *bear straddle* and *butterfly spread*.

Butterfly spread: A butterfly spread is the combination of a bull straddle (q.v.) and a bear straddle (q.v.). One of the futures contracts (q.v.) in the bull straddle overlaps with one of the contracts in the bear straddle, so that a butterfly spread has, for example, one long (q.v.) contract for May delivery, two short (q.v.) contracts for July delivery, and one long contract for September delivery. If plotted, these positions would look like the shape of a butterfly from the front.

Call: A type of option (q.v.), a call gives its taker the right, but not the obligation, of buying from another party at a price specified in the contract. If the privilege is exercised, however, the maker of the call has the obligation to sell. Contrast with *put*.

Carrying charge: See *spread*.

Cash: Cash refers to prompt payment with currency or its equivalent. Because most contracts call for payment on delivery, a purchase with immediate delivery is often said to be at the "cash price." Sometimes, however, cash price refers to deals with neither immediate delivery nor immediate payment. In this sense, however, cash, as well as its synonym actuals (q.v.), is meant solely to contrast with futures contracts (q.v.).

CIF: CIF is an abbreviation meaning a good has arrived with "cost, insurance, and freight" paid by the seller of the good. The buyer, however, must assume the additional charges of getting the good into his warehouse or on board a vessel. Contrast with *FOB* and compare with *on track*.

Clearinghouse: Begun as central locations where the the clerks of the members of clearing associations met to balance accounts, clearinghouses have evolved into adjuncts of exchanges dealing in futures contracts (q.v.). An exchange's clearinghouse settles transactions executed on the floor of the exchange through a process of matching sales and purchases. It also oversees delivery procedures, including the recording of delivery notices (q.v.) and the passing of warehouse receipts (q.v.).

Clearing member: Some futures commission merchants (q.v.), in addition to being members of a commodity exchange, are members of the exchange's clearinghouse (q.v.). All trades of nonclearing members must be registered and eventually settled through a clearing member.

Commission merchant: A commission merchant buys and sells for others. His function could involve little more than executing a transaction on the floor of an exchange of which he is a member. On the other hand, he might assume the responsibility of handling goods on consignment (q.v.), overseeing in turn their arrival in town, inspection, placement into storage, and sale or transshipment depending on the owner's instructions. In all cases, he is acting as the agent for his principal (q.v.) and does not himself take title to the goods, except in the case of negotiable instruments like warehouse receipts (q.v.), which belong to the party in physical possession.

Consignment: A consignment is a good given over to another's care. See *commission merchant.*

Contango: Of British origin, contango describes the situation where the price of a good for later delivery is higher than that of the same good for earlier delivery. The term arose from the practice of continuing obligations from one accounting period to another. Contrast with *backwardation.*

Contract grade: For each futures contract (q.v.), an exchange designates a particular grade of the commodity eligible for delivery. Some exchanges set premiums and discounts for delivery of grades other than the contract grade, which in consequence is sometimes known as the "par grade." Sometimes several grades are eligible as the contract grade, although shorts (q.v.) will usually find it advisable to use only one. Delivery must be made at one of the official delivery points (q.v.).

Corner: A corner occurs when a few people gain control of all available supplies of a good, thereby being in a position to sell at inflated prices and to force other parties who had promised to deliver that good, but who can no longer do so, to pay heavy damages to the cornerers. See *squeeze.*

Crush: Far from implying romance, crush refers to the process by which soybeans are converted to soybean meal and soybean oil. To "put on the crush" is a complex spread (q.v.) among futures contracts (q.v.), specifically multiples of long (q.v.) 10 soybean contracts, short (q.v.) 12 meal contracts, and short 9 oil contracts. This complex spread amounts to the forward sale of the service of crushing. A "reverse crush," which reverses these three positions, long and short, amounts to a forward purchase of the service.

Day trader: A day trader holds a position only during the day, liquidating it before the close of trading in order to have no exposure overnight. Thus, a day trader hopes to profit from moves in price over the course of several hours. A scalper (q.v.), in contrast, holds positions for a matter of minutes.

Delivered: See *FOB.*

Delivery month: The delivery month on a futures contract (q.v.) is the span of time during which the short (q.v.) must make delivery, the exact day being at the short's option. As commodity markets have evolved, the first notice day and the last notice day do not always span an exact calendar month, although the span is called "May," "June," etc., for convenience. See *delivery notice.*

Delivery notice: A short (q.v.) in a futures contract (q.v.) makes written notice to the clearinghouse (q.v.) and through the clearinghouse to a long (q.v.) of his intention to make delivery of the physical commodity in order to settle his contract. Usually a day or two following his delivery notice, the short passes the commodity or warehouse receipt (q.v.).

Delivery points: Commodity exchanges designate the locations delivery can be made in order to settle a futures contract (q.v.). For example, the soybean contract of the Chicago Board of Trade can be settled with delivery at either Chicago or Toledo, Ohio.

Exchange for physicals: An exchange for physicals, often abbreviated EFP, is a transaction in futures contracts (q.v.) between two dealers in commodities conducted away from the trading floor of the futures market. For example, a dealer in copper may have a quantity of scrap and a short (q.v.) position in a futures contract. Another dealer, wanting to buy copper scrap, might hold a long (q.v.) position in the same contract. As the first dealer delivers the scrap to the second, they cancel their futures contracts themselves. In grain markets, this type of transaction is called "ex pit," while in some other markets it is an "exchange for product."

Ex pit: See *exchange for physicals.*

Floor traders: A floor trader, a member of a commodity exchange, trades for his own account, rather than acting as a broker for others as does a futures commission merchant (q.v.). Most floor traders are scalpers (q.v.) or day traders (q.v.). They are also referred to as "locals."

FOB: FOB abbreviates the phrase "free on board." It means that the charges for placing a good on board ship are assumed by the seller of that good. When the buyer assumes title, he is responsible only for the price of the good. "Delivered" is much the same as FOB except that the seller would be responsible for the charges of getting the good into a warehouse rather than on board a ship. Contrast both with *CIF* and *on track.*

Forward contract: In its most general sense a forward contract is any agreement calling for the execution of some act in the future, including, but not limited to, futures contracts (q.v.). Sometimes the term is used to refer to those contracts containing conditions tailored to the particular needs of the contracting parties rather than to the standardized terms of a futures contract.

Full carrying charges: When a spread (q.v.) exactly covers the warehouse fees, insurance premiums, and capital expenses of holding the commodity, it is said to be at full carrying charges.

Futures commission merchant: A futures commission merchant specializes in buying and selling futures contracts (q.v.) for his clients. See *commission merchant.*

Futures contract: Futures contract abbreviates the phrase "contract for future delivery." It usually refers to one of the standardized contracts traded in high volume on a central exchange. Compare and contrast with *forward contract.*

Hedge: A hedge is the position taken in futures contracts (q.v.) by a dealer in commodities. When a dealer buys a futures contract, his position is called a long hedge. When he sells a futures contract, he has a short hedge.

Hedger: Hedger is the term applied to dealers in commodities who take a position in futures contracts (q.v.).

Inverse carrying charges: Also known as backwardations (q.v.), inverse carrying charges occur when the nearby delivery months (q.v.) have higher prices than those of futures contracts (q.v.) for later delivery.

Leg: A leg refers to one of the two positions constituting a spread (q.v.) or straddle (q.v.).

Limit move: Commodity exchanges and the Commodity Futures Trading Commission limit the maximum advance or decline in price from the closing price the previous day. When prices are "limit up" or "limit down," either sellers or buyers find the price unrealistic, and trading ceases. Limit moves have nothing to do with the term limit order (q.v.).

Limit order: In contrast to a market order (q.v.), a limit order specifies conditions under which a broker may execute a trade. For example, a broker executes a limit order to sell at $1.10 only if the price rises that far or higher. Contrast with *stop order.*

Margin: Margin is a deposit, usually of money or exceptionally safe and liquid assets like Treasury bills, that secures the execution of a contract. With a contract for future delivery, there is a chance that either the buyer or seller might default if the market price moves against him, so it is customary for both parties to the deal to deposit a set sum called "original margin." When the price changes, a margin call (q.v.) is made. Additional funds called "variation margin" are required from the party against whom the price has moved so that the contract remains secure.

Margin call: If prices move against his customer, the futures commission merchant (q.v.) demands additional funds, otherwise known as margin (q.v.), in order to ensure the performance of futures contracts (q.v.) that the broker has initiated on the customer's behalf. If the customer fails to meet the margin call, the broker can close out the position.

Market order: A market order instructs a commission merchant (q.v.) to buy (or sell) as soon as possible with no restrictions, except that he make a reasonable effort to obtain the best price. Contrast with *limit order.*

Marking to market: (1) Marking to market is a practice adopted to ensure that in the face of volatile prices the obligations of buyers and sellers are met. The effect of marking to market is to renegotiate a contract by readjusting the margin (q.v.) to equal the difference between the original price of a contract and its current market price. (2) Marking to market is also used to refer to the accounting convention of relisting all assets or liabilities at their current worth.

Offset: To offset means to eliminate a position in futures contracts (q.v.) by an opposite transaction. The sale of a contract for the same delivery month (q.v.) offsets a long position previously taken, just as a purchase offsets a short (q.v.) position.

On track: On track refers to goods in which the buyer must assume the tranfer fees for moving the good from the rail yard to its destination. Compare with *CIF* and *FOB.*

Open interest: Open interest refers to the number of futures contracts (q.v.) outstanding at a particular moment, that is, the number of contracts that have not been canceled by an offsetting trade. The official figures give the open interest at the close of each day's trading.

Option: An option is a contract allowing one of the parties to choose whether he proceeds with the agreement. Thus, an option is a conditional contract. Although futures contracts (q.v.) are unconditional contracts, they are sometimes, as was the case especially in the late nineteenth century, referred to as options, because the short (q.v.) has the option of the exact day of delivery during a delivery month (q.v.). See *privilege.*

Original margin: See *margin.*

Pit: A trading pit is a specially constructed set of steps, usually hexagonal, on the floor of a commodity exchange. On some exchanges this area is called a "ring" after the circular restraining bar.

Principal: A principal is the individual ultimately responsible for paying for a purchase or delivering on a sale. He will often appoint a commission merchant (q.v.) to act as his agent.

Privilege: A privilege is a contract in which one of the parties may choose whether or not to proceed with the rest of an agreement. Option (q.v.), a term synonymous with privilege, is more common in modern usage. For examples of privileges and options, see *put, call,* and *put-and-call.*

Put: A type of option (q.v.), a put gives its taker the right but not the obligation of selling to another party at a price specified in a contract. The maker of the put, on the other hand, has the obligation to buy if the privilege is exercised. Contrast with *call.*

Put-and-call: A put-and-call is a type of option allowing its holder to call a commodity from or to put the commodity to the person selling the option. Because a call (q.v.) is the right to buy and a put (q.v.) the right to sell, a put-and-call gives the right, but not the obligation, to buy or sell at a price specified in a contract.

Repurchase agreement: A repurchase agreement (repo, for short) is a type of contract in which a party sells a commodity (or bonds, or shares of stock) to another, and commits himself to buy the commodity or its equivalent back at a later date at a stipulated price. The purchase and repurchase prices need not be the same. In essence, a repurchase agreement amounts to a double loan, one party obtaining temporary use of the commodity, the other temporary use of money.

Ringing up: Ringing up is a method of settling (q.v.) contracts. If a person has sold to another, and he to another, who in turn has sold to the first person, their transactions form a ring. The members of a ring agree, in the interest of economy since the good will come right back to where it started, to cancel their contracts and pay only the differences in their obligations.

Rollover: A rollover postpones an obligation either to take or make delivery, most often in the case of futures contracts (q.v.). The existing position is liquidated and simultaneously reinstated in another delivery month (q.v.). This is accomplished either by (1) taking a position in a contract that offsets, and in effect cancels, an immediate obligation while opening the equivalent in the more distant delivery month, or by (2) arranging the appropriate straddle (q.v.). In this most common sense, rollover implies the special class of a "roll forward," namely rolling a nearby futures contract into a more distant contract. "Roll back," contrary to natural usage, means to roll a futures contract for distant delivery into a nearer month. A transfer (q.v.) is a rollover when the contract is just about to expire.

Scalper: A scalper tries to buy just a little below the market price and to sell just a little above it by anticipating the direction of price changes. At other times, scalpers act as wholesalers, buying (or selling) a large order and then breaking it into smaller amounts. A scalper holds his position for only a few minutes and hopes to make a small amount of money on each of many trades.

Settlement price: A settlement price is a price selected to be typical of prices at a particular time of day, which provides a standard for the payment of differences, the application of variation margin (q.v.), and the invoice price for physical deliveries. Usually the settlement price is the closing price.

Settling: In its most general sense, settling refers to the actions taken to fulfill a contract. For example, the delivery of warehouse receipts (q.v.) settles a contract for future delivery of grain.

Short: Short describes the market position of someone who has sold something, usually a futures contract (q.v.).

Short selling: Short selling is the selling of a good that has not yet been bought. A short seller hopes that the price of the good will fall, so that when he buys the good to deliver, it will be at a price lower than that at which he has sold it.

Speculator: In commodity markets the term speculator is a catchall for anyone who does not handle the commodity and who hopes to profit from movements in price. In practice some dealers do, in fact, speculate.

Spot: The term spot refers to a good that is right at hand, and so available for immediate delivery. When the good is delivered immediately, the price paid for that good is said to be the "spot price."

Spot month: Spot month refers to the futures contract (q.v.) whose delivery month (q.v.) is closest to the present. It is the next contract to expire. Because not all twelve months are covered in, for example, the wheat futures market, there being only March, May, July, September, and December, in early April the contract for May delivery is designated as the spot month. See *spot.*

Spread: A spread is the difference between the price of a good for two different dates of delivery or at two different locations. The term is also used to describe the trades necessary to achieve such an implicit position in the market, for example, by the purchase of a near-term futures contract (q.v.) along with the sale of a distant-term futures contract. The difference in price between later delivery and earlier delivery is the "carrying charge" for that commodity, which in the extreme is at full carrying charges (q.v.). See *straddle.*

Stop order: A stop order is put in place to protect a profit or limit a loss. Owning a commodity currently selling for $1.00, a trader might place a stop order at $.90 in order to liquidate his position if prices fell. A limit order (q.v.), in contrast, would be above the current price. If the trader were a short (q.v.) instead of a long (q.v.), the limit order would be below the current price and the stop order above it.

Squeeze: A squeeze is a form of corner (q.v.) that involves the long (q.v.) taking advantage of his dominant position in futures contracts (q.v.) quite apart from his holdings of the physical commodity itself.

Straddle: Straddle is a synonym for spread (q.v.), which refers to the simultaneous taking on of both a long (q.v.) and a short (q.v.) position in futures contracts (q.v.). In options markets (q.v.), straddle has the quite different meaning of a put-and-call (q.v.).

Switch: Switch is a synonym for rollover (q.v.).

Transfer: When a futures contract (q.v.) comes due, the seller can postpone delivery by transferring his obligation into a later month. Often in practice he buys back his contract and sells one calling for delivery in a later month. By this operation, he pays (or receives, as the case may be) the difference between the prices for these two delivery dates. See *rollover*.

Transitu: Transitu describes the sale of a good while en route from one place to another.

Variation margin: See *margin*.

Warehouse receipt: A warehouse receipt is the acknowledgment a warehouseman gives when he accepts goods into his warehouse. The receipt lists the good's condition and quantity, as well as the time it was placed in storage. Often these warehouse receipts become fungible and negotiable, allowing the owner to sell his good simply by passing his warehouse receipt to someone else.

Reference list

Books and articles

Aigner, D. J., and Sprenkle, C. M. 1973. "On Optimal Financing of Cyclical Cash Needs." *Journal of Finance* 28: 1249-1254.

Anderson, Ronald W., and Danthine, Jean-Pierre. 1980. "Hedging and Joint Production: Theory and Illustrations." *Journal of Finance* 35: 487-501, with discussion.

Anderson, Ronald W., and Danthine, Jean-Pierre. 1981. "Cross Hedging." *Journal of Political Economy* 89: 1182-1196.

Anderson, Ronald W., and Danthine, Jean-Pierre. 1983a. "Hedger Diversity in Futures Markets." *Economic Journal* 93: 370-389.

Anderson, Ronald W., and Danthine, Jean-Pierre. 1983b. "The Time Pattern of Hedging and the Volatility of Futures Prices." *Review of Economic Studies* 50: 249-266.

Armstrong, William. 1848. *Stocks and Stock-Jobbing in Wall Street.* New York: New York Publishing.

Arrow, Kenneth J. 1978. "The Future and the Present in Economic Life." *Economic Inquiry* 16: 157-169.

Arthur, Henry B. 1971. *Commodity Futures as a Business Management Tool.* Boston: Graduate School of Business Administration, Harvard University.

Baesel, Jerome, and Grant, Dwight. 1982. "Optimal Sequential Futures Trading." *Journal of Financial and Quantitative Economics* 17: 683-695.

Baltensperger, Ernst. 1980. "Alternative Approaches to the Theory of the Banking Firm." *Journal of Monetary Economics* 6: 1-37.

Batlin, Carl Alan. 1983. "Production under Price Uncertainty with Imperfect Time Hedging Opportunities in Futures Markets." *Southern Economic Journal* 49: 681-692.

Benninga, Simon; Eldor, Rafael; and Zilcha, Itzhak. 1984. "The Optimal Hedge Ratio in Unbiased Futures Markets." *Journal of Futures Markets* 4: 155-160.

Benston, George J., and Smith, Clifford W., Jr. 1976. "A Transactions Cost Approach to the Theory of Financial Intermediation." *Journal of Finance* 31: 215-231.

Bisbee, Lewis H., and Simonds, John C. 1884. *The Board of Trade and the Produce Exchange: Their History, Methods and Law.* Chicago: Callaghan.

Black, Fischer. 1976. "The Pricing of Commodity Contracts." *Journal of Financial Economics* 3: 167-179.

247

Blau, Gerda. 1944. "Some Aspects of the Theory of Futures Trading." *Review of Economic Studies* 12: 1-30.

Blau, Leslie A., and Barber, James S. 1981. "Proposed Amendment of Section 4d(2) of the Commodity Exchange Act: Concerning Investment of Customer Funds." *Journal of Futures Markets* 1: 657-658.

Bobst, Barry W. 1979. "The Effects of Location-Basis Variability on Livestock Hedging in the South." In Raymond M. Leuthold (ed.), *Commodities Markets and Futures Prices*, 171-201. Chicago: Chicago Mercantile Exchange.

Bonney, C. C. 1885. *Higgins & Gilbert* v. *McCrea, Statement of the Case with Brief and Argument for Plaintiffs in Error*. Chicago: Chicago Legal News.

M. C. Brackenbury & Co. 1968. *Dealing on the London Metal Exchange*. London.

Brannen, Pamela P., and Ulveling, Edwin F. 1984. "Considering an Informational Role for Futures Markets." *Review of Economic Studies* 51: 33-52.

Bray, Margaret. 1981. "Futures Trading, Rational Expectations, and the Efficient Markets Hypothesis." *Econometrica* 49: 573-596.

Breeden, Douglas T. 1979. "An Intertemporal Asset Pricing Model with Stochastic Consumption and Investment Opportunities." *Journal of Financial Economics* 7: 265-296.

Breeden, Douglas T. 1980. "Consumption Risk in Futures Markets." *Journal of Finance* 35: 503-520.

Brennan, Michael J. 1958. "The Supply of Storage." *American Economic Review* 47: 50-72.

Britto, Ronald. 1984. "The Simultaneous Determination of Spot and Futures Prices in a Simple Model with Production Risk." *The Quarterly Journal of Economics* 99: 351-365.

Burns, Joseph M. 1979. *A Treatise on Markets: Spot, Futures, and Options*. Washington, D.C.: American Enterprise Institute.

Callier, Philippe. 1981. "One Way Arbitrage, Foreign Exchange and Securities Markets: A Note." *Journal of Finance* 36: 1177-1186.

Campbell, Tim. 1978. "A Model of the Market for Lines of Credit." *Journal of Finance* 33: 231-244.

Carlton, Dennis W. 1977. "Equilibrium in Markets where Price Exceeds Cost: Uncertainty, Production Lags, and Pricing." *American Economic Review* 67: 244-249.

Carlton, Dennis W. 1979. "Contracts, Price Rigidity, and Market Equilibrium." *Journal of Political Economy* 87: 1034-1062.

Carlton, Dennis W. 1983a. "The Cost of Eliminating a Futures Market, and the Effect of Inflation on Market Interrelationships." University of Chicago Law School Program in Law and Economics Working Paper No. 18.

Carlton, Dennis W. 1983b. "Futures Trading, Market Interrelationships, and Industry Structure." *American Journal of Agricultural Economics* 65: 380-387.

Carlton, Dennis W. 1984. "Futures Markets: Their Purpose, Their History, Their Growth, Their Successes and Failures." *Journal of Futures Markets* 4: 237-271.

Carter, Colin A.; Rausser, Gordon C.; and Schmitz, Andrew. 1983. "Efficient Asset Portfolios and the Theory of Normal Backwardation." *Journal of Political Economy* 91: 319-331.

Castelino, Mark G., and Vora, Ashok. 1984. "Spread Volatility in Commodity Futures: The Length Effect." *Journal of Futures Markets* 4: 39-46.

Chicago Board of Trade. 1972. *Introduction to Hedging.*

Chicago Board of Trade. 1982. *Grains: Production, Processing, Marketing.*

ContiCommodity. 1983. *Seasonality in Agricultural Futures Markets.* Chicago.

Cootner, Paul H. 1960. "Returns to Speculators: Telser vs. Keynes;" and "Rejoinder." *Journal of Political Economy* 68: 396-404, 415-418.

Cootner, Paul H. 1961. "Common Elements in Futures Markets for Commodities and Bonds." *American Economic Review* 51: 173-183.

Cootner, Paul H. 1968. "Speculation, Hedging, and Arbitrage." *International Encyclopedia of Social Science* 15: 117-120.

Cornell, Bradford, and Reinganum, Marc R. 1981. "Forward and Futures Prices: Evidence from the Foreign Exchange Markets." *Journal of Finance* 36: 1035-1045.

Cowing, Cedric B. 1965. *Populists, Plungers, and Progressives: A Social History of Stock and Commodity Speculation 1890-1936.* Princeton: Princeton University Press.

Cox, Charles C. 1976. "Futures Trading and Market Information." *Journal of Political Economy* 84: 1215-1237.

Cox, John C.; Ingersoll, Jonathan E., Jr; and Ross, Stephen A. 1981. "The Relation between Forward Prices and Futures Prices." *Journal of Financial Economics* 9: 321-346.

Cukierman, Alex. 1980. "The Effects of Uncertainty on Investment under Risk Neutrality with Endogenous Information." *Journal of Political Economy* 88: 462-475.

Dansby, Robert E. 1978. "Capacity Constrained Peak Load Pricing." *Quarterly Journal of Economics* 92: 387-398.

Danthine, Jean-Pierre. 1978. "Information, Futures Prices, and Stabilizing Speculation." *Journal of Economic Theory* 17: 79-98.

Deardorff, Alan V. 1979. "One-Way Arbitrage and Its Implications for the Foreign Exchange Markets." *Journal of Political Economy* 87: 351-364.

Dewey, T. Henry. 1886. *A Treatise on Contracts for Future Delivery and Commercial Wagers.* New York: Baker, Voorhis.

Dewey, T. Henry. 1905. *Legislation against Speculation and Gambling in the Forms of Trade.* New York: Baker, Voorhis.

Dow, J. C. R. 1940. "A Theoretical Account of Futures Markets." *Review of Economic Studies* 7: 185-195.

Duddy, Edward A. 1931. "Grain Elevator Storage and the Interior Terminal Markets: Chicago." *Journal of Business* 4: 1-25.

Dusak, Katherine. 1973. "Futures Trading and Investor Returns: An Investigation of Commodity Market Risk Premiums." *Journal of Political Economy* 81: 1387-1406.

Economist Intelligence Unit. 1958. *The London Metal Exchange.* Tonbridge: Whitefriars Press.

Ederington, Louis H. 1979. "The Hedging Performance of the New Futures Markets." *Journal of Finance* 34: 157-170.

Edwards, Franklin R. 1983. "The Clearing Association in Futures Markets: Guarantor and Regulator." *Journal of Futures Markets* 3: 369-392.

Ellison, Thomas. 1905. *Gleanings and Reminiscences.* Liverpool: Henry Young.

Emery, Henry Crosby. 1896. *Speculation on the Stock and Produce Exchanges of the United States.* New York: Columbia University Press. Reprinted, New York: Greenwood Press, 1969.

Exxon Corporation. 1981. *World Oil Inventories.* New York: Exxon Corporation Public Affairs Department.

Feder, Gershon; Just, Richard E.; and Schmitz, Andrew. 1980. "Futures Markets and the Theory of the Firm under Price Uncertainty." *Quarterly Journal of Economics* 94: 317-328.

Feiger, George M. 1978. "Divergent Rational Expectations Equilibrium in a Dynamic Model of a Futures Market." *Journal of Economic Theory* 17: 164-178.

Fisher, Anthony C. 1981. *Resource and Environmental Economics.* Cambridge: Cambridge University Press.

Frenkel, Jacob A., and Levich, Richard M. 1975. "Covered Interest Arbitrage: Unexploited Profits?" *Journal of Political Economy* 83: 325-338.

Frenkel, Jacob A., and Levich, Richard M. 1977. "Transactions Costs and Interest Arbitrage: Tranquil versus Turbulent Periods." *Journal of Political Economy* 85: 1209-1227.

Gardner, Bruce L. 1975. "The Farm-Retail Price Spread in a Competitive Food Industry." *American Journal of Agricultural Economics* 57: 399-409.

Gibson, George Rutledge. 1888. *The Stock Exchanges of London, Paris, and New York.* New York: Putnam's Sons.

Gibson-Jarvie, Robert. 1976. *The London Metals Exchange.* Cambridge: Woodhead-Faulkner.

Goldberg, Victor P. 1980. "Relational Exchange: Economics and Complex Contracts." *American Behavioral Scientist* 23: 337-352.

Goss, B. A. 1970. "A Note on the Storage Market Equilibria of Brennan and Telser." *Australian Economic Papers* 9: 273-278.

Gray, Roger W. 1960. "The Characteristic Bias in Some Thin Futures Markets." *Food Research Institute Studies* 1: 296-313.

Gray, Roger W. 1961. "The Search for a Risk Premium." *Journal of Political Economy* 69: 250-260.

Gray, Roger W. 1976. "Risk Management in Commodity and Financial Markets." *American Journal of Agricultural Economics* 58: 280-285.

Reference list 251

Gray, Roger W. 1979. "The Emergence of Short Speculation." *International Futures Trading Seminar* 6: 77-100. Chicago Board of Trade.

Gray, Roger W. 1984. "Commentary." *Review of Research in Futures Markets* 3: 80-81. Chicago Board of Trade.

Gray, Roger W., and Peck, Anne E. 1981. "The Chicago Wheat Futures Market: Recent Problems in Historical Perspective." *Food Research Institute Studies* 18: 89-115.

Grossman, Sanford J. 1977. "The Existence of Futures Markets, Noisy Rational Expectations and Informational Externalities." *Review of Economic Studies* 44: 431-449.

Gupta, Manak C. 1973. "Optimal Financial Policy for a Firm with Uncertain Fund Requirements." *Journal of Financial and Quantitative Analysis* 8: 731-747.

Gustafson, Robert L. 1958. "Carryover Levels for Grain: a Method for Determining Amounts That Are Optimal under Specified Conditions." U.S.D.A. Technical Bulletin 1178.

Hartman, Richard. 1976. "Factor Demand with Output Price Uncertainty." *American Economic Review* 66: 675-681.

Hayenga, Marvin L., and DiPietre, Dennis D. 1982. "Hedging Wholesale Meat Prices: Analysis of Basis Risk." *Journal of Futures Markets* 2: 121-130.

Hecht, Felix. 1884. *Die Warrants*. Stuttgart: Ferdinand Inke.

Heifner, Richard G. 1966. "The Gains from Basing Grain Storage Decisions on Cash-Future Spreads." *Journal of Farm Economics* 48: 1490-1495.

Hicks, J. R. 1946. *Value and Capital*. 2d ed. Oxford: Clarendon Press.

Hieronymous, Thomas A. 1971. *Economics of Futures Trading*. New York: Commodity Research Bureau.

Higinbotham, Harlow N. 1976. "The Demand for Hedging in Grain Futures Markets." Ph.D. dissertation, University of Chicago.

Holthausen, Duncan M. 1979. "Hedging and the Competitive Firm under Price Uncertainty." *American Economic Review* 69: 989-995.

Horsefield, J. Keith. 1977. "The Beginnings of Paper Money in England." *Journal of European Economic History* 6: 117-132.

Houthakker, Hendrik S. 1959. "The Scope and Limits of Futures Trading." *The Allocation of Economic Resources: Essays in Honor of Francis Haley.* Stanford: Stanford University Press.

Houthakker, Hendrik S. 1968. "Normal Backwardation." In J. N. Wolfe (ed.), *Value, Capital, and Growth: Papers in Honour of Sir John Hicks,* 193-214. Edinburgh: Edinburgh University Press.

Howell, L. D. 1956. "Influence of Certified Stocks on Spot-Futures Price Relationships for Cotton." U.S.D.A. Technical Bulletin 1151.

Irwin, H. S. 1935. "Seasonal Cycles in Aggregates of Wheat Futures Contracts." *Journal of Political Economy* 43: 34-49.

Jaffee, Dwight M. 1984. "The Impact of Financial Futures and Options on Capital Formation." *Journal of Futures Markets* 4: 417-447.

Johnson, Leland L. 1960. "The Theory of Hedging and Speculation in Commodity Futures." *Review of Economic Studies* 27: 139-151.

Jones, Frank J. 1981. "Spreads: Tails, Turtles, and All That." *Journal of Futures Markets* 1: 565-596.

Kaldor, Nicholas. 1939. "Speculation and Economic Stability." *Review of Economic Studies* 7: 1-27.

Kallard, Thomas. 1982. *Commodity Spreads.* New York: Optosonic Press.

Kaplan, Robert S. 1970. "A Dynamic Inventory Model with Stochastic Lead-Times." *Management Science* 16: 491-507.

Kawai, Masahiro. 1983a. "Price Volatility of Storable Commodities under Rational Expectations in Spot and Futures Markets." *International Economic Review* 24: 435-459.

Kawai, Masahiro. 1983b. "Spot and Futures Prices of Nonstorable Commodities under Rational Expectations." *Quarterly Journal of Economics* 98: 235-254.

Keynes, John Maynard. 1930. *A Treatise on Money: Volume II: The Applied Theory of Money.* London: Macmillan.

Keynes, John Maynard. 1936. *The General Theory of Employment, Interest, and Money.* London: Macmillan.

Klein, Benjamin; Crawford, Robert G.; and Alchian, Armen A. 1978. "Vertical Integration, Appropriable Rents, and the Competitive Contracting Process." *Journal of Law and Economics* 21: 297-326.

Labys, Walter C., and Granger, C. W. J. 1970. *Speculation, Hedging and Commodity Price Forecasts.* Lexington, Mass.: Heath.

Leuthold, Raymond M., and Mokler, R. Scott. 1979. "Feeding-Margin Hedging in the Cattle Industry." *International Futures Trading Seminar* 6: 56-68. Chicago Board of Trade.

Liberatore, Matthew J. 1977. "Planning Horizons for a Stochastic Lead-Time Inventory Model." *Operations Research* 25: 977-988.

Lurie, Jonathan. 1979. *The Chicago Board of Trade, 1859-1905: The Dynamics of Self-Regulation.* Urbana: University of Illinois Press.

Maccini, Louis J. 1973. "On Optimal Delivery Lags." *Journal of Economic Theory* 6: 107-125.

Marcus, Alan J. 1984. "Efficient Asset Portfolios and the Theory of Normal Backwardation: A Comment." *Journal of Political Economy* 92: 162-164.

Marcus, Alan J., and Modest, David M. 1984. "Futures Markets and Production Decisions." *Journal of Political Economy* 92: 409-426.

Martin, Larry; Groenewegen, John L.; and Pidgeon, Edward. 1980. "Factors Affecting Corn Basis in Southwestern Ontario." *American Journal of Agricultural Economics* 62: 107-112.

Mayers, David, and Smith, Clifford W., Jr. 1982. "On the Corporate Demand for Insurance." *Journal of Business* 55: 281-296.

Mayers, David, and Thaler, Richard. 1979. "Sticky Wages and Implicit Contracts: A Transactional Approach." *Economic Inquiry* 17: 539-574.

Meeker, J. Edward. 1932. *Short-Selling.* New York: Harper.

Miracle, Diane S. 1972. "The Egg Futures Market: 1940 to 1966." *Food Research Institute Studies* 11: 269-292.

Mishimura, Shizuya. 1971. *The Decline of Inland Bills of Exchange in the London Money Market 1855-1913*. Cambridge: Cambridge University Press.

New York Cotton Exchange. 1891. *Charter, By-Laws and Rules of the New York Cotton Exchange*. 13th ed.

Oldfield, George S. 1981. "Forwards Contracts and Futures Contracts." *Journal of Financial Economics* 9: 373-382.

Paul, Allen B. 1966. "Pricing below Cost in the Soybean Processing Industry." *Journal of Farm Economics* 48 (Part II): 2-22.

Paul, Allen B. 1970. "The Pricing of Binspace—A Contribution to the Theory of Storage." *American Journal of Agricultural Economics* 52: 1-12.

Paul, Allen B.; Kahl, Kandice H.; and Tomek, William G. 1981. *Performance of Futures Markets: The Case of Potatoes*. U.S.D.A. Technical Bulletin 1636.

Paul, Allen B., and Wesson, William T. 1966. "Short-Run Supply of Services—The Case of Soybean Processing." *Journal of Farm Economics* 48: 935-951.

Peck, Anne E. 1975. "Hedging and Income Stability: Concepts, Implications and an Example." *American Journal of Agricultural Economics* 57: 410-419.

Peck, Anne E. (ed.). 1978. *Views from the Trade*. Chicago: Chicago Board of Trade.

Peterson, Richard L. 1977. "Investor Preferences for Futures Straddles." *Journal of Financial and Quantitative Analysis* 12: 105-120.

Phaup, E. Dwight. 1981. "A Reinterpretation of the Modern Theory of Forward Exchange Rates." *Journal of Money, Credit and Banking* 13: 477-484.

Pindyck, Robert S. 1980. "Uncertainty and Exhaustible Resource Markets." *Journal of Political Economy* 88: 1203-1225.

Plisker, Stanley R. 1973. "Supply of Storage Theory and Commodity Equilibrium Prices with Stochastic Production." *American Journal of Agricultural Economics* 55 (Part 1): 653-658.

Powers, Mark J. 1967. "Effects of Contract Provisions on the Success of a Futures Contract." *Journal of Farm Economics* 49: 833-843.

Protopapadakis, Aris, and Stoll, Hans R. 1983. "Spot and Futures Prices and the Law of One Price." *Journal of Finance* 38: 1431-1455.

Richards, R. D. 1929. *The Early History of Banking in England*. London: P. S. King.

Rockwell, Charles S. 1967. "Normal Backwardation, Forecasting, and the Returns to Commodity Futures Traders." *Food Research Institute Studies* 7 (Supplement): 107-130.

Rolfo, Jacques. 1980. "Optimal Hedging under Price and Quantity Uncertainty: The Case of a Cocoa Producer." *Journal of Political Economy* 88: 100-116.

Rutledge, David J. S. 1972. "Hedgers' Demand for Futures Contracts: A

Theoretical Framework with Applications to the United States Soybean Complex." *Food Research Institute Studies* 11: 237-256.

Sandor, Richard L. 1973. "Innovation by an Exchange: A Case Study of the Development of the Plywood Futures Contract." *Journal of Law and Economics* 16: 119-136.

Saving, T. R., and De Vany, Arthur S. 1981. "Uncertain Markets, Reliabilty and Peak-Load Pricing." *Southern Economic Journal* 47: 908-923.

Scammel, W. M. 1968. *The London Discount Market.* London: Elek Books.

Schrock, Nicholas W. 1971. "The Theory of Asset Choice: Simultaneous Holding of Short and Long Positions in the Futures Markets." *Journal of Political Economy* 79: 270-293.

Shefrin, H. M. 1979. "Spot Trading, Efficiency, and Differential Information." *Journal of Economic Theory* 20: 281-299.

Shefrin, H. M. 1981. "Transactions Costs, Uncertainty and Generally Inactive Futures Markets." *Review of Economic Studies* 48: 131-137.

Silber, William L. 1975. "Towards a Theory of Financial Innovation." In William L. Silber (ed.), *Financial Innovation,* 53-85. Lexington, Mass.: Heath.

Silber, William L. 1981. "Innovation, Competition and New Contract Design in Futures Markets." *Journal of Futures Markets* 1: 123-155.

Smith, Courtney. 1982. *Commodity Spreads.* New York: Wiley.

Smith, Gordon W. 1978. "Commodity Instability and Market Failure: A Survey of Issues." In F. Gerald Adams and Sonia A. Klein (eds.), *Stabilizing World Commodity Markets,* 161-188. Lexington, Mass.: Heath.

Sraffa, Piero. 1932. "Dr. Hayek on Money and Capital." *Economic Journal* 42: 42-53.

Starr, Merritt. 1886. "The Clearing House in the Grain and Cotton Exchange." *American Law Review* 20: 680-697.

Stein, Jerome L. 1961. "The Simultaneous Determination of Spot and Futures Prices." *American Economic Review* 51: 1012-1025.

Stein, Jerome L. 1979. "Spot, Forward and Futures." *Research in Finance* 1: 225-310. Greenwich, Conn.: JAI Press.

Stoll, Hans R. 1979. "Commodity Futures and Spot Price Determination and Hedging in Capital Market Equilibrium." *Journal of Financial and Quantitative Economics* 14: 873-894.

Stonham, Paul. 1982. *Major Stock Markets of Europe.* New York: St. Martin's Press.

Taylor, Charles H. 1917. *History of the Board of Trade of the City of Chicago.* Chicago: Robert O. Law.

Telser, Lester G. 1955. "Safety First and Hedging." *Review of Economic Studies* 23: 1-16.

Telser, Lester G. 1958. "Futures Trading and the Storage of Cotton and Wheat." *Journal of Political Economy* 66: 233-255.

Telser, Lester G. 1960. "Reply." *Journal of Political Economy* 68: 404-415.

Telser, Lester G. 1980. "Reasons for Having an Organized Futures Market." *Livestock Futures Research Symposium,* 11-31. Chicago Mercantile Exchange.

Telser, Lester G. 1981. "Why There Are Organized Futures Markets." *Journal of Law and Economics* 24: 1-22.

Telser, Lester G., and Higinbotham, Harlow N. 1977. "Organized Futures Markets: Costs and Benefits." *Journal of Political Economy* 85: 969-1000.

Teweles, Richard J., and Bradley, Edward S. 1982. *The Stock Market.* 4th ed. New York: Wiley.

Thiessen, G. Willard. 1982. "Spread Trading in the Grains." *Review of Research in Futures Markets* 1: 189-194. Chicago Board of Trade.

Tomek, William G., and Gray, Roger W. 1977. "Temporal Relationships among Prices on Commodity Futures Markets: Their Allocative and Stabilizing Roles." *Selected Writings on Futures Markets* 2: 137-189.

Treat, John (ed.). 1984. *Energy Futures.* Tulsa: PennWell.

Tsiang, S. C. 1969. "The Precautionary Demand for Money: An Inventory Theoretical Analysis." *Journal of Political Economy* 77: 99-117.

Turnovsky, Stephen J. 1983. "The Determination of Spot and Futures Prices with Storable Commodities." *Econometrica* 51: 1363-1387.

Vaile, Roland S. 1948. "Inverse Carrying Charges in Futures Markets." *Journal of Farm Economics* 30: 574-575.

Venkataramanan, L. S. 1965. *The Theory of Futures Trading.* Bombay: Asia Publishing House.

Vollink, William, and Raikes, Ronald. 1977. "An Analysis of Delivery-Period Basis Determination for Live Cattle." *Southern Journal of Agricultural Economics* 7: 179-184.

Ward, Ronald W., and Dasse, Frank A. 1977. "Empirical Contributions to Basis Theory: The Case of Citrus Futures." *American Journal of Agricultural Economics* 59: 71-80.

Ward, Ronald W., and Fletcher, Lehman B. 1971. "From Hedging to Pure Speculation: A Micro Model of Optimal Futures and Cash Market Positions." *American Journal of Agricultural Economics* 53: 71-78.

Weymar, F. Helmut. 1966. "The Supply of Storage Revisited." *American Economic Review* 56: 1226-1234.

Weymar, F. Helmut. 1974. "The Effects of Cocoa Inventories on Price Forecasting." In R. A. Kotey, C. Okali, and B. E. Rourke (eds.), *The Economics of Cocoa Production and Marketing,* 432-449. Legon: University of Ghana.

Williams, Jeffrey C. 1980. "The Economic Function of Futures Markets." Ph.D. dissertation, Yale University.

Williams, Jeffrey C. 1982. "The Origin of Futures Markets." *Agricultural History* 56: 306-316.

Williams, Jeffrey C. 1984. "Fractional Reserve Banking in Grain." *Journal of Money, Credit, and Banking* 16: 488-496.

Williamson, Oliver E. 1979. "Transaction-Cost Economics: The Governance of Contractual Relations." *Journal of Law and Economics* 22: 233-261.

Working, Holbrook. 1934. "Price Relations between May and New-Crop Wheat Futures at Chicago Since 1885." *Food Research Institute, Wheat Studies* 10: 183-228.

Working, Holbrook. 1948. "Theory of the Inverse Carrying Charge in Futures Markets." *Journal of Farm Economics* 39: 1-28.

Working, Holbrook. 1949. "The Theory of Price of Storage." *American Economic Review* 39: 1254-1262.

Working, Holbrook. 1953a. "Futures Trading and Hedging." *American Economic Review* 43: 314-343.

Working, Holbrook. 1953b. "Hedging Reconsidered." *Journal of Farm Economics* 35: 544-561.

Working, Holbrook. 1954. "Whose Markets? Evidence on Some Aspects of Futures Trading." *Journal of Marketing* 19: 1-11.

Working, Holbrook. 1962. "New Concepts Concerning Futures Markets and Prices." *American Economic Review* 52: 431-459.

Wright, Brian D., and Williams, Jeffrey C. 1982. "The Economic Role of Commodity Storage." *Economic Journal* 92: 596-614.

Yamey, B. S. 1971. "Short-Hedging and Long-Hedging in Futures Markets: Symmetry and Asymmetry." *Journal of Law and Economics* 14: 413-434.

Yamey, B. S., and Peston, M. H. 1960. "Inter-Temporal Price Relations with Forward Markets: A Method of Analysis." *Economica* 27: 355-367.

Cases cited

Beveridge v. *Hewitt.* 8 Ill. App. 467 (1881).

Board of Trade of the City of Chicago v. *Christie Grain and Stock Co.* 198 U.S. 236 (1905).

Clarke v. *Foss.* 5 Fed. Cas. 955 (1878).

Clews v. *Jamieson.* 182 U.S. 461 (1901).

Corbett v. *Underwood.* 83 Ill. 344 (1876).

Gettys v. *Newburger.* 272 Fed. Rep. 209 (1921).

Gregory v. *Wendell.* 39 Mich. 337 (1878).

Higgins & Gilbert v. *McCrea.* 23 Fed. Rep. 782 (1885); 116 U.S. 671 (1886).

Lyons Milling Co. v. *Goffe & Carkener, Inc.* 46 Fed. Rep. (2d) 241 (1931).

Melchert v. *American Union Telegraph Co.* 11 Fed. Rep. 193 (1882).

Oldershaw v. *Knowles.* 4 Ill. App. 63 (1879); 6 Ill. App. 325 (1880).

Palmer v. *Love.* 80 S.W. (2d) 100 (1934).

Sawyer, Wallace & Co. v. *Taggart.* 77 Ken. 727 (1879).

Seligson v. *New York Produce Exchange.* 394 Fed. Supp. 125 (1975).

Union National Bank of Chicago v. *Carr.* 15 Fed. Rep. 438 (1883).

Ward v. *Vosburgh.* 31 Fed. Rep. 12 (1887).

Williar v. *Irwin.* 30 Fed. Cas. 38 (1879); 110 U.S. 499 (1884).

Index

257

258   **Index**

Edwards, Franklin R., 11, 165n5
eggs, futures market in, 224
Eldor, Rafael, 92
Ellison, Thomas, 169
Emery, Henry Crosby, 169
Exxon Corp., 117n5

Feder, Gershon, 100
Feiger, George M., 35
financial futures markets, 3, 35, 197,
    215-218
financial intermediation, 2, 112, 145
Fisher, Anthony C., 20n25
Fletcher, Lehman B., 91n12
forward contracts, 162-163, 166-168,
    216, 241
Frenkel, Jacob A., 44n1
futures commission merchants, 13, 15,
    177, 178, 242
futures contracts, definition of, 2-3,
    242

Gardner, Bruce L., 102
Gibson, George Rutledge, 53n6
gold, futures market in, 197
Goldberg, Victor P., 152n1
Goss, B. A., 137n29
grain banks, 154-156
Granger, C. W. J., 225
Grant, Dwight, 92
Gray, Roger W., 38, 85, 94, 170, 200n10
Groenewegen, John L., 108
Grossman, Sanford J., 225-227
Gupta, Manak C., 144n30
Gustafson, Robert L., 33n35

Hartman, Richard, 149
Hayenga, Marvin L., 107n21
Hecht, Felix, 56
hedgers
    behavior under risk aversion of,
        95-97, 100-103, 106-111
    behavior under risk neutrality of, 144,
        145-148
    definition of, 18-19, 81, 242
    and lifting a hedge, 103-106
    practices of, 41-42
    speculation by, 98-100, 104-106
hedging operations, 19, 65-70, 74-75,
    82, 88-90, 93-96, 130, 163, 173,
    230, 236-237
Hicks, J. R., 80n2
Higinbotham, Harlow N., 33-34, 222
Holthausen, Duncan M., 100
Horsefield, J. Keith, 141

Houthakker, Hendrik S., 87
Howell, L. D., 38

implicit markets, 42-48, 159-162, 186-
    187
Ingersoll, Jonathan E., Jr., 166n7
insurance, 1-2, 77, 80, 81, 124
interest rates, commodity specific, 134-
    135
inventory
    control theory, 123, 124
    demand for, 112, 115-118, 119-122,
        127, 135-137
inverse carrying charge, *see*
    backwardation
Irwin, H. S., 4

Jaffee, Dwight M., 217n27
Johnson, Leland L., 90, 100-101
Jones, Frank J., 18n23
Just, Richard E., 100

Kahl, Kandice H., 71
Kaldor, Nicholas, 82, 137, 163, 167-168
Kallard, Thomas, 31n32
Kansas City Board of Trade, 199-202
Kaplan, Robert S., 123
Kawai, Masahiro, 35, 227
Keynes, John Maynard, 80, 82, 83-88,
    134
Klein, Benjamin, 152n1

Labys, Walter C., 225
Leuthold, Raymond M., 92
Levich, Richard M., 44n1
Liberatore, Matthew J., 123
line of credit, 121, 129
liquidity theory, 162-167, 222
Liverpool Cotton Exchange, 166-167,
    169, 207n13, 228
loan markets
    for commodities, 39-40, 129-130,
        143-145, 158-159, 205-206
    equilibrium relation for, 48-50, 62,
        74-75, 227
    for grains, 57-60, 169, 172-173,
        236
    for pig iron, 56
    for shares of stock, 51, 53, 169
    for uranium, 56-57
    see also money: market for
Lombard-Wall, Inc., 61
London Metal Exchange, 66-67, 165-
    166, 180, 197-198
London Stock Exchange, 53-55, 170